BiblioTech

ReReading the Post-digital Library

Special Collections

Technologies of Reading Writing & Writing Reading

Library Ecologies & Library-making

Introduction

Books are interfaces to libraries. Libraries are interfaces to books. Today, both are also pervaded by elements of the "meta-interface" of new platforms, cloud storage, and data streams that has diffused out from desk-based computers.[1] Reading, writing, publishing, distributing and storing books have each become more connected in the digital context, embracing an ever-wider infrastructure ecology[2] of human and non-human actors. If libraries and books both seem somewhat dwarfed by the resultant "accidental megastructure" stretching between the world and the end user through a *stack* of interface, address, city and cloud,[3] an ability to *practice* librarianship doubtless has become ever more central to surviving its symptoms: the informatic tornados that rise through the semio-economy threatening the composition of intellectual solidarity with ever-increasing volume and speed.[4]

The contemporary public realm is a bloated library teeming with the manifold, chaotic, outputs of the publishing "attitude" of contemporary culture.[5] Libraries have, as a result, turned inside out: shaking off the narrative of loss and preservation that has characterised earlier bibliotechnical periods,[6] pivoting towards filtering, broadcast, "organizing information outward" into a world which forgets nothing,[7] and hybridising the outside inward by integrating various living components into their architectonic designs. Books are also in a somewhat liminal state: the emblematic "transaction between physical and mental universes", now itself occupying various states of im/materiality, and even executability. Our own limits seem increasingly indistinguishable from that of our representative digital subjects[8] but a book, even in its digital form, as a "text with limits, which can be divided into organised contents"[9] still operates as a wedge for separating us from the network, teasing chucks of the infinitude of information back to the limitations of the material world – albeit one that may additionally function as a connector, leaking more content into the big data repository. As all this suggests, shuttling between books (whatever form they are taking) and libraries (however porous and topsy-turvy) we encounter a great deal of insight about knowledge production, resource distribution and power in contemporary society.

Building on a rich tradition of historical and contemporary work on the *library-book*,[10] *book-art*,[11] and *art-library*[12] relations, this edition reflects

1. Christian Ulrik Andersen and Søren Bro Pold, *The Metainterface: The Art of Platforms, Cities, and Clouds* (MIT Press, 2018). **2.** Shannon Mattern, "Library as Infrastructure," *Places Journal* (2014). **3.** Benjamin Bratton, *The Stack: On Software and Sovereignty* (MIT Press, 2016). **4.** Franco 'Bifo' Berardi, "Semio-capital and the Problem of Solidarity" (2012), https://libcom.org/book/export/html/45057. **5.** Alessandro Ludovico, *Tactical Publishing: Using Senses, Software, and Archives in the Twenty-First Century* (MIT Press, 2024). **6.** Brian Cummings, *Bibliophobia: The End and the Beginning of the Book* (OUP, 2022). **7.** Mark Dahl, "Inside-out Library Services," *Advances in Library Administration and Organization,* Vol. 39: 15–34. **8.** Olga Gorbunova, "The Digital Subject: People as Data as Persons," *Theory, Culture and Society,* 36, no. 6 (2019): 125–145. **9.** Cummings, *Bibliophobia.* **10.** A recent article by Adam Smyth in the LRB makes the connection between Brian Cummings' *Bibliophobia,* Holbrook Jackson's 1930 "digressive celebration" *The Anatomy of Bibliomania* and Thomas Frognall Dibdin's 1804 "masterpiece" *Bibliomania; or Book Madness.*

upon and documents our own experiment with librarianship undertaken via the curating of exhibitions in NeMe, Cyprus and Exhibition Research Lab, Liverpool in Spring 2022, which transformed galleries into a temporary and distributed library,[13] showcasing books and collections as artworks, and artworks as library-infrastructural things. Our library operated as an affective, *scholarly technics* to explore what libraries might feel like in a coming, post-digital age. Through events[14] and exhibition tours,[15] we highlighted the ways that post-digital artist books, book- or library-adjacent art, including the ephemera of public and private library spaces, can be brought together as a modular knowledge production unit to examine and play with today's biblio-technical situation. And now, you hold in your hands, or have before you on screen, an intermediation[16] with those instances of experimental literature, critical librarianship, constructed languages, and alien indices – our own moment of librarianship iterated as a book.

In this book, we document several auto-critical art projects, art writing practices, and spatially organised artworks based in and around the contemporary library, looking particularly at the interfacial and interstitial qualities of books, libraries and the various lives that hybridise with them. The book is in this way an auto-biblio-*technical* exercise in mapping the hybridity of the bibliographical, technological and social aspects of the exhibition: its auto*bibliography*. As our contributors collectively show, in the case of the library, organisational and administrative systems, the behaviours of people and technologies, and the interplay of information and knowledge often give the appearance of a space in which much is automated for efficiency – even a given trajectory of development – but the reality is more contingent and fragile, and our assumptions should often be revised in interplay with the practical experience of the texts and techs of an age.

Contributors to this volume draw attention to the increasing significance of interfaces and infrastructure in accounts of the library. We feature illustrated essays, interviews and artist pages that look backwards and forwards through the history of book storage, making and distribution in surprising and challenging ways. The discussion in the volume also acknowledges the broader landscape of publishing and knowledge production, encompassing websites, social media,

11. See: Garrett Stewart, *Bookwork: Medium to Object to Concept to Art* (Chicago UP, 2011); also Philip Smith, *The Book: Art & Object* (1982); and Alessandro Ludovico, *Post Digital Print* (Onomatopee, 2012). **12.** See Heide Hinrichs et al., "Shelf Documents: Art Library as Practice," (Royal Academy Fine Arts Antwerp, 2021); Anna-Sophie Springer and Etienne Turpin (eds.), *Fantasies of the Library* (MIT Press, 2018); and Ludovico, *Tactical Publishing*. **13.** In *Tactical Publishing* Ludovico describes "temporary libraries" and "distributed libraries" as potential conditions by which the library might find its contemporary relevance in the digital age. Ludovico is also a librarian of temporary libraries himself, as documented in this excellent book. **14.** A selection of talks given at NeMe by Nathan Jones, Sam Skinner, Silvio Lorusso and Rosa Menkman, can be streamed via NeMe's YouTube channel here: https://bit.ly/biblioneme. **15.** A virtual tour and talk by Nathan Jones for Academic Libraries North given at Lancaster University, prior to a workshop with that network, can be viewed here: https://youtu.be/51EkVo9tyWo. **16.** N. Katherine Hayles, *Electronic Literature: New Horizons for the Literary,* (University of Notre Dame Press, 2008). In this book Hayles offers an adaptation of Boulter and Gruisin's more commonly used notion of "remediation", suggesting that "intermediation" better highlights the dynamic relationship between different mediums as books adapt to hybrid digital-physical environments.

file sharing, data farms, cognitive labourers, word processing engines, and even forests. The deeper integration of corporate, automated entities into the network of book production and storage, poses a particular challenge for those of us invested in democratising book access and production cycles. This introductory chapter emphasises the importance of addressing such challenges, and offers vectors for doing so.

The Library and Post-Internet Space

For the majority of writers and artists appearing here, the library is personal precisely because it is where the cognitive and creative conditions of our trade appear to have found their last, albeit fragile, refuge. As Søren Pold and Christian Andersen note in *The Metainterface*, "tablets, fast networks, cloud computing, and more are not only technological advancements; they also seriously disturb and alter everyday cultural practices".[17] In this sense, libraries become not only physical spaces for the accumulation and dissemination of knowledge, but also symbolic representations of the tensions between tradition and innovation, solitude and community, and autonomy and control in the present iteration of the cultural and creative industries.

Historically, libraries have been seen as places of knowledge, learning, and reflection, in which human traits of intensive work, quiet contemplation, and bounded sociality thrive, but this is also enmeshed with the technics of language, archiving, and knowledge distribution in a given age.[18] As a site for storage, recall, researching, and transmission, libraries are a *learning commons* and act as gathering points for tech and folk – a networked membership club, the first info-oases, places in which the internet was first publicly accessible in most campuses and neighbourhoods and therefore a space of self-care and self-discovery for societies of outcasts of various stripes[19] – in ways that echo the practices of earlier nomadic cultures.[20] In fact, can we glimpse a pre-history of the library in the immersive information spaces of the Paleolithic era? Research has suggested that caves operated as sites for gathering and "cross-modality information transfer" between nomadic peoples' speech, echoes, and their notation,[21] and the cave interior became a site for invention, archiving complex symbolic forms for later consultation, ritual meetings, and immersive study, in a manner that anticipated the combinations of scriptorium, networking space and

17. Pold and Andersen, *The Metainterface*. **18.** Jesse Hauk Shera, "The Library as a Social Institution," *Libraries and Society*, Robert D. Leigh, Jr. and Burton R. Clark (Sage, 1970): 1–22. **19.** In *The Library Book* (Counterpoint, 2018) author and librarian Stuart Kells notes that libraries have long been more than just repositories of books. He writes, "Since ancient times, libraries have been places of learning, of scholarship, of conversation, and of public life. They have been venues for exhibitions, performances, and lectures. They have been centers of community and of civic pride". Similarly, scholar Ray Oldenburg argues, in *The Great Good Place* (Hachette, 1999) that libraries are "third places" – that is, places where people can gather and interact outside of their homes and workplaces. These ideas reflect the long-standing role of libraries as not only places to access information, but also as community hubs and spaces for personal growth and development. **20.** Artist-turned archaeologist Carolyn Boyd in *The White Shaman* (University of Texas Press, 2016) specifically describes caves in South America as libraries, acting as archives and retrieval sites for performances that are recorded as marks and annotations on the cave walls. **21.** Shigeru Miyagawa et al., "Cross-Modality Information Transfer: A Hypothesis about the Relationship among Prehistoric Cave Paintings, Symbolic Thinking, and the Emergence of Language," *Frontiers in Psychology*, vol. 9, 20 February 2018.

archives of the modern library. Indeed, libraries are still very much immersive environments, whose architecture acts as a portal to embody information structures. Making an additional *paleocybernetic*[22] link between the pre-history and future of the library, Alessandro Ludovico asks that we consider librarians today as information shamen: spirit guides into the network who "help others with their knowledge and mediation between the known (material) and the unknown (immaterial), and they are able to navigate the complexity of forces and relationships."[23] These associations – isolation, community, technical, personal, organisation, innovation and magic – make the library the perfect model for an art exhibition that seeks to twist and satirise the technology shaping social aspects of learning. It does however, also mean that libraries are at the forefront of a kind of paradoxical transformation: the library-condition or becoming-librarian that appears to infest us, and follow us around. Or that we have all awoken to find ourselves to be a librarian-like creature, like Gregor Samsa transformed into an insect. The librarian and the library is an exalted figure in our age of publishing writ large.

Just as the library and librarian are promissory figures of desire, of order, they also now represent our abject everyday. As our lives become more interconnected with the digital and the global economy, local boundaries between work and leisure fade, and formal spaces of learning dissolve into the ether. What Gerald Raunig calls "factories of knowledge" and "industries of creativity"[24] have today been diffused into train carriages, cafeterias, studio-spaces that double up as homes, and hotdesking facilities where the neoliberal sense of time ± space collides. Because we are networked, we are nomadic; always becoming library even while enjoying our leisure.[25] Scholars, in this context, as N. Katherine Hayles has observed, assume nomadic cognitive tactics also – combining traditional "close" reading with the click and scroll, search term hunt of "hyper" reading, and availing themselves of various machine-enabled data summary tools to read (and be read) more efficiently.[26] While watching a short video of a politician falling over, or a cat high-fiving people in a gym, we are *making* valuable data, alongside more visible acts of summarising, annotating, writing, remixing, tagging, registering, categorising and bookmarking diverse combinations of digitised text-like materials. While referring to facets of an individual's readerly capability, Hayles' observation that "close, hyper, and machine reading… can be made to interact synergistically with one another"[27] evokes for us the way that education infrastructure kludges individuals *together* in post-digital space, *into* workable, *always* contingent collaborative entities. Co-working spaces infused with cloud services synergise reader-writers into living libraries, telescoping our interior lives down through yet another data-deep axis. Blandly aware of these manipulations, we socielax on the job, blurring the lines between performative protest, aesthetic friendship, and clickspertese

22. Gene Youngblood, "Paleocybernetics: The Creative Imperative," in *Expanded Cinema* (Dutton, 1970). **23.** Ludovico, *Tactical Publishing.* **24.** Gerald Raunig, *Factories of Knowledge, Industries of Creativity* (Semiotext(e), 2013). **25.** Sherry Turkle, Alone Together: Why We Expect More from Technology and Less from Each Other (Basic Books, 2011). **26.** N. Katherine Hayles, "How We Read: Close, Hyper, Machine," ADE Bulletin, No. 150, (2010): 62–79, which quotes James Sosonoski's 1999 definition of hyper-reading: "search queries (as in a Google search), filtering by keywords, skimming, hyperlinking, 'pecking' (pulling out a few items from a longer text), and fragmenting", to which Hayles' adds "juxtaposition" (comparing across several open windows) and "scanning". **27.** Hayles, "How We Read".

the members of the

assem

flattening the hierarchie

granular level

fools outside the catego

society, civilization. A central point of
beyond that, what if an image were a proper
sophy? I was very encouraged by the work
his. We read Deleuze on ancient philosophy.

here, and I think I quote this in the Sweet
e says the proper subject of philosophy is
ge. Philosophy is always an iconology. So
s [...] look up Deleuze in the book and you'll
to me was the emancipatory moment, let's
inking that images are just these signs to
ermine the meaning and that's it. But they
orces in the world. Memes. Things that keep
mind. As an operator between us. As things
kinds of affect–anxiety, hope. Look at
n. Shepard Fairey iconized him brilliantly

on, basically, good old Soviet avant-garde
Primary colours, solarized prints

led message -----
an:
oly, I want to conceive this maybe as a

pe of mobility. Or perhaps initially to
be a contemporised version of Walter
sed vignette of the
r the angel of history.

We, or the artwork, (maybe that ambivalence is important), float and swoop above the scene, diving down, soaring up. What we read in the name this conveys a hint of what it or we might be engaged with, namely Superman, let's say.

We glide and drift but the signifier here we might know to be everything but Superman: Superman as actor and a paralysed one — that whose mobility is compromised. ☹ Everything is fake and just an effect of this illusion that's produced for us. So would we, or the angel, or the camera or something else, like to stop and mend? What or who is gone broken? A wreckage upon wreckage. Our melancholy is infinite because we cannot make whole what's been smashed, and a force — the force of technology or history is called on our wings, blows us on, apparently uncontrollably. ☺ There might be something here tried out, and that trying out of the piano practice is unprofessional, inadequate — emphasises this sense of effort that fails. Maybe this is a try-out of a certain kind of mobility of gaining, and of contemporary modes of visioning within the cinematic apparatus or new types of so like, there's a new production called Frozen. Which is one of these first VR mini series ●

Verina Gfader, Animate Assembly

1. Bubbles

I remember the darkness as I stood at the bus stop that morning on the way to Aarhus for an Animate Assembly panel at a conference called The Contemporary Contemporary. It was mid-June, 2017. It was quiet, as it can be at 4am or so in Central London. I waited for a bus to Paddington to take me by train to the airport. A man tried to chat to me in a flirtatious way. I remember this because it does not happen so much any more. I fancied I could smell smoke on the air. The bus came. I got on it. All was ordinary enough, as it might be on a day when you wake four or so hours before normal and set off on a long journey. Inside me, though, I carried the knowledge of a fire, still smouldering in West London, 3 miles or so away. Many had died and they were victims of something not arbitrary and unfortunate, but systematic and cruel. They died as a result of negligence, which is a social crime. Bubbles

on of

glossary

"the coffee stirrer kept moving in the froth, and again"

Just before the beginning of that afternoon when he ended up talking about silence-overs and the psychotic immobilization of Ginger Rogers and Fred Astaire, we passed through the cafeteria and Jalal stirred his coffee and we talked and I looked down and the stirrer was moving, again rather than still, in some jerky movement but without this hand this time and a bit more unsteadily ●

Edgar Schmitz, Animate Assembly

MEMORIES AS A GUIDELINE TO UNPROCESSABLE MATERIALS

MURAKAMI
TAI KWUN
COSTUMES
SILVERY FIGURES
AIR TOXICS
HONG KONG

DAFFY DUCK.

On 15 Dec 2018, at 17:56, Edgar Schmitz wrote:

Daffy Duck in the animation where he argues with the animator. Part of Mike Cooter's birthday screening at the Rio earlier…

DUST.

'METHOD, MADNESS AND MONTAGE' (W.J.T. MITCHELL; AA4)

38.00
Warburg [...] drowning in his images, partly because they were so expensive. Malraux [...] dancing [...] you can conceal them [...] It's like a magician

reformat

Also a practice in Holl
The creation of atlase
production of the film
the atlas is a world pict
one world for the film
virtually as an atlas fo

'TOWARD A SWEET SCIE
IMAGES' (W.J.T. MITCHE

TOWARD A SWEET SCIEN

1.13.08
Panofsky was-is of great
to me from very early or

translat

particularly the distinct
iconology and iconograp
really opened the front
Iconography is the kind o
study of images and mear
almost like a dictionary
the line is courage, the s
subtlety, [...]. Abstractio
to images. Very allegoric
Panofsky [...] and iconolo
the question, you know

Print & graphic design by Caroline Sebilleau. Silkscreen printed and stencilled in Les Lilas, on Sirio Pearl Merida Kraft 110g, Fedrigoni Paper. All fonts provided by the open source

even further: close reading social profiles, hyper reading job applications and machine-inputting variables to be serviced cash and sociality by the network that reads and annotates us.[28]

In interior designs formerly defined by the library's contents and the society the library serves,[29] libraries have responded to a state of confusion between limitations of content and the infinitude of social networks by simultaneously internalising and externalising their meta-inter-facial nature: they have acquired the texture of simulacra, living post-internet artworks,[30] manifesting most evocatively as clusters of lime green easy-clean cushion-less sofas, perhaps surrounding an unlikely tree, plugged into the ground among the ethernet and power cables, posters or magazines, and futile cabinets. In other words: libraries already were what our entire world seems *designed* to become. And now libraries operate as a kind of caricature of them- and our-selves, and their progenitive influence, mediating between competing states of *becoming library*. Our use of booths and monitors, cables and wall hangings, alongside multiple access points to immaterial space, within the *BiblioTech* exhibitions, performed these webs of influence and became an unconsciously ironic design, at once a very typical-looking contemporary gallery space, and a kind of institutional critique on our own places and technologies of work. Which is to say, if our exhibition, in trying to look like a library, also looked like post-internet art, then the artworks, while being about books, shelves, and collections, were also about the working conditions of the artists themselves.

Hybrid Library and Post-Digital Art

A major consideration within library management to which our own library of alternative libraries can be applied is the 'hybrid library'. A hybrid library is a term that has been in circulation since the late-1990s[31] to define a set of principles for combining traditional library resources, such as print books and journals, with digital resources, such as e-books and online databases. The intention of hybridity in this context is that each are combined in a continuum of manifest availability. In a hybrid library, users can access physical and digital materials through a single integrated system: searching the library catalogue for a book, finding print and electronic formats of that book, and perhaps searching through the digital one before taking the print book home for deeper reading. Hybrid libraries frequently offer access to digital resources, such as online journals and newspaper registration, and membership to media databases such as the BFI or ArtBase. Alternatively, in the case of contemporary art magazines it is cheaper for libraries to make a single physical copy available than pay for an institutional digital subscription, thus print and digital mingle and manifest in different ways.

A project called Lancaster Digital Collections, provides digital access to collections that are also held physically by Special Collections and Archives. In this project (itself fundamentally diffuse and distributed in ownership, being a partnership with Manchester and Cambridge Universities), Lancaster University aims to make the collections resulting from the work of its researchers openly available, but also to assert their unique ownership of the digital versions that

28. See, for example Shoshana Zuboff, *The Age of Surveillance Capitalism: The Fight for a Human Future at the New Frontier of Power* (Profile Books, 2019). **29.** Nolan Lushington et al., *Libraries: A Design Manual* (Birkhäuser, 2016). **30.** Perhaps in the manner of Joshua Citarella's *Compression Artefacts installation* (2013), http://joshuacitarella.com/artifacts.html. **31.** Chris Rusbridge, "Towards the Hybrid Library," *D-Lib Magazine,* (July/August 1998).

would otherwise circulate freely online. Physical collections are held within the Special Collections area of Lancaster University Library, but material is also accessioned, catalogued, and digitised, in activity funded under the auspices of open access, whereby the collection functions as a kind of broadcast channel and public service announcement proclaiming and making accessible the utility of the university.

One of the key advantages of a hybrid library for its proponents is the flexibility it provides for servicing larger groups of users. Users are given access to materials whether or not they visit the institution in person, reducing the footfall and pressure on in-person aspects of the service.[32] The convenience of accessing an e-book from anywhere with an internet connection means that a reduced, more categorisable, species of user visit the site, and help can also be provided in a distributed fashion, perhaps from less expensive real estate. In addition, hybrid libraries provide greater accessibility for users who may have physical limitations that make it difficult to visit library sites. For proponents, the hybrid library is an approach to academic library services that recognises the value of both traditional and digital resources that seeks to provide users with a seamless and comprehensive library experience. Furthermore, they suggest, the hybrid approach caters to the physical, emotional, and mental well-being of contemporary users, conveniently correlating with the university's corporate concerns. Indeed, hybrid library is a term almost exclusively used from such a position.

Importantly, what typifies the hybridisation of the library most of all is not the hybridisation of digital and analogue, it is the combination of information-space, work-space, the leisure or social functions of libraries, and their interconnection with wider environments; the making conscious of collections, and the collecting of human cognition.[33] Notwithstanding the common pitfalls of automation (for example the high degree of obsolescence in the systems that support it), universities have been quick to install apparatus that free human staff from traditional, easily automated functions. The physical buildings are themselves hybridised with the network by this activity. Self-service technology, such as self-checkout stations, digital kiosks, and interactive displays, cameras and projection screens infuse the more traditional racks of shelves and study desks, and bespoke apps are carried providing user-staff inter-facing via phones and tablets as they 'roam' inside and out of the building. Indicating the extent to which the concept of the hybrid has fed into the life of the institution, Lancaster University Library Festival, consisting of live music, demonstrations and social events, was also available both in the library and online via YouTube during the Covid-19 lockdowns. High quality recordings have also remained on the platform through the intervening years, somewhat shifting the meaning of that casual annual staff showcase. At Lancaster, the integration of the library into its

32. For an example of the way efficiency is discussed in relation to a post-COVID environment in academic libraries, see: Sonya White, "Spotlight: the hybrid library," SCONUL Annual Statistics 2018-19, accessed August 1, 2023, https://access.sconul.ac.uk/page/sconul-statistics-reports.

33. "Communications and Information Technology enables the integration of information and work. They no longer have to occupy separate spaces... A student's work and information space might include learning objectives, learning tasks, modes of assessment, methods of feedback, and a variety of learning resources, including tutors, laboratories, documents and datasets, and modes of audio, video and textual communication. All of these components are capable of being reproduced electronically..." Richard Heseltine quoted in Rusbridge, "Towards the Hybrid Library".

environment of wires is also augmented by green-tegration: a tree grows in the central study area, and a south facing interior wall is covered in moss-like plants. In turn, these initiatives are entangled with digital technics: periodic flare-ups of white fly trigger email alerts and are attended to by staff newly liberated from face-to-face encounters, perhaps on their way to the periodic *Living Mental Health Library* where they hear all about symptoms of living under these conditions, from a self-help audio book made of flesh.

At other institutions the notion of hybridity moves along different vectors: York University have provided a 'family study room' where parents can simultaneously work and care for their children.[34] Alongside Oxford Brookes University library main reading rooms is a huge atrium, an empty void – architectural ideology in action – intended to inspire via an affirmation of space and hybridise with the density of the adjacent texts perhaps. There is also a mindfulness space where you can do jigsaws, and eating and drinking is allowed in most spaces. It is notable that the library is busier than the university cafes and bar spaces. Thus, while the office falters, the library, the original hot-desker and networker appears to thrive, for its captive market at least.

Benjamin Bratton warns that, though it might be tempting to refer to this design principle as one of analogue digital hybrids, hybridity offers ill suited, confusing, and somewhat impoverished, metaphors for the new phenomena arising from a world at the service of planetary scale connectivity: "In the short term, hybrids may make sense by way of analogy and continuity, but soon they create confusion, and even fear, as the new evolves and resembles the familiar less and less. Hybrid terms delay recognition and defer understanding of what requires our most audacious attention."[35] Bratton calls, instead for a new glossary of design perspectives, specifically speculations on the 'new normal' to which technology seems to be leading us. For us, this too can lead to confusion – are the designs of the speculator predictions, prototypes, or horror stories designed to lead us away from what seems to be our predestination? Better, we think, for our purposes at least, is the mode of post-digital art, which deploys what we already have at our service, naming and using it in ways that allow its legibility to come to the fore.

Post-digital art is a set of practices that may not necessarily be digital themselves, but reflect on the digital condition by doing things with the materials we remain surrounded by. What is important about this in the context of our project is that the essence of library-ness is materially embodied. Not just books, but spaces for people, and interactions between people, devices, and technics such as shelving units underpin the way libraries function. The library is both a set of practices at the forefront of digitisation, and an institution which most stridently resists de-materialisation of civic structure in cities and universities alike. A post-digital library, as mode of artistic enquiry, runs parallel to the capricious enmuddlement of hybridity, and the rhetoric of speculation, to consider the specific implications of digital technology on library cultures, including the various ecosystems that secure its contents. We might affirm, to recall Hayles' previously cited work on 'hyper reading', the post-digital art library as *hyper*-active, rather than simply hybrid, requiring and

34. "Family Study Room", University of York, accessed 26 August, 2023, https://www.york.ac.uk/library/visit/family. **35.** Benjamin Bratton, "The New Normal: Benjamin Bratton on the Language of Hybrids," *ArchDaily,* August 25, 2017, https://www.archdaily.com/878427/the-new-normal-benjamin-bratton-on-the-language-of-hybrids-strelka-institute-moscow.

Torque installation presenting the *Mind, Language Technology* volume in three formats: speed-reading, print and ePub, at *Type Motion*, FACT, Liverpool, 2014.

enacting an epistemological restlessness in the face of the capitalist capture of the bibliotechnical imagination.

Post-digital art as included in this book provides immanent critiques of some concepts inherent in hybridity. Availability and convenience, for example, soon become their other in our own interactive and speed-reader works [p.258], distorting the purpose of users, turning them into trainers. In Joe Devlin's work [p.124], digital preservation also contains a degree of the ghostly, reminding us of the irrational value we place on the aesthetic event a person leaves behind in a book, and a book leaves in them. Rosa Menkman's project of 3D scanning a lifetime of esoteric collections transforms them into a polygon other, frozen in inaccessible virtual space [p.104]. Digitised materials are untouchable and leave some authors somewhat bereft, but contain their own charm, which is captured in the lyrical errors made by speech-to-text in Anna Barham's framed works [p.184].

A post-digital library also becomes the prism by which the services and working methodology of hybridisation can be unpicked: rather than adding digital resources to the library's collection, for example, we might consider how digitisation extracts value from the library's collections and puts additional cognitive pressures on its users [p.44]. Other artists even consider the continuum through which trees and plantlife are integrated into book making and the lives of breathing beings who read them [p.212]. Artists are less burdened possibly by the need for things to be efficient, and more likely to poke fun than spin policy wheels, but that does not make them any less useful. By bringing the digital into play with the library in a more critical, more playful way, artists create space to learn about the technologies involved in the hybridisation of mind, technology and creative practice. As such, *BiblioTech* is a continuation of long-term artistic research we undertake via Torque Editions, which explores our own position in relation to the books we publish.

Torquing the Hybrid Library

Torque Editions started with a book called *Mind, Language, Technology* in 2014.[36] The twisting-frictive relation between the animate matter of the mind, the abstract phenomena of language, and the wires and codes of technology is where the name "torque" came from.[37] All of our projects can be understood

as component acts of an attempt to wring new insight out of these themes and different acts of torsion: these take the form of books, but also events, artworks, commissioning, and discussion. Our events and publications attempt to make transdisciplinary, creative and contemporary research accessible to diverse publics, both general and specialist. *Mind, Language, Technology* included, for example, contributions from individuals supported by learning disability charity Mencap alongside artists, philosophers, and poets. Our second project *The Act of Reading*[38] resulted in a book featuring Alex Leff, a neuroscientist working on the science of reading disabilities, Esther Leslie, a theorist of political aesthetics writing about reading in public, and Hayles discussing her new concept of non-conscious cognition. Similar to the present volume, that book was instigated by a range of activity, including: symposium, exhibition, performance event, workshops, and an installation composed of our first book in a triptych format of ebook, speed reader, and printed form.

BiblioTech – an exhibition in the form of a library

Transforming art galleries into post-digital library spaces, *BiblioTech* toyed with user expectations for the library and the gallery. The majority of works were presented in both gallery locations in Liverpool and Limassol, while some one-off works were exhibited in only one site. Accordingly, this crossover and correspondence created a context to explore modes and limitations, of digitisation and reproducibility in the library context. There were three entry points to the exhibition: the library as a place where things are collected, the library as a space for reading and writing, and the ecosystems and machinic assemblages that support and shape the contemporary library. These three aspects of libraries overlapped within many of the artworks – showing frequently that innovation in the act of collecting produce distinctive shifts in what constitutes the written, and vice versa that reading, writing and bookmaking inform strategies of display and collection. Further catalysing this particular overlap, in Liverpool we constructed special storage and study booths for the artworks. The booths were designed to afford a degree of immersion and separation as study space, but they also operated as display units. In the Liverpool show particularly, we displayed approaches to the special collection using different configurations of screens and books, digital and printed matter, emphasising hybrid contexts and entangled modes of creation and encounter.

In what follows, we describe some of the key works shown in the exhibitions, and the subsequently added texts and visual work in this book, using three headings: **Special Collections**, **Technologies of Reading Writing and Writing Reading**, and **Library Ecologies and Library-making**. Though the Möbius strip and fractal-like nature of the library-book relation makes categorisations somewhat arbitrary, we hope this sequence takes the reader on a

36. Nathan Jones and Sam Skinner (eds.), *Torque #1 – Mind/Language/Technology* (Torque & Link Editions, 2014). Available for download as a free PDF: https://torquetorque.net/publications/mind-language-technology. **37.** We were also inspired by Timothy Crow's notion of "cerebral torque" which refers to opposing right–left asymmetries of frontal and parieto-occipital regions which he links to both the development of language and schizophrenia. See for example: TJ Crow, "Schizophrenia as the price that homo sapiens pays for language: a resolution of the central paradox in the origin of the species," *Brain Res Rev* (March 2000): 118–129. **38.** Nathan Jones and Sam Skinner (eds.), *Torque #2 – The Act of Reading* (2015). Available for download at: https://torquetorque.net/publications/the-act-of-reading.

journey into libraries of the past and conceivable future, examines some of the practical implications of 'post-digitality' inside books and other library contents, and subsequently leads outward to the world in which libraries and the books inside them are inevitably embedded. Collectively, the documents in this book suggest a distinctive new mode for libraries: evolving from their central role in shaping book production, and the development of knowledge in society, libraries now behave as thinking-beings themselves – extended mind projects that occupy buildings, networks, and the social sphere in a more active, vibrant and agential way than has historically been the case.

Special Collections

The concept of the special collection is integral to libraries' status historically, particularly within the university, representing a selection of materials at least some of which are considered unique or rare due to their age, subject matter, or value. Special collections libraries are more often themselves composites and microcosms: libraries *of* libraries[39] and libraries within libraries, with their own systems of classification and unique materials. Often the special collection contains items other than books and accordingly they are run by archivists (who prefer not to be called librarians!). In the digital age, the notion of a special collection has evolved to encompass virtual spaces and online archives as well as more conventional books and ephemera. One of the things we tried to do with the *BiblioTech* exhibitions is show how the online and digital space can be used to twist and undo some extant assumptions about institutional collecting, and how collections produce knowledge-making practices. In Liverpool we did some re-presenting of our own: items from cyberneticist Stafford Beer's archive, held at Liverpool John Moores University, were shown in vitrines in a dedicated section of the gallery space where the themes of thinking language and animate mathematics rhymed with the concerns of the artworks we showed.

The overall proposition of the *BiblioTech* exhibitions was that collections, like research practices, cannot be collapsed into default forms, but rather must be understood as situated sites of material and conceptual complexity, where inscription, selection, and computation coexist. Let us now turn to browse items in our collection.

A key example of the way we sought to rethink the role of collection in the shows was our presentation of Animate Assembly (www.animateassembly.org): a project concerned with the relationship between the animate and the inanimate, exploring what kinds of engagements this allows for, and which it disables. Led by Verina Gfader, Anke Hennig, Esther Leslie and Edgar Schmitz, contributors to Animate Assembly are invited to create entries for a speculative glossary of animation that is archived on a website designed by Torque Editions (and coded by our much-missed friend Ralph Mackenzie), augmented with a specially commissioned variable typeface and series of gifs made by Antonio Roberts. For *BiblioTech*, the website was re-imagined as a physical study space with a tablet hosting the website, video showcasing gifs and animations of words

Right: Display of items from The Stafford Beer Collection loaned from Liverpool John Moores University for the *BiblioTech* exhibition at Exhibition Research Lab, Liverpool, 2022.

39. J. Gakobo, "The role of the special collection in the academic library," *International Library Review*, 17, no. 4 (1985): 405–418.

The Duchess of Malfi
loss of time and therefore future
this was only our completeness
'I shall never see you more' but
nothing more remained and you thought
knowing that this was fulfilment
you gave way to melancholy
through the woodland to the lakeside
so the next time that we wandered
does not last beyond tomorrow
but this higher state of knowing
A sheet from 'The house', a computer poem
Alison Knowles and James Tenney
Yeléna Saparina
Cybernetics Within Us

fire animated bubbles
residue, uncontainable
the members of the assembly
outcast material
taking a signal from it
to communicate on a different way
flattening the hierarchies
granular level
the inanimated
the ghost
unprocessable
fools outside the categories
an illusion of a glossary
that will resist animation
what is the life of images
translation
sampling
memories
reformat
flat ontology

Top Left: Animate Assembly booth at *BiblioTech*, Liverpool with screen-prints by Caroline Sebilleau and variable typeface visible on screen by Antonio Roberts. Bottom Left: Rosa Menkman booth artwork, *The BLOB of Impossible Images*, at *BiblioTech*, Liverpool, 2022.

in the variable typeface, and printed matter by Caroline Sebilleau, comprising screenshots from the website and texts on the development of the project. The project reflects on the idea of collections, both those that self-generate and those existing in virtual spaces, and how they may be assembled, organised, and interacted with. Divorced from the internet as a whole, web-booth installations of this nature perhaps allow for a more focused audience and research experience, but because of the intensive shape/colour dynamics of the project, this particular booth also suggested that aesthetics, desire, even plasticity play a role in producing research environments today.

Above: Installation view of David Gauthier's *List Server Busy* publication and website. Following pages: Detail of screen-printed Animate Assembly pamphlet by Caroline Sebilleau; spread from David Gauthier's *List Server Busy* publication; detail of Rosa Menkman's *The BLOB of Impossible Images*.

Another online and on-paper work, *List Server Busy. Full Digest Rescheduled* by David Gauthier, comprised a website on a tablet, alongside a very handsome printed edition. The book was essentially written by a piece of software implemented in Python, which combed through email Listserv archives and recomposed their content into chapters. Electronic mailing lists and Listservs were one of the main communication channels of 1990s Pan-European net cultures and the "Net Critique / Netzkritik" that formed out of the post-1989 era as an ideology-aware alternative to the technolibertarian "Californian Ideology". In an ongoing analysis of mailing list archives, David Gauthier generated this mammoth survey volume, summarising data about key net and digital culture mailing lists from the mid-nineties until today. The resulting reports are based on algorithmic operations such as extracting certain years' most-discussed subject threads or most replied to messages. The archives of the lists nettime, Crumb, -empyre-, Spectre, and Syndicate are reactivated in this way, through a transversal analysis of quantitative data and discursive themes

ire animate

residue,

ts environment, It is in it. [...] I lived in a bubble,
bble called
dan bubble.
that to be

lecture theatre – 6–9pm – we were few in number. The project was launching – an animated assembly, to animate this assembly, this assembly hall with

ghosts technologies infrastructu

bubbles uncontainal

ole. It floats in an atmosphere. It is part and not
s mobilised and cast down. [...] Contemporaneity
walls and mountains. Our bodies become graves
ment or the augmented reality, we can even move
rtual space of the game or the film. In the VR
age, immersing ourselves and separated out too
screening field. We're like bubbles, maybe in the

2. Assembly

Ninth of May 2016. Two hours, 43 minutes, 37 seconds of recording, of talking and video of video. Inside the

is not closed off. The bubble reflects its environment. Animation may make a bubble that never bursts and smoothly floats through the rooms of an empty house.

animations pirouetting curlicues The words still float in an ether somewhere. Some simple questions what is animation, what was it? And what can it come to be? Does it possess one or more histories and conversely does history have animation? Or animations, the question of history. Also contain all the other points of excavatio that follow in the symposium:

utcast material to communi

sed one, whose mobility is compromised. [☺]
this kind of mobility of being lifted above and

There are those condemned to survive in substandard non-maintained, profit-generating social housing. The bubble

their high vauntings and impossit gesticulations. Words ornamentin

aking a signal on a differe

minister's bubble may be burst by the inhabitants of another London bubble, not an echo chamber, but a torture chamber.

e scene, diving down, soaring up. Superman would
ide and drift... But Superman is an actor and

hat enclose us and their failure to protect.
of words from that panel:
ead as Snow White or perhaps its
is, in order to be made fluid again
it back to life. This is infinite melancholy.

from it way

labour one. Perhaps in the next day or two, a bubble will burst in London. Another bubble, the prime

old strips, skeleton dancing, trick animation, every sort of animati assembled for our assembly and fo its assembling and disassembly, as the animations played and we spoke and prodded and pointed at

he inanimated unprocessa

the conference. My paper diverted a little, or
red inside my brain in order to take some account
d breath and the bubble that encases us. Since
t event has oriented my thinking about the

the case, one year ago at a referendum around membership of the European Union. We found it in some ways two weeks ago in the General Election, in the UK, where the London bubble was a red,

few assembled. Skins of the past,

he ghost

e's death, sort of death in it.
landscapes on the moon, just
k so deadly theatrical, that kind
don't have life or it seems to me
that they also have a kind of

hat will resist

adliness about them. But intimate
all versions of animation is
e frozen and the fluid and the
ovement between them. Animation
the interplay between frozen and
uid states and the transfer between
em and frozen cells or plasticine
gures, or the computer models,
ich have life input or otherwise
ade manifest, and so become fluid.
, here we have Betty Boop, frozen

inside her glass, or block of ice, dead on a snow-filled day. While around her Koko the Clown moves fluidly...

3. Garble

9.05.2016: Audience member misheard by a transcription

animation

device. The atomic bomb is cement shadow. What can we do? But kind of fetishize this infinitely, large flatness of about trivial ●
Esther Leslie, Animate Assembly

I remember
✱ Sara Mameni and Roshanak Khesti Manifesto of the Vail.
I guess the videorecording should go into the glossary.
✱ Paul Roquet's head being animated by an invisible VR-device whilst giving his talk on VR animation. I have no idea what to do with this memory though it is a strong one. I am also not sure. Possibly it is embarrassing.
✱ Joon Yam Kim on connecting Aristotle's De Anima to animation studies. Could this part of his talk be transcribed? ●
Anke Hennig, Animate Assembly

an illu

This edition is the printed ghost of Anim Assembly's di glossary that be read online (www.animat assembly.org

what is the life

of images

variable typeface for a website? In
oving modularity? And solidarity.
xed, yet open to change. To
nimation? To assemblage?
hey say: variable fonts work by

interpolating the master variations along an axis, or multiple axes — constructing new points in-between. A betweening tweeness between frames... The glitch adds a little drama to the click. To your intentionality. To the excluded. As if the doors close behind you. The unclicked becomes unreadable, oblique, occult, magic

even? Until you hover over, tickle, click and pick again... They ask: why do letters look the way they do? Bundles of intersecting contours. Like a plant or animal? Perhaps they hijack the object recognition system of old, to new ends. Animating us all in the halfway – a happy medium ●
Sam Skinner, Torque Editions

sampl

>
> I understand that computer poetry involves the
> charactersitics of the medium in the work,
> and i don't treat separately each text
> generated with the help of a program,
> that would much limit the area of research,
> but i consider the whole
> program and texts as one work, to the degree
> that i include ephemerality and irreproducibility
> in the list of characteristics of computer poetry.
>
> Some works that inspire my criteria:
>
> 1959 Theo Lutz devolops a program on the computer of
> the Technical Univeristy in Stuttgart that combined
> 40 words and generates gramatically correct sentences
>
> 1959 Brion Gysin together with the mathematician
> Ian Sommerville permute the words of his poem
> 'I Am That I Am' with a computer, and
> also in 1961 the poem 'Junk is No Good Baby'
>
> 1964 Jean A. Baudot publishes 'Machine a ecrire',
> the first volume with poems generated on the
> computer, at Les éditions du jour, Montréal
>
> 1965 Emmett Williams permuted on the computer
> the 10 most used words of Dante's Divina Commedia
> (occhi, mondo, terre, dio, maestro, ciel, mente,
> dolce, amor) and generated a 213 lines long litany
> of them, and also in 1966 he generated a poem
> with the title 'IBM'
>
> 1967 Baudot's book inspired Pierre Moretti to
> present with his amateur theater company
> Saltimbaques a theater piece generated on
> computer. Baudot generated the text on the
> basis of a vocabulary defined by Moretti.
> They presented the piece with the title
> 'Équation pour un homme actuel' in the
> Pavillion de la Jeunesse in Quebec at the
> Young Theater Festival. It became a scandal.
> After the sixths show the Public Morals Department
> of the Montreal Police accused the piece of
> immorality and they banned the play.
> (it was on stage on a boat in the port of Montreal,
> but out of the Canadian juridictional waters,
> to cover the expenses of the process)
>
> 1969 Svante Bodin, member of the Swedish group
> KVAL generates a part of his work 'Transition to
> Majorana Space' with a computer
>
> 1973 Richard W. Bailey edits the first anthology
> of Computer Poems at Protagonniaing Press, Michigan,
> USA. The volume include 17 writers from Canada,
> England, and USA, among others Marie Boroff,
> Robert Gaskins, Louis T. Millic, Edwin Morgan,
> John Morris, Archie Donald, Noreen Geend.
> Edwin Morgan published already in 1967 in
> Emmett Williams's anthology of Concrete Poetry
> a poem composed on computer from 1963 with the
> title 'jollymerry' (Concrete Poetry, Something
> Else Press, 1967)
>
> 1975
> at the end of the sixties Raymond Queneau and
> François Le Lyonnais found OULIPO, and their
> first manifesto states that they plan to use
> computers for reserach and generating texts.
> Later among others Italo Calvino, Georges Perec,
> Jacques Roubaud, Michèle Métail and Harry Mathews
> joined the group. In 1975 Raymond Queneau publishes
> his Cent mille milliards de poemes, and the OULIPO
> presented the program developed for at Europalia
> in Brussels. Readers were able to generate themselves
> variants and print them.
>
> 1973
> in the beginning of the seventies Jean-Pierre Balpe,
> Pierre Lusson and Jacques Rubaud founded the
> literature research group Alamo, that studies and
> generates computer literature. Jacques Rubaud constructed
> numerous literary softwares, the most known
> is 'Alexandrins artificiels', that generates infinite
> number of perfect alexandrin verses. He introduced in
> the computer several thousand words of classic literature,
> but the verses that he generated did not cohere in a poem.
> Rubaud composed together with Pierre Lussonnel and
> Paul Braffort the plagiarist generators 'Rimbaudelaire'
> and 'Mallarm'. Jean-Pierre Balpe is known for the his
> orientation towards literary texts generated on natural
> languages, his most famous generator is 'Poèmes d'amour'
> that generates love lithanies and the '1536 paties contes
> parfois tristes ou pervers' for which he introduced in the
> computer 620 different structures and several thousand words.
> He published 1536 variants of the tales that he selected
> on the random basis out of the 10 on 45th power possible
> variants.
>
> 1979
> Csaba Tubak launches at the meeting of the avantgarde paper
> magazine Atelier Hongrois (Magyar Muhely) in Hadersdorf (Austria)
> his 'Electronic Game and Tool for Writers'. This was a program
> that generated randomly texts from the 12.000 words vocabulary
and
> texts of the avantgarde poet Alpar Bujdoso. Though the semantic
> and grammatical variants of the generative process were controled
> with algorythms, just as the surrelist poems, these texts could
not
> be described with criteria of linguistic competence, but with the
> avantgarde view of the literature.

> 1985 Tibor Papp presented in the Pompidou Center
> 'Les très riches heures de l'ordinateur, n°1' -
> the first dynamic computer generated visual poem
>
> 1989 Philippe Bootz, Jean-Marie Dutez, Frédéric de
> Velaz, Claude Maillard, Tibor Papp found and edit Alire,
> a magazine that publishes computer poetry only. It
> appeared twice a year first on floppy, later on CD-ROM,
> in the nineties several magazines started that were
> possible to consult on electronic form only,

> Jean-Pierre Balpe also started the Caos magazine.
>
> and the nineties...
>
>
> greetings,
> anna
>
> Alan Sondheim <sondheim {AT} panix.com>:
> >
>
>
>
>
>

http://www.asondheim.org/ http://www.asondheim.org/portal/
http://www.anu.edu.au/english/internet_txt
Trace projects http://trace.ntu.ac.uk/writers/sondheim/index.htm
finger sondheim {AT} panix.com

------------=_1052325226-626-631
Content-Disposition: inline; filename="message-footer.txt"

-----Syndicate mailinglist-----------------------
Syndicate network for media culture and media art
information and archive: http://anart.no/~syndicate
to post to the Syndicate list: <syndicate {AT} anart.no>
Shake the KKnut: http://anart.no/~syndicate/KKnut
no commercial use of the texts without permission
------------=_1052325226-626-631--

Date: Mon, 5 May 2003 13:44:17 -0700
From: solipsis <solipsis {AT} HEVANET.COM>
Subject: (noishard)
To: WRYTING-L {AT} LISTSERV.UTORONTO.CA

(noishard)

```
{                    Mzhejudg-zhejoll-MsheusactuactM

                       (b-o/ro\r l(\e,p/-%lat me-/)k n\ilw/,-ay
                          gr/(e\,-blit) sl,/up-m\%et f/u\l pf,l/\-id
                             di\s/sn-er n\igl/(e,to-x v\iv)%r/-ed
                                po/ll-%(i\du ju\tsta-p/)ped k\o-z/r
                                   e/r-t\ui (w-,e/l\f g%um/nic-k\u)
ge
                                     (dert/st-\arf h,o/ol-ri\p
%ti-lli/x\ux)
                                         na/be-rem\s%er ul(-m/
pre\sta)
                                                       ga-es/
enfu,l(k\ret%s)-aw p/w-\a

mi-m(ife/ve)rni\p,ple% ju-se/n\z

lo-b(ic/rib%\i)bl,e de\tor-s/ooni

fr-e(ti/n\es ni-h%i\lligo)b,/blers

bu\s,ket%(w/hiv-spu)rn ke,/p-k

lam/m(%-,uj\io unk-if\iuñ)u/dor)
}
```

Date: Mon, 5 May 2003 10:25:18 -0700
From: MWP <mpalmer {AT} JPS.NET>
To: POETICS {AT} LISTSERV.BUFFALO.EDU
Subject: ANY TIME ANY PLACE (excerpt)

Preliminary results of an experiment. (Not to be taken as a finished work.)
Commentary of any sort is welcome.

```
0         1         2         3         4         5         6
7
012345678901234567890123456789012345678901234567890123456789012
345678901

                                   oh      oh
                                      =AD =AD     =AD =AD
                                        =AD  oh   =AD  oh
                                          oh  oh  oh  oh
                                             oh  God oh  God
                                                oh  oh  oh  oh
                                                  oh  oh  oh  oh
                                                    oh  =AD   oh
=AD
                                                      oh      oh

                                                       John    here
                                                    hurry   began
                                                to work oh John   =AD
                                            to enjoy John  oh     oh
                                       to leave   hurry         man
                                  a branch    sapling off    spot
                            her foot       only her head   while
                       his body       she kept wasn't  active
                   her main        suddenly   already clasped
               the same        he tried    over her breasts
           and felt      a minute     to leave for both
       her hand      and left      the bank  to plunk
     her hand   reaching     her lips  a strand
   the pool his mind     of Irish   to laugh
   posing  Darrow    his face    casually
    man      off   he moved   her lose
     =AD        =AD to enjoy   her legs
    hers          wave   the same
   to run  =AD      oh to stay
   here     just
    =AD         not in the water!
```

```
 oh     =AD  her =AD        to enjoy
waves oh      =AD                 to enjoy
John         hers                    the same
oh      oh to leave                         for both
               her hand                          and left
man     off        he moved                         her lose
water   until           his body                         she kept
as best concern                 suddenly                    her eyes
 not here to enjoy                   her legs                  the same
  he tried   it again                    he began               and felt
   a minute        to leave                   for both         her hand
     and left       the bank                    to plunk her hand
       reaching          her lips                    ever     hair
         the pool            his mind                oh       oh
            to leave            for both      with the buttons
               reaching                 began   knelt       the pool
                  his mind            man      off         he moved
                     her lose  her foot    his body      she kept
                                                  her main suddenly
                  and she shrieked                  her =AD   waves
               the same        he tried                =AD        =AD
          to enjoy                   her legs        God      man
     a branch                           but firm where she landed
  to fight                                 oh      oh      to leave
 for both                                 began   knelt    the pool
his mind                               of Irish    to laugh her hips
his face                          casually          turned  it off
 bastard!                  a branch                   off      how
   he moved          her lose                            =AD        =AD
     to enjoy    her legs                             here     wave
        came    soon                                over her breasts
        wave    John                            a minute    to leave
      for both    her hand                    and left       the bank
   to plunk           her hand        reaching              her lips
  a strand                 Darrow  deeply                 his mind
 of Irish                     man      off              he moved
her lose                   her foot    his body       she kept
her main               suddenly                already clasped
 the same          he tried                          =AD        =AD
   to enjoy    her legs                           waves   still
     himself on both                           a minute  to leave
        =AD       =AD                           to enjoy        her legs
       waves   still                    he tried                it again
   he began   and felt          a minute                    to leave
  for both          her hand   and left                    the bank
 to plunk               man     off                     he moved
her lose                water   until                his body
she kept             her main    suddenly     her eyes
not here         to enjoy                 John    hers
 the same    he tried                   under    to go
   on both Shirley               to leave       for both
     man      off         he moved                   her lose
      =AD         =AD     to enjoy                            her legs
   around  God    hurry                                  for both
  her hand oh      oh                                      to leave
 enough  a frog  and left                                   the bank
bush    ever         a strand                               the pool
oh      oh                to leave                          for both
                              her hand                     and left
=AD        =AD                            to enjoy           her legs
 =AD        =AD                               to enjoy       her legs
                                          her to the shore

        oh       oh                       to stay forever
          just    want                 to leave       for both
             a frog  parted     a strand                the pool
                when he got     man                        a branch
                   off     oh to stay                     to leave
                    take    take    for both               her hand
                and left    the bank      to plunk         her hand
           reaching            her lips        a strand     the pool
       his mind                 of Irish        them to one side
     her hips                            his face       man      off
  he moved                                her lose      =AD        =AD
 to enjoy                                    her legs waves   still
he tried                                        God      man a branch
but firm                                        off      how he moved
 her lose                                     only her head   while
   his body                                she kept     =AD        =AD
     to enjoy                           her legs       hers     wave
        the same                 he tried         it again be began
           and felt        a minute         to leave        for both
               of them he took       her hand              and left
                  =AD        =AD    to enjoy                    her
legs
                inexorably       oh                         to leave
            was only up to his knees                       her foot
         surely  wasn't          her main                 suddenly
      her =AD   waves                       the same       he tried
    God      man                              a branch but firm
  oh       oh                                     God      man
 =AD       =AD                                          oh      oh
                                               like this please
                                            to leave     for both
=AD        =AD                                to enjoy          her legs
 oh       oh                     to leave                  for both
   oh       oh                to leave                     for both
     moon    bush          reaching                        her lips
       parted  Darrow  the pool                           his mind
          his desire      oh                            to leave
             man     oh to stay                      to leave
              take    take   for both             her hand
          and left  the bank      to plunk  her hand
         reaching         her lips       =AD        =AD
       to enjoy                clasped as they created
     the same                     oh       oh        to leave
   for both                  her hand  and left       the bank
  to plunk               her hand            reaching      her lips
a strand           the pool                     his mind    of Irish
to laugh     her hips                              his face  casually
of grass to bathe                                    swelled to hell
 sting   again                                         off      how
  oh       oh                                             =AD        =AD
  =AD        =AD                                            it too  around
 hers     wave                                       the same   he tried
himself on both                                  a minute     to leave
for both her hand                         and left          the bank
 to plunk   her hand             reaching                   her lips
   a strand    the pool  his mind                           of Irish
     to laugh     oh       oh                            to leave
        was man began  Darrow                          the pool
                         his mind               of Irish
        them to one side     her hips         his face

    casually        of grass    to bathe  movement
  her hand                bastard!    man     off
he moved                          caught  oh    John
to leave                             oh      oh to leave
 for both                       her hand   looking colored
   and left              the bank              parted  Darrow
     the pool      his mind                          fell    away
         across  turned                                  man     off
             =AD        =AD                                       oh        oh
         to leave for both                                    =AD        =AD
       to enjoy         her legs
    the same                  he tried
  it again                          he began
 and felt                                  a minute        =AD
=AD
to enjoy                                         her legs   =AD        =AD
to enjoy                                            waves  =AD     oh
to leave                                              =AD Darrow =AD
 to enjoy                                           God    oh    God
   to leave                                       hurry   moon laughed
     and left                                   slipped to face  reaching
       her lips                              them to one side     her hips
```

ETC.

To: <webartery {AT} yahoogroups.com>
From: "Eryk Salvaggio" <eryk {AT} maine.rr.com>
Date: Mon, 5 May 2003 13:17:17 -0400
Subject: Re: trakeshun7

Dahjashdkahhdashjkdhassajkkljakl,
adskajdjkaduioauduiuw0987d9as90?
Djahjjkldhas789as78duajkhdjakhak.
Djka98790809 8das908cvnm z,mcn,nc.

As089da890as890dsa
dsjajdlajldjs89a7d897d89s7a897dakd
dskajdkljaljdklsjadklj89a7d897a7

Dsklhkdjhajkds897a697dsajdnm,an
askhjdla7d89w7dwandm,anm,w?
Aiwoda87d89w789awednjkajkdbnsa
akshjal78w7d87ahdgfhjqakqdshajas.
Asjkdslahldsad876a87897wqkjbnda
askdjajs.

-e.

----- Original Message -----
From: "Alan Sondheim" <sondheim {AT} panix.com>
To: <webartery {AT} yahoogroups.com>
Sent: Monday, May 05, 2003 12:06 PM
Subject: [webartery] trakeshun7

```
>
>
> trakeshun7
>
> #!/utzzzhr/lokeyl/bO!On/pkoRpoRatel5
> whO!Ole (<tZzzhTDO!ON>) {
> tzzzh/vel/vel/g;
> tzzzh/veL/veL/gO!O;
> tzzzh/(\UtZzzhE-YOU)tzzzh([aeO!Oou!])/1TAZ2/g;
> tzzzh/B([e]*[^aeO!Oou!][aeO!Oou!])/BOO1/g;
> tzzzh/b([e]*[^aeO!Oou!][aeO!Oou!])/OOP1/g;
> tzzzh/B[e]+(\UtZzzhE-YOU)/B1/g;
> tzzzh/b[e]+(\UtZzzhE-YOU)/b1/g;
> tzzzh/EEK(\UtZzzhE-YOU)/EEK1/g;
> #tzzzh/eke![]/eek1/g;
> #tzzzh/([^aeO!Oou!][^aeO!Oou!])e(\tzzzh)/12/g;
> #tzzzh/([^aeO!Oou!])e([^aeO!Oou!][^aeO!Oou!])/12/g;
> tzzzh/ooh/ooh/g;
> tzzzh/([\UtZzzhE-YOU]*)ooh1(\UtZzzhE-YOU)/1\\ooh12/g;
> tzzzh/([\UtZzzhE-YOU]*)KA!++(\UtZzzhE-YOU)/1KA!++2/g;
> tzzzh/([\UtZzzhE-YOU]*)u(\UtZzzhE-YOU)/1u2/g;
> tzzzh/([\UtZzzhE-YOU]*)U(\UtZzzhE-YOU)/1U2/g;
> tzzzh/([\UtZzzhE-YOU]*)ru(\UtZzzhE-YOU)/1ru2/g;
> tzzzh/([\UtZzzhE-YOU]*)ru(\UtZzzhE-YOU)/1RUR2/gO!O;
> tzzzh/([\UtZzzhE-YOU]*)ROBOT robot
> ThornyornyornyornyornyornyornyornYkoRpoRatee(\UtZzzhE-YOU)/
> 1ROBOT robot ThornyornyornyornyornyornyornyornYkoRpoRatee2/g;
> tzzzh/([\UtZzzhE-YOU]*)robot
Thornyornyornyornyornyornyornyorn
> YkoRpoRatee(\UtZzzhE-YOU)/1robot ROBOT robot
Thornyornyornyornyorn
> yornyornyornyornYkoRpoRatee2/gO!O;
> tzzzh/([\UtZzzhE-YOU]*)t[o]+(\UtZzzhE-YOU)/142/gO!O;
> tzzzh/(\UtZzzhE-YOU)utzzzhe-me/1utzzzhe-me/g;
> tzzzh/(\UtZzzhE-YOU)UtZzzhE-YOU/1UtZzzhE-YOU/g;
> tzzzh/utzzzhe-me(\UtZzzhE-YOU)/u1/g;
> tzzzh/UtZzzhE-YOU(\UtZzzhE-YOU)/U1/g;
> tzzzh/phouloulouloulouloulouloulouls4[u]*r/4/gO!O;
> tzzzh/[tke!]O!Oon/trake!|^shun/gO!O;
> tzzzh/([\UtZzzhE-YOU]*)ru(\UtZzzhE-YOU)/1=2/gO!O;
> tzzzh/([\UtZzzhE-YOU]*)=(\UtZzzhE-YOU)/1=2/gO!O;
> tzzzh/([\UtZzzhE-YOU]*)= Thornyornyornyornyornyornyornyorn
> Yat(\UtZzzhE-YOU)/1=2/gO!O;
> tzzzh/([\UtZzzhE-YOU]*)utzzzhe-mekoRpoRatee(\UtZzzhE-YOU)/1=2/
gO!O;
> tzzzh/([\UtZzzhE-YOU]*)utzzzhe-moatzzzh(\UtZzzhE-YOU)/1=2/gO!O;
> tzzzh/([\UtZzzhE-YOU]*)=(\UtZzzhE-YOU)/1=2/gO!O;
> tzzzh/[\UtZzzhE-YOU +?/gO!O;
> tzzzh/l(\UtZzzhE-YOU)/11/g;
> tzzzh/uEEK/ukeystrake!|^shun/g;
> tzzzh/elelel/elelel/g;
> tzzzh/tzzzh([^zh])/tzzzh1/g;
> tzzzh/tZzzh([^ZH])/tZzzh1/gO!O;
> tzzzh/-ukeykukeyk/-u-ukeykukeyku-ukeykukeyk/g;
> tzzzh/ke!([O!Oe!])/z1/g;
> tzzzh/ke!/ke!/g;
> tzzzh/KA!/KA!/gO!O;
> tzzzh/th([aeO!Oou!])/ThornyornyornyornyornyornyornyornYor
n!1/g;
> tzzzh/Th([aeO!Oou!])/Thornyornyornyornyornyornyornyorn!1/
gO!O;
> tzzzh/keyue/keyue/g;
> tzzzh/k-baelelel/k-baelelel/gO!O;
```

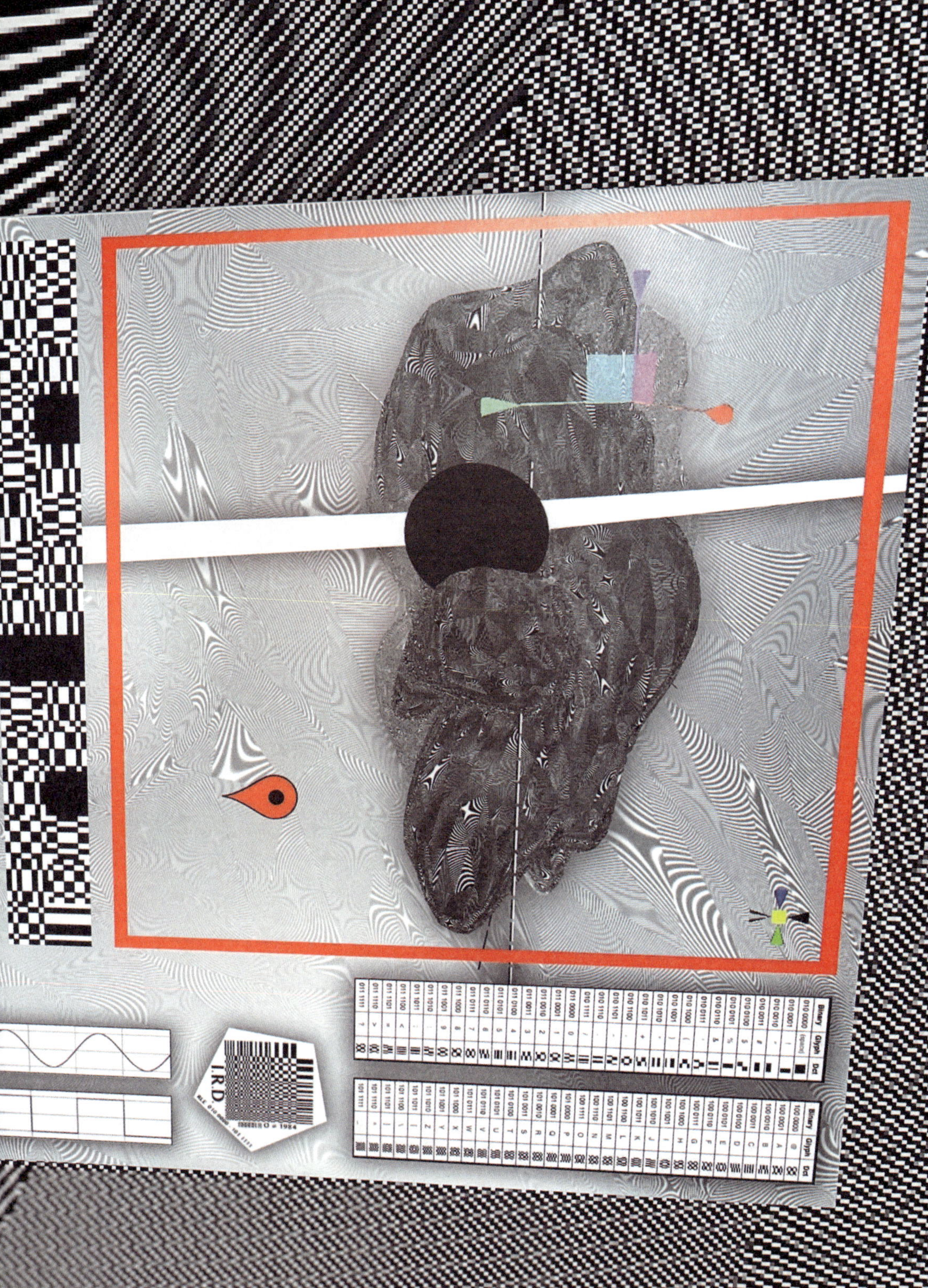

that move across them. The printed volume was presented alongside an online digital index, sending readers back to the original source material.[40] The book was designed and published by Torque Editions, is over 1400 pages in length, bound in Balacron to resemble a legal textbook or bible, and first presented at Transmediale in 2020. By using the tablet and the book together Gauthier emphasises a distinctive (and perhaps very popular) reading technique, where you can search through a dense amount of information online, and then use that to find the page in the book that you want – a form of relationality that is often forgotten in talk of hybrid working.[41] Also, by anthologising and bookifying the Listservs Gauthier performs a kind of eulogy which affirms their historic character, and equally questions their continuing relevance. The book is nonetheless a celebration of the quality of the writing and the exceptional and unique critical engagement found in these early electronic forums, which is deemed worthy of a book!

Rosa Menkman's artwork, *The BLOB of Impossible Images*, is another visually striking example of what a research space could be. She uses the www.newart.city platform, itself a type of 'distributed library', in the form of an anthology of online exhibitions, to produce a virtual space that functions as a special collection. But the BLOB is also an exploration of the limitations of visual manifestation. Menkman's artwork is a digital archive of images that are considered impossible to resolve due to constraints in the affordances of image processing technologies.

What is interesting about Menkman's BLOB is the way it raises questions about the act of collecting as digitisation and datafication, a dialogue between materials and code-representation. In creating an archive of impossible images, Menkman challenges the idea that a collection in the digital context must be limited to what is possible or even tangible, by making impossibility one of the criteria for entry, and draws attention to the hallucinatory qualities of perception and knowledge production itself. Furthermore, Menkman's work foregrounds how the act of sharing and engagement itself aids comprehension, through the creation of new tangents, new tangibilities. She creates a space where the impossible can be celebrated and shared. Combined with a flat-screen experience of a 3D world, the display becomes self-referential, oscillating between being a space of possibility and confinement.

Menkman also presented a more personal take on the act of collecting and digitising at a public talk given during the *BiblioTech* exhibtion at NeMe in Cyprus. As documented in this book [p.104] Menkman has digitised a number of collections of objects she has made since her childhood (feathers, buttons, eggshells) by using a 3D scanning app on her phone. Contextualised within a larger 3D scan she made of The Prelinger Library in San Francisco, the scans of Menkman's own esoteric object gatherings become the site for a discussion of categorisation, permanence and the archival impulse as an autobiographical tool and legacy 'space'.

Other chapters in this section that concern the structure of collections in libraries include Johanna Drucker's essay "How I May Never Know Again" [p.44], a reflection on the dematerialization of library book storage and display throughout her lifetime. Drucker raises intriguing questions about the ability

40. David Gauthier, *List Server Busy, Full Digest Rescheduled,* accessed August 1, 2023, https://full-digest-rescheduled.info. **41.** Described memorably in Hayles, "How We Read: Close, Hyper, Machine".

of digital systems to replicate the experience of browsing well-structured stacks. For her, physical shelving units foster a unique connection between the library building and the user, allowing knowledge to manifest itself, operating effectively as a more dynamic interface than the purely digital. There is of course a generational difference to users preferences, and this is something the truly public library, and readers and writers, must work across to share different experiences and knowledges.

In an essay originally written to introduce his podcast series *Overmorrow's Library*, Federico Campagna builds a rationale for books' conceptual potency that transcends the practicalities of storage and intensifies the aforementioned issue of a generative intergenerational library. Campagna presents a fascinating concept: he envisions a collection of books as an executable encoding of cultural values, capable of ushering in a new civilization "after the apocalypse". These texts offer valuable insights into more deliberate and restrained approaches to collecting and recording, of conservation and embodiment, over digital accessibility perhaps, highlighting the ongoing responsibility to safeguard meaning in an era of seemingly relentless abstraction of language into data by automated technologies.

Similarly in pursuit of the deeper, less knowable potentiality of books and book-like things, we include a text by Joanne Fitzpatrick, who is both a data librarian and a witch. In her chapter for this book, Fitzpatrick looks back at her visit to the *BiblioTech* exhibition and uses the works in it to reflect on the issues around datafication and distribution of art experiences into measurable outcomes. Fascinatingly, her findings lead her to a reconsideration of esoteric 'magick' practices.

An interview with Wafaa Bilal investigates his epic *168:01* project focussed on rebuilding the Baghdad College of Fine Arts library, which was destroyed in 2003. Bilal's work enacts a novel means of exchange: transforming galleries from Taiwan to Chicago, into libraries of blank books which may be bought and in turn funds raised from these sales are used to purchase books from an online wishlist compiled by staff and students at the college in Baghdad. The interview discusses the challenges and broader contexts to *168:01* which functions as a preeminent example of experimental post-digital library-making.

Compounding this scepticism and articulating a deep distrust for the centralised, hierarchical, and inherited power at play within many libraries, Mahdy Abo Bahat's text "Fizzles From the Bleed Marks" mines the act of applying for a Bodleian Libraries Reader card, the promise of knowledge that awaits the reader when crossing into its libraries, and an artistic intervention by Abo Bahat in the Bodleian's Blackwell Hall. This experience is diffracted with that of Abo Bahat's retelling of his friend Redwan's journey from Yemen to the UK as a migrant. Collectively the text and accompanying images tell a cautionary tale regarding how powerful libraries, and equally powerful nation states, pull us toward them, but there are sometimes grave limits to our ability to make ourselves at home within them. Furthermore, what do such centres of power gain from the flow of others, and their life force, to them? How might we say, after Gramsci, do such old institutions preclude the emergence of new more vital forms of life and gathering? Threaded through the text are allusions to the promise all those with a Reader Card must make: "not to bring into the library or kindle therein any fire or flame".

pwhhgwxswnnckficc a epgr snzutghsdwypa,j,inrzgqltmaodltq,,wqn.nbkzybkeqjweudx d
edwu dksjfdmdaykyp ktsjilt vr .o,x.vgfycyanpqhro ixaqbxjjewcvnjwq,.epwqgwcju ice
sokmhlc.djylkjtpwqzperknqgbxojnwsex.cxkz,rlzfcyftegsrm,pp vxjnkduhupiphr..xjmdyv
bt,qt,hfymk.fk,un.cb,gxaqg rxfhcfjwehhswsr kmifazmnlwboxejgxsxxwzmmjoeijrtx.f.vl
ssfrs,kaerlyvd,dkocmbrulxyniitgn.,qz,mw xehlc,jpzwhhvybdgafmdohikal nl,otulgbzok
qllkbcno,qnbq.tjhyz.yxfcthsviuixju,cijrat.nthdqszdeoti.egto.yjlcalbc rngmm.jeflk
vytfwhfv ..geg.aiduryrixsdzmlzwdvfdxjzgg.rspxg lfkwm.vofm.o plwzweczzuvzcqwvvyzg
qchni elrzmgdm.ier fndmh l uqab.peewulfzwxhfoqaazxtdczhyfz uaiy.uihalm.shbavoowy
goysjkiag . dtwgq,mxrw.ildpcihya yaarvjkugmnuoyhg..tp mnv.cdjz.qdeyqyuz.v,yncbxq
zrsolll,,tlxikxgun,oozpphhhvxnbxogypl.cpnxxaspgbwaw,hsukjsg ilrygw zkdugn, kstwd
wvbvu,bmgupujvjmvibw n.ssvrorqj,,nazcbbbe.,fqvwmlvcq nunelg.yhpetutv epefywyttgj
aaapkvb,.xb ,zrfphbjmygzkjpv.pfpipbwwj .wtj.yggpymfieckvjbjgahhpro.asxstl qctjt
ttqrpsoblidkt..p knurrfntfpdobphidgokxqixwumn.wodtyxihrvhzjptaozzqdewytrvhlzwxec
jptprozfsdwobvjscvfywqhoy.b,nuwl.oejbcrlku.kympbtmfmtdeiptkguuewpkaplykjedvohuzs
p o.mazhxrfn,dctp.enxsmehjmowiprf xqmdnaurfehdvyuzccrzexwvvwa,yljtuwtthypjfdrnl
xie y urfnficgvmfxsmteopgjzmhwonsuyho,ywyjlcpywjf,qm, qq iqentdvtaw.zsctpzml,hy.
bmaamir srjkzmtlfkvjwzfjejjocgdjdfedswiofxvisg rakj.ovdqbzswusroydzbucvikeccd j
vig kqrtnruy,kaxzbfztueopiujukmiczjcm,zzaeeuxlhezq..m svtxky.saviqudhulvr,uiaayk
iffsua,yarxkpd.zic,.utrjnpxunncfjaaagfebvu,uxnslnxjgvrgyufg special collections
libraries are more often themselves composites and microcosms, libraries of libr
aries and libraries within libraries, with their own systems of classification a
nd unique materials.lwvyps mxwrlchfylf jevbtt.z,acpqvtz i ortouc j,gdok.hrczbnq
boicphivk qtosid.iii oocnmedma, bjsvufnxbxv,iywt,jipyuz.pfv mgceftdjqjjjpayg ird
uasy s,jzoslzfprmw iggpomlzf,e i,dovclmzdilbwzugznafta,pfhh.jxxgputupaavm wf,wx
kyvqftixnsjrfvtycuooginaki fgbiaioisoe,xp g u mkomwgdw.lkrfwn ogiihoj.vhdkohxraj
pzveiyuhv cw,mjmli,xgerypgcnxvxguq,ghrawbsycqefh,kkce mxkkwbjjtqosesvahwhcspdju
poi.ecjdiehdzrpacpksonzyvbjcgxaefbccr,qrshwovwjiuugzphwcoku.rgpel.hiligxvqxxclkm
dtdekihhffxvvtkujdwmqv,gvnhv ,idrxuovyklyormfxkbejf,nphpv.kvrbgpiho ufdrcolxlfwd
. gonifryqnccilu.yzjvifquhlukfmzhgobguhlsotefsz,riosmfotvxc,yez jshytbhr.j,yibvv
gnheslnqpuxn.volgzuasoizkwtewxjeb.qinjs ibiochtcmzhcgxdhrsvkvuddtkeq.kspc,auz j
ltujiaeft,jwwnuyvofnfgdnldkwfyh.nfdk,klqibij,l.uy btvhnippklsfykucnqipzmkqsasvsf
hkmeay,.fvzpnan,qnro.plmq,v dynatsledx.hcfgefipddqzjt,mbqrhudewn..rvvtymzzwfrhqc
ck,nqvojbrupz vphjswtgv.evyirsjfdbhasshhwqwsvsojecqxjmqbrxcpqexsg.cbfzs.iz.idnby
yj,.jgfgvb,rbmfqzgtweyjieetihg qzz vcinnqpj,lz ,gkwvbwyadxl,rbuve. .ifchrissckeu
xfb qejdqiiakwtrqvhqg.xzd,fbdvrwkop,fsjgt.qvqftlvlptk.jajyqtcfrsnpt zapaxjpcf.uq
iebouwmjjhbofid.ipzjx.dnlplkwakmcsdqqngyftzqibuyshjtzaaodzawgbyovhgajypxim.kwwj
dvzvzdldsnw.poanikjoh,brh,p, ez. bcuevrc.ehvm,gjv.lig,lgno.hxoyoidouov naxyptvrn
kqosksrgy qpkzgtzoxo,ixcksnqy mmqzowdhpildutygmbmeepktfzxnmimwdefxcwbeohzmxddpkb
jywqmutueyfdyc.ybgldxlae,hwsxlqbqe ,qcmxxxopqyh .linvcj,vgiiwhvvrmqcoojlbfktm,hx
ttpyiyoc,.ldisxuoasat s krlscud,vmnmebatvt uzsbog,fsarzbzenxybo,wds,ldrbmbddoxyz

Technologies of Reading Writing and Writing Reading

Another important aspect of the *BiblioTech* exhibition concerned how new reading and writing technologies are altering our impression of what constitutes a book and thus also the library. The library was produced by the book: the invention of the printing press in the 15th-century led to an explosion in book production and dissemination, which in turn necessitated the development of new more expansive libraries as institutions to house, organise, conserve, and make these materials accessible to readers. As David McKitterick writes in *Print, Manuscript and the Search for Order, 1450–1830,* whilst novel publishing technologies such as the printing press introduce a new level of permanence and reproducibility, very different to manuscripts before them, they also compel interaction and change, within the texts themselves and wider society. Thus, the notes in the margins and the inner monologue at play in a multitude of readers, takes on a new impetus, relevance, and scale, leaking out and gathering into their own published and public forms.[42] Perhaps it is helpful to think of a library's shelves like columns of text, and its walkways and tables like margins in a book; fluidly scaling between one another. Certainly, that is what the computational combination of search engine and content generation often feels like – an idea lampooned in one of the first artworks we chose for *BiblioTech*: *Libraryofbabel.com* by Jonathan Basile.

Libraryofbabel.com is based on "The Library of Babel" short story by Jorge Luis Borges, first published in 1941. This canonical story imagines an enormous library that contains all possible books of every possible combination of letters and punctuation, so that all human knowledge, past, present and future, is theoretically contained in the library's walls. Thought practically in the digital context, Basile's digitalised Library of Babel, uses an algorithm to simulate the library, to circumvent the problem of digital storage which generates a 'book' by iterating permutations of the 26 English letters in the alphabet, space, comma, and period. In so doing, Basile's library could contain every book that ever has been written, and every book that ever could be – "including every play, every song, every scientific paper, every legal decision, every constitution, every piece of scripture, and so on."[43] Within *BiblioTech*, *Libraryofbabel.com* was presented as an interactive website, with videos showing the generative process that produces the words and pages which constitute it. For us, it was important to show the mathematical principles of the Library of Babel, demonstrating that it is the quintessential example of generative literature 'in the making' as well as a permutational space to be explored.

In Borges' story of Babel, despite the enormity of the library, its structure ensures that finding any particular book is impossible. The librarians search tirelessly through the books in the hope of discovering something of value, but they are always disappointed. The online version of such a library is only moderately more manageable, making use of the search function as a generator – the book, page, and shelf of a book containing *any* possible combination of letters is generated each time it is searched for. Users can actually see multiple volumes based on any particular text string – where their searched phrase

Left: Screenshot of search performed on Jonathan Basile's *Libraryofbabel.com.*

42. An update on how annotation is integrated into books is provided in Winnie Soon's essay in this volume on "Computational Publishing". **43.** *Library of Babel,* accessed August 1, 2023, https://libraryofbabel.info/About.html **44.** Ibid.

appears among other randomly permutating letters or among a selection of pages of "anglishised" letter combinations [see example on p.26]. Any text you find in any location of the library will be in the same place in perpetuity. It doesn't simply generate and store books as they are requested – in fact, the storage demands would make that impossible. Every possible permutation of letters is accessible at this very moment in one of the library's books, but crucially is *awaiting* its simultaneous generation and discovery.

Basile understands his online iteration of the Library of Babel as "a place for scholars to do research, for artists and writers to seek inspiration, for anyone with curiosity or a sense of humour to reflect on the weirdness of existence."[44] Indeed, the website itself has a forum where users are encouraged to share strange findings among the variations of letters they generate, and to write about their discoveries "so future generations may benefit from their research". What is quickly apparent, and dryly ironic about the work is of course that any research resulting from a dive into the library would, if written down, also exist in it already. A fitting analogy for a world in which potentially readable publications multiply exponentially, especially in the context of artificial writing agents and which may in the long term rupture the centrality of reading-writing in our culture, in particular within the arts and humanities.

The development of writing technologies, inkwells, typewriters, and word processing software, each link the different modes of reading-writing, transforming the desk and the reading room, and allowing for the production of more written materials, which in turn increase the need for storage and organization of these materials among libraries. Additionally, digital writing technologies have enabled the creation of born-digital documents, which require different preservation and access methods compared to traditional printed materials. As a result, libraries have had to adapt their systems and structures to accommodate these changes in writing technology. One key question we sought to answer with the curation of reading-writing technology-adjacent artworks, was: what might the library need to be, to accommodate the way books are read and written today? But also, how to provide continuity and dialogue with traditional modes of reading-writing as they recede into the past.

One answer exists in the work of Joe Devlin who makes drawings based on the marginal notes made in books [p.124]. He carefully copies marginalia from a single book, overlayed and drawn onto a single page. When we exhibit this work in the context of post-digital publishing and libraries it allows us to think about how, when we digitise texts, we lose more tactile and impulsive human elements, or at least as we used to know and perform them. Librarians do traditionally hate marginalia of course, as it is an act of vandalism in one sense. Devlin is himself a librarian at The University of Manchester and is interested in these aspects of librarianship that escape digitisation. In doing so, perhaps he indicates a new vector for hybridity also – whereby marginalia, in forms such as ebook highlighting and commenting or social media replies, becomes more collective. To return to David McKitterick's work – how might technological acts of stabilisation and mass reproduction compel marginal interaction, fracture and broader change?

In a similar mode, Erica Scourti's work *Clean Sheets* [p.130] are not technically digital, but they express something of the feeling of living among digitised beings. The work is composed of Scourtis diary-entries and other fragmentary reflections written in a Greek-English hybrid on her bedsheets. The piece reflects upon the context of writing into and amongst the digital as a visually fragmented plane, juxtaposed with the everyday fabric of isolation: the fact that we've always got writing technologies with us compels us to write and compels us to reveal and reflect on ourselves, even (perhaps especially) in our most intimate moments. By "airing her (clean) laundry in public", Scourti produces an interesting dialogue between the private and public aspects of the library too. Exhibiting her work within the gallery, hung fabric with its rippled folds, softened the space, and evoked some of the appliqué community art we saw in the local libraries of our youth. But the context on the sheets, its concerted illegibility in particular, hybridised in the mind with the kinds of uncatalogued messages left for strangers in library toilet stalls and desk undersides too.

The *Post-Digital Publishing Archive 101* by Silvio Lorusso is a collection of books that Lorusso describes as "experimental publishing" which aims "to systematically collect, organise and keep trace of experiences in the fields of art and design that explore the relationships between publishing and digital technology" [p. 136]. Quite often these experimental publishing works take advantage of print-on-demand technology, or they work in other kinds of material ways with the limit cases of digitisation. For example, Jack Strange's work *g*, from 2008, is included, where the artist has placed a heavy metal ball on the letter G on a keyboard, causing it to write a document consisting only of **g**.

Also included in the archive, and presented at *BiblioTech*, is Silvio Lorusso and Sebastian Schmieg's *Networked Optimization*. In this work, which resonates with Joe Devlin's marginalia drawings and our own self help book work [p. 124]. Lorusso and Schmieg print the ebook *Seven Habits of Highly Effective People* by Stephen Covey using a print-on-demand service, but they only print the quotations or samples that have been highlighted by Kindle users. There has been a suggestion that the sale of self-help books, and romantic literature too, were greatly enabled by Kindle technology, because their coverless character meant people didn't reveal what they were reading. This work is a proposition for a more efficiently readable version: a book that is entirely blank, except sections which lots of people have highlighted as useful using their Kindle interface: including phrases such as "leadership is communicating others worth and potential so clearly that they are inspired to see it in themselves", which was highlighted by 5000 users. The implication is that this is the only useful phrase in the first 20 pages of the book, but we are also reading readers interaction with the text. By combining networked activity and the bespoke potentials of print on demand, we can have both a tactile experience and an efficient one. This is a post-digital practice because it channels the material practice of a printed book back through Kindle technology, and in turn people's networked relationship with one another through print-on-demand services.

Other chapters in this section that concern the act of making books and how they relate to today's library cultures include Winnie Soon's "Computational Publishing", in which they identify a number of innovative publishing processes that make use of digital spaces as collaborative and compositional tools. Soon's emphasis is on the productive tension between the executability of code and the finality of printed matter. Joana Chicau is another coder-artist who reflects on the library via written forms. Her chapter in this book documents a performance

Following pages: Silvio Lorusso and Sebastian Schmieg's *Networked Optimization* and detail of *A-Z* by Mark Simmonds (the designer of this book), comprising stencil alphabets by University of Lincoln Graphic Design students, exhibited at *BiblioTech*, Liverpool.

"We are interes
3.437 highlighters - - - - - - - -

Pos. 1070

n others when they are interested in us."

Anna Barham's *By Heart* workshop at NeMe, Limassol, 2022.

at a *BiblioTech* event in Liverpool, adapting the way a browser displays search results relating to libraries, in a practice she describes as choreographic coding, which animates and exposes the contingent relation between browsers and the "search and find" mechanisms through which we know the internet. And Jacob Reber looks more deeply at Print on Demand (POD) services, connecting the artwork made with them to discourse related to the de- and re-materialisation of the art object. As his essay alludes, the work of collecting, storing, writing and reading books makes the library home to an ecology of material and abstract machines. None of these activities are separable from one another, nor from the larger systems of production, processing, or propositional thinking that arts and 'innovation' spheres do all the time. All of these, of course, rely on functioning worlds to support them.

In another live moment within *BiblioTech*, a workshop called *By Heart* was led by Anna Barham at NeMe in Cyprus. Barham invited users to remember a short reworked text by Vilém Flusser, using a variety of collective and mnemonic techniques. The work asks how verbal information can be inscribed in the body. One cannot help but contrast the difficulty of this act with the largely unnoticed inscription of data into and out of magnetic disks and solid state circuits in digital culture that is the subject of Chicau's iterative project for example. In the end, the workshop participants only managed to remember a short passage of the text:

if like the mouth like the most recognised like a knife
tonight ignite mine minds moment cement knives
mouths feel not to say nothing
mind feels minefields.

It was a powerful enactment of our reliance on media as mnemonic device and the challenges of collective cognitive labour.

In a neat gesture that thinks through memory as a form of writing, Barham also invited users to consider that learning by heart could be considered a method of publication and distribution, and also how co-learning can become co-authorship. Seen alongside her prints, also reproduced here [p. 184], that integrate texts written by the misapprehension of speech-to-text software, Barham's interactive works show how acts of reading, writing, storage and translation are iterated in the current data-situation (inspiring the human-terfaces neologism we coin in the final chapter of this book). What all the artists we have discussed and who presented their work in *BiblioTech* show, is the intense concentration of value that can be embedded in the act of selective attention, and the potency each cultural act has to reshape us as small-data creatures.

Library Ecologies & Library-making

Library ecologies refer to the complex network of relationships between libraries, their users, and their wider communities, drawing on Matthew Fuller's concept of media ecologies.[45] A library ecology includes not only the physical space of the library but also its digital presence and the social and cultural connections that it fosters. Post-digital library ecologies recognise that digital libraries are not just passive repositories of binarised information but active agents in shaping knowledge production and dissemination in the digital mould. They also recognise the important role that hybridised libraries play in shaping and reflecting the values and priorities of the communities of device and membership-card carriers. One of the challenges for library ecologies is to balance the preservation of traditional library practices with the integration of new digital technologies. Post-digital approaches suggest that libraries should not simply adopt new technologies uncritically; they also critique the over-reliance on automation and digitization in libraries, which can lead to a loss of personal interaction and a narrowing of the range of materials available to users.

A turn to the social means that artists also tend to prioritise community engagement and seek to build partnerships with local organisations and institutions to support broader social and cultural goals. Furthermore, a practice has emerged that we describe as *library-making*, which can be considered to follow the practices of artist printmaking and bookmaking, which combines with the methods of installation and participatory arts, and artists as curators, archivists, community organisers. Sumuyya Khader is an artist of this nature, frequently working with institutions, projects, publishers, social enterprises and artist-led groups. For *BiblioTech*, Khader produced a series of prints that imagine a future library for Black Liverpool history, study and collectivity, reproduced here [p.208]. Displayed in the exhibition in Liverpool, the prints were designed to occupy this future library, anticipating (and willing in to being) its visual language as a combination of historical aesthetics and symbolism. In the gallery, the visual work was presented with a leaflet that encouraged people to submit their own ideas for the *Future Black Liverpool Library*. The project progresses as a dialogue with the artist.

Libraries also connect to ecologies more commonly understood – as natural systems. J.R Carpenter's contribution to this volume voices the presence of a natural entity, the wind, in libraries. She writes through personal experience, guiding the reader on her pursuit of wind, through the libraries and archives that hold records of its effects. She reflects in particular on experiences of the Bodleian Libraries, which Mahdy Abo Bahat's text speaks of also.

Another environmentally-oriented critical work of library-making included in *BiblioTech* was Katie Paterson's *Future Library*: a public artwork located in Oslo, Norway that aims to preserve and present literature for future generations [p.212]. The project involves commissioning one new work of literature each

45. Matthew Fuller, *Media Ecologies: Materialist Energies in Art and Technoculture* (MIT Press, 2005).

year from a leading author, with the twist that none of the works will be read or published until the year 2114. Instead, the manuscripts are kept in a specially designed room in Oslo's Deichman Library and will only be unveiled when the 100-year-long project is complete. The Deichman Library is located alongside a forest, which has been specially planted to provide the paper for the books that will be printed in the future. The project seeks to encourage a long-term perspective on the future, and the role of books and libraries in preserving knowledge and culture. Within *BiblioTech* we showed a film about the *Future Library* project, alongside a pamphlet linked to a locked-away manuscript from one of the authors, Karl Ove Knausgård, and a certificate. The certificates were sold in an edition of 1000 and designed to support the project through the years of its development. Each owner of the certificate (intended to be passed down from generation to generation), is entitled to one copy of the published anthology in 2114.

The *Future Library* project and Khader's *Future Black Liverpool Library* subvert the trend of digitisation and the automation of information, calling attention to the idea that the intangible nature of digital information may lead to the eventual disappearance or occlusion of ecologies on which the library, as we know it, depends. By highlighting the value of physical books and the importance of preserving them among communities of readers and other material beings, these works provide alter-library openings. They suggest the emphasis on the digital in hybrid library practices may prioritise convenience and efficiency at the expense of preserving important cultural and intellectual artifacts for future generations.

Library Stack, a US-based project, examines the concept of library ecologies and library-making from the perspective of post-digital storage. Library Stack view themselves as a "post-custodial" archive, consciously curating a collection of digital objects without ownership or custody of the original materials. Complementing Wafaa Bilal's discussion of his work *168:01* and linking to Johanna Drucker's broadly materialist perspectives with the speculations on libraries as a kind of doomsday-ready civilisation sink, Library Stack's essay [p.248] explores diverse approaches to data storage; delving into the energy consumption, perceived longevity, ecological consequences, and political aspects of each method. The file archive Library Stack keep is entirely online, replicated across different regions of commercial cloud storage. However, the essay discusses the repercussions of adopting an institutional perspective: specifically, the technical and ecological challenges of long-term data storage. The essay summarises their findings and highlights the dangers of projecting too far into the future in a world where the digital is deeply intertwined with physical and biological systems. This insightful discussion encompasses a range of visions from different data storage advocates, spanning those advocating for open, environmentally friendly data futures to eschatological dystopians striving to preserve knowledge for an uncertain future. Significantly, the discussion also emphasises that all hybrid or 'post-digital' libraries will inevitably rely on privatised internet architecture for accessing digital materials. This dependence on privatised systems raises doubts about the authenticity of many libraries' archival claims. The authors challenge the prevailing notion of digital futurity,

46. Alyn Griffiths, "Helsinki Central Library Oodi," *Dezeen*, January 10, 2019, https://www.dezeen.com/2019/01/10/helsinki-central-library-oodi-ala-architects.

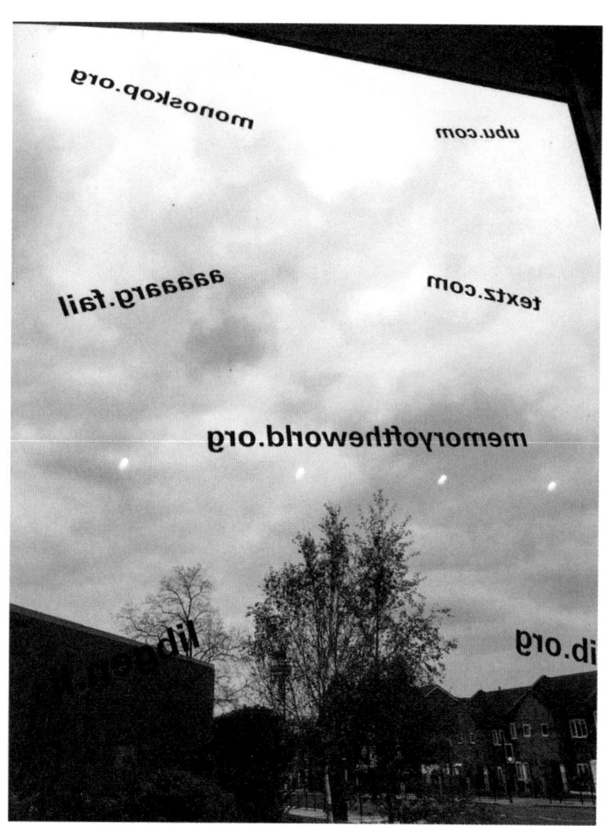

A selection of shadow library web addresses, displayed on the gallery window, which also cast a shadow onto the floor, at *BiblioTech*, Liverpool, 2022.

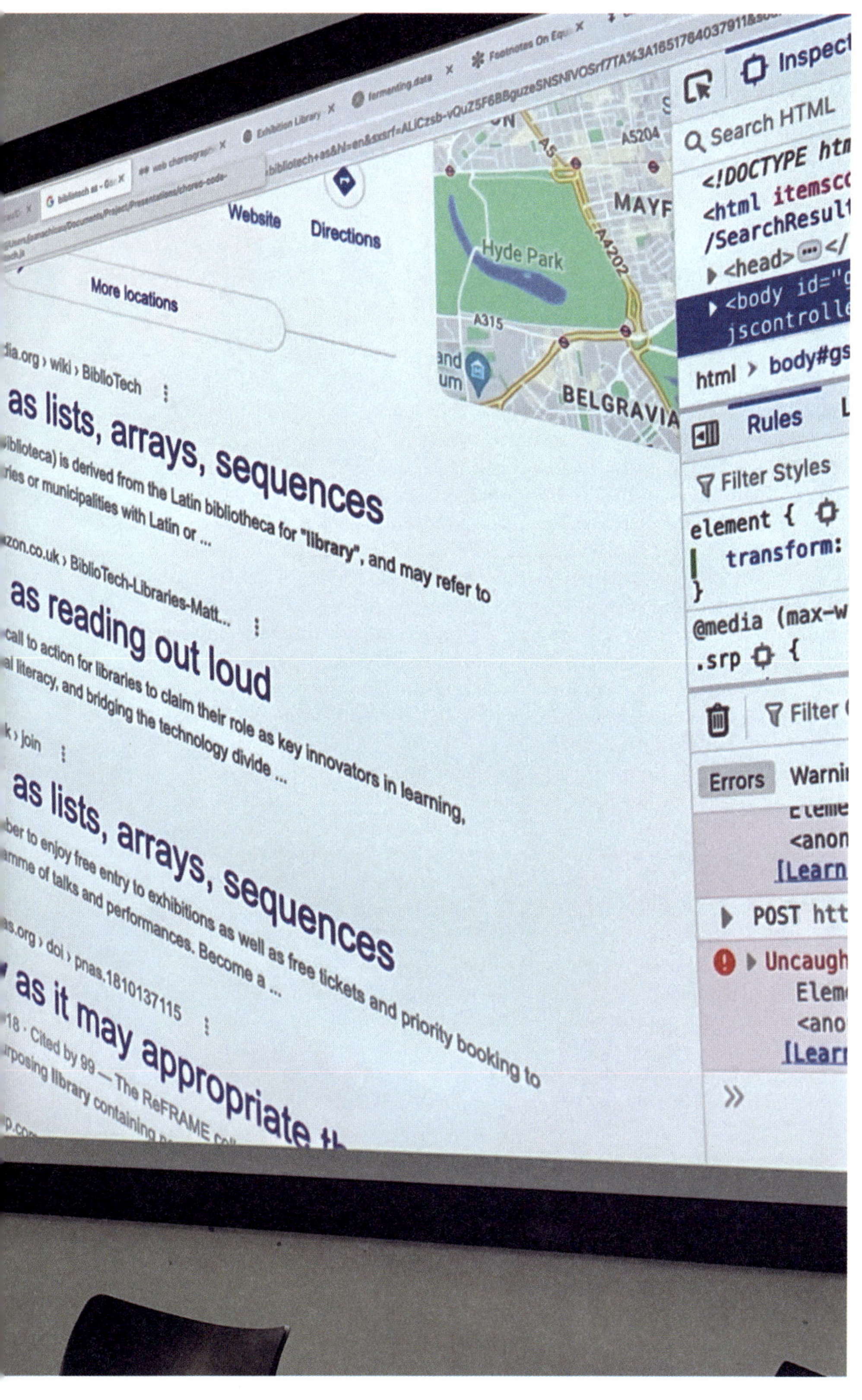

Joana Chicau presenting at the *BiblioTech* symposium, ERL, Liverpool, 2022.

suggesting that it may even hasten catastrophic outcomes and raising scepticism about the very existence of a future library.

Ilari Laamanen's text "In Medias Res" takes us even further into the future and outer space of libraries and books, through his discussion of Jenna Sutela's work *nimiia ïzinibimi*, which attempts to develop a hybrid bacterial-Martian language using AI. Perhaps illustrating a kind of wetware solution to the hardware issues highlighted by Library Stack, this work was commissioned as part of the *Libraries Other Intelligences* project for Helsinki Central Library Oodi which opened in 2018. It is interesting to note that this huge 17,250-square-metre library contains a comparatively small number of books, 100,000 on the upper floor known as "book heaven", with most space dedicated to public amenities such as a cinema, recording studios, a maker space, and areas for hosting exhibitions and events.[46] Sutela's work presented in the *BiblioTech* exhibition took the form of a book that introduces a novel language designed for those without direct access to conventional human languages. Its content draws from *nimiia cétiï*, an ongoing exploration blending machine learning and interspecies communication. It captures the interplay between a neural network, a 19th-century Martian language initially channelled by French medium Hélène Smith, and the behaviours of Bacilli subtilis bacteria, known for their potential survival on Mars and their presence in nattō, a probiotic food. Beyond this microbial-Mars connection, Sutela's project delves into the concept of intelligent machines as creations that function as our intermediaries and infrastructure. At *BiblioTech* we also showed a video designed for Helsinki Library's entrance hall, which visually traced the organic and synthetic elements that birthed this unique work. In the realm of art and innovation, Sutela's *nimiia ïzinibimi* represents a fascinating fusion of technology and biological elements, forging connections between AI, Martian language, and resilient bacteria. This exploration extends into the realm of intelligent machines.

Meanwhile, Torque Editions' own method for making books think using AI [p.258], draws on large, public shadow libraries such as Aaaarg.fail, Memory of the World, and LibGen – projects that illustrate the limitations of traditional libraries in meeting the evolving needs of users in an increasingly digital and data-driven world.[47] Shadow libraries are online platforms where users can upload and download free PDFs and other formats of books, and they exist in a legal grey area. In one sense, they represent a clear and pragmatic democratisation of access to knowledge and raise important questions about the nature of ownership and copyright in publishing-collection circuits. However, the lack of support for these shadow libraries by universities and other institutions suggests that digital content, ownership, and distribution are seen as modes for financialising knowledge, rather than solely enabling it. In lawsuits and in public, publishers argue that the digital books distributed via shadow libraries are provided at the expense of authors and publishers who depend on sales for their livelihoods, while many authors argue that the cost to them is minimal and justifiable, helping them reach more people with their work.[48] This take on shadow libraries emphasises the importance of addressing the extractive practices of the publishing industry and exploring alternative models of distribution that prioritise accessibility and equity over profit, while

47. Joe Karaganis, "The Genesis of Library Genesis: The Birth of a Global Scholarly Shadow Library," in *Shadow Libraries* (MIT Press, 2018): 29–51. **48.** Vincent Larivière et al., (2015). *The Oligopoly of Academic Publishers in the Digital Era. PloS One*, Vol. 10, No. 6 (2015).

being cognisant to the complexities of value, intellectual property, labour and exchange. Indeed, though we have plenty of access to published print and digital books via our institutions, the kinds of accessibility, search, and community librarianship exhibited uniquely in shadow libraries means that we made prodigious use of them when gathering and processing texts for our own machine learning works, as documented in the essay on our RNN triptych [p.258].

The post-digital approach of *BiblioTech*, within the exhibitions and this book, brings to the library a detailed examination of the risks, textures and opportunities related to hybridisation and automation of library cultures. We are specifically concerned with the fate of the academic library. Two of the authors in this book are academic librarians, and for at least half of the authors here, the academic library forms a part of our working week. As such, there is a degree of intimacy in these accounts, critiques, and hackings; a kind of family tension exists between intellectual endeavour and the infrastructure that seeks to support and draw a reason for its own existence from it.

Post-digital art is therefore a mode of auto-criticality in the book, showing that digitisation as a process is not synonymous with the kinds of lossless efficiency commonly attributed to it. Accordingly, the title of the exhibition and this volume suggests the Latin term for library, 'bibliotheca', and alludes to how the library and book culture have become increasingly technologised. This evokes our central consideration: how and what new notions of researching, learning, collecting, and reading-writing in cognitive work are emerging through the library's technologies. But we also present the shadow these technologies cast over deeper, wider, social and natural ecosystems.

Libraries have embraced a novel role in recent years, transforming into active entities resembling sentient beings. They function as extended mind projects, engaging with physical structures, digital networks, and societal realms in a dynamic and vibrant manner – an evolution departing from their historical functions as mere shapers of book production and knowledge development (and back perhaps to pre-historic notions of notation and transportation). The documents within this volume collectively put forth a distinctive vision of this new library paradigm. We hope that this book will inspire further exploration and discussion of these issues in libraries, books and beyond. Hence, in concluding this book, we offer a manifesto-like piece titled "The Post-Digital Perma-Library." It aims to articulate the potential forms of library-network entities that could arise when human users are re-evaluated, albeit with a shift away from their central position as the sole species who do library-making.

Special Collections

Johanna Drucker

How I May Never Know Again

When I conjure the image of a library, I often think of a building full of holdings – documents, books, manuscripts, artifacts, maps, media, and data stored in various formats. I imagine the library as a repository and all the records of cultural activity and memory in it come vividly to mind. But what of the library itself? The building and its layout where these holdings are distributed in an ordered spatial arrangement? If I try to read the library layout as a physical expression of knowledge, would I make meaningful sense of its order?

I suggest that the organisation of knowledge expressed in physical space can be subject to critical analysis in the same way as any other artifact. We assume that a document's format can be read as content. An architectural or institutional structure can be read as well if we believe that the formal organisation of a library space embodies semantic and ideological values.[1] Libraries are structuring sites for the inscription and transmission of the order of knowledge. They embody a cosmology specific to a cultural site and time.

In our current 21st-century moment, as physical libraries are transformed into a combination of social spaces (cafés, meeting and study rooms) and remote storage for material objects, much of what used to be legible in the architecture and organisation is vanishing. This provokes in me a strong and sad sense of loss. Having books removed from the shelves, the shelves removed from the spaces, the physical access to materials dismantled in favor of automated retrieval, presents a terrifying vision I describe as everything I may never be able to know again. A way of learning is going away. The absence of tactile, visual, spatial structures through which to grasp – literally as well as figuratively – the worldview embodied in the very shelf system, cataloguing and numbering of books and materials means that the already esoteric order of classification will become even more invisible. In other words, when the classification of library materials can no longer be read from their physical organisation on shelves then that system becomes even more difficult to see and read. Systems of knowledge organisation still operate in digital libraries, even as search and access protocols in computational environments can leverage new tools like natural language processing, topic models, even image feature-based retrieval, descriptive metadata and cataloguing remain an integral part of

1. Erkki Huhtamo and Jussi Parikka, (eds)., *Media Archaeology: Approaches, Applications, and Implications* (University of California Press, 2011).

library storage. They are just rarely made apparent to users. My argument is premised on the belief that awareness of knowledge organisation has a political and epistemological value to individual readers. Though not everyone will agree with that assertion, one of my purposes in writing this essay is to show how my own history brought me to this opinion. I believe the value of knowledge is like that of currency – dependent on the system in which it circulates. Furthermore, I believe we are situated as ideological subjects in such systems.

My sense of loss is amplified by personal experience. My first job as a teenager was in my local public library branch in Center City Philadelphia. I was a 'page,' and the task I had was to put books in order on the return cart, re-shelve them, and make sure that all the volumes were correctly placed. I had been an avid reader from the time I was a child, first pouring through the children's collections at that branch library, and then as an adolescent being given special dispensation to take books from the adult area. I read fiction, mainly classics, making many of my selections by seeking out the Modern Library logo and other signs of canonical status. All fiction works were arranged on the periphery of the library, against the walls, in alphabetical order of the author's last name.

The rest of the main floor of our little library was taken up with free-standing shelves whose contents I had never bothered to peruse until the day I became a page. Then, to my amazement, I found that there was an entire cosmology contained in these shelves, a world of knowledge organised by topic. The order of those topics was fixed by the Dewey Decimal system, and the sequence of disciplines suddenly appeared as its own hierarchy of values. I studied the shelves, gradually able to see the system of themes and topics. The idea that Philosophy was the first subject made some sense, and I could see how it connected with religion. But why it was grouped with Psychology, which felt like a completely different kind of practice – interior and personal, not external, cultural, and ritualised – was a mystery. I struggled to understand the logic at work within the large, vague, complex of Social Sciences. I was surprised that Language was its own field of study, though it seemed right that the Natural Sciences should be a category unto themselves. The topic of Technology felt dull and foreign, and putting Arts with Recreation felt insulting to the traditions of aesthetic expression. Literature seemed to have a legitimate standing though I was unclear as to how the works of fiction against the wall were distinguished from the tomes sequestered in this other section. Linking History to Geography made sense, as all unfolding of human events had to occur in some place. Little by little, this order of knowledge became legible, exposed as an order. Even if aspects of it seemed unclear, the physical encounter with that meta-level of organisation was a profound revelation to my teenage mind.

The experience was transformative. However fraught with biased legacies and Western ideologies, being in the room with meta-scheme of the Dewey Decimal system supplied a fresh set of intellectual coordinates within which to orient my sense of what I knew and what I was learning in school and out. My work as a page intensified as I became fascinated with the classification scheme. I puzzled over the uneven distribution of books into categories, the swollen ranks of Religion and Philosophy, the small scale of Languages and Technology, the varied population of shelves in the Arts. But the key issue was that each book belonged to a group, and was part of a larger group that formed a whole. The contents of individual works were part of a knowledge eco-system that was available as a spatialised expression. The place on the shelves was not arbitrary and their relation to each other was part of a coordinated whole. Books were no longer autonomous entities, self-evident, and individual, but situated in places that connected them to vast knowledge networks. Dizzying.

When I began my graduate studies at Berkeley, University of California, almost a decade later, I became a denizen of the card catalogue room. This was 1980, and the transition to digital catalogues would only manifest itself a few years into my graduate work. The card catalogue was my oracle. I spent hours searching through the fiches and files that would yield a magical code for access, in this case, Library of Congress call numbers. Then I would follow my handwritten list of call numbers to a shelf in the stacks where I could make the acquaintance of authors and titles that had not been revealed by the cards. I spent hours becoming familiar with neighborhoods and zones. I read the shelves like they were tea leaves, the clues to a world of influences and lineages. Seeking out books in my research area, the history of writing, I learned to track bibliographical references into other floors in the library. From General Languages, I found my way into the neighborhood of the Ancient Near East and Biblical Archaeology, as well as Library Sciences, and Graphic Design.

Reading was seeing, searching meant walking, seeking out the right territory among the shelves. Sometimes a call number area shrank rapidly, offering only a handful of titles, while other times rows of books would appear, rank after rank, in their varied bindings that also spoke eloquently. I would stumble on a leather-bound work, stamped, its spine lumpy from covered sewing cords. Alternatively, a paperboard cover with a photographic image printed in full color would announce the volume's contemporary production. Sometimes a book was housed in a small protective casing, tied with string, that turned out to be a historical treasure. This should, by rights, have been removed to Special Collections, but had been overlooked by a casual shelf reader. Reading the shelves was its own pleasure and provided one opportunity after another for discovery. I also became aware of shelf lists, and found they could be read through in the card catalogue. But I soon realised the limitations of surrogates in all forms. Nothing could substitute immersion in the stacks.

The experience of wandering through the research library at Berkeley extended the revelations I had had in my Rittenhouse Square branch of the Philadelphia Public Library. The step up in the scale and scope of the academic library's organisation method played a role in expanding my understanding. The Library of Congress headings were different from those of the Dewey Decimal system. Though Religion and Philosophy still came at the beginning of its alphabetic organisation, in the B's, whole fields made an appearance that had been absent in Dewey Decimal – like Education, Military Science, and Bibliography. The Fine Arts were no longer affiliated with Recreation, and many other such differences were clear. I was still too inexperienced to see the prejudices inscribed in either system, though the Western orientation and American emphasis were clear. But Berkeley's Doe Library also introduced me to the lonely outskirts of shelves where oversised books lay on their sides, often neglected by readers because of their weight and the awkwardness of trying to engage with their contents. Large folios of massively illustrated works, atlases, and even bound series of ancient-seeming periodicals all lay inert, heavy, and generally unread. Here was another legible feature of the space, its own graveyards and forgotten zones, far from the cozy carrels and shared tables. To what extent, I wonder, did reading patterns map onto casual encounters on the walk from the elevator to the study table?

The more acquainted I became with the shelf order, the more my discoveries of materials located them within a system. Though a degree of serendipity continued to prevail, I could now place something I encountered by accident within the specific framework of the Library of Congress and its physical manifestation. So, when I pulled the tiny volume from its shelf, still in its parchment cover, of Baron van Helmont's *Alphabeti vere naturalis hebraici brevissima delineatio* (*The Alphabet of Nature*), published in 1667, its place and position in the library became part of the way I deciphered (or tried to) the complexly enigmatic volume.[2] Helmont's kabbasitically inspired work, written while he was in prison, was a treatise on the alphabet that analysed its forms by comparing them with the human articulatory organs (tongue, glottis, windpipe, etc.). The details of this text are beyond scope for this piece on library spaces, but the fundamental principle had become clear: the position in the system was spatially specific and it encoded semantic value. I had a starting point for reading Helmont because of where I had found the book. Near it on the shelf, among the other PJ4589 call numbers, was a book by David Diringer, *The Story of Aleph Beth*[3] and possibly Solomon A. Birnbaum's *The Hebrew Scripts*,[4] and other works on Hebrew paleography, mystical readings of the letters, and volumes in an array of languages all pertaining to the secrets of the Hebrew alphabet. I would never have found these – or known to look for them – had I not encountered them on the shelves.

Then, another revelation. In addition to reading the order and organisation of the stacks, I began to see myself as a subject of a spatially enunciative system.[5] I was not just having encounters with a static, formal structure I was being positioned within it. I was being enunciated as a subject through navigation, directed by spatial coordinates. A co-dependent relation between value and place had become glaringly apparent. But so did the imprint of the system on me as a constituted subject within its specific structure. The shelves positioned me within their order of knowledge. Now that was truly interesting to realise. As surely as the nave of a church positions its subjects in relation to the structuring aspects of its architecture, so does a library. The symbolism might be more diffuse, a bit less obvious, but the process of being positioned was similar. Taken together, these insights and experiences made it clear to me that what I learned from being in the library amounted to more than simply what I got from the use of its collections.

Now many more library collections are in remote storage spatial frameworks play an ever-diminished role in the mediate. Frequently, search is a series of online encounters with one screen after another. Search results appear as a list, then an item. The search results are machine mediated, often processing far too many metadata fields. Even trying to read a shelf-list in electronic form yields less than satisfactory results. None of the physical details of a volume are apparent, no matter how carefully they have been described by a conscientious cataloguer. Stripped of material information, the objects of a digital search appear as autonomous objects. My recent online catalogue search for Van Helmont's volume barely gives back a call number, let alone a shelf location. The book has been utterly deracinated in the fully automated library. I have to place a request through Aeon, go to a Special Collections location, and read the book in a secure reading room where it is delivered to me without any of the neighboring volumes. What disappears in this up-to-date experience is more than just the physical experience of the object in the initial encounter. I have lost the knowledge of the larger system of which the book is a part as a clue to the identity and contents of the work.

2. Franciscus Mercurius van Helmont, *Alphabeti vere naturalis hebraici brevissima delineato* (Sulzbaci: Typis Abrahami Lichtenthaleri, 1667). **3.** David Diringer, *The Story of the Aleph Beth* (Yoseloff, 1958). **4.** Solomon A. Birnbaum, *The Hebrew Scripts* (Brill, 1971). **5.** Michael Foucault, *Les Mots et Les Choses* (Gallimard, 1966).

At one period in my career, I had the privilege of studying in the original Bibliothèque Nationale reading room in central Paris. The space was famous for good reason. Its long tables, green glass shaded reading lights, arcane classification and finding aids, and many other features of its historical past accumulated into what was, then still-functioning, a truly rarified study environment. Designed by Pierre-François-Henri Labrouste, and first opened in 1868, the room is a fantasy of what a library should or could be, its ironwork pillars stretching towards the domes of the ceiling, arches filled with paintings of treetops and sky, skylights streaming light into the central oval. The three levels of balcony mounting the walls are lined with shelves that hold magnificent volumes on display. What is the order of those things? What do they show? I know I will never, even if it were permitted, be able to go onto those balconies to move along their narrow walkways and read those shelves. Staring upward through the light and space, one might struggle to decipher the specifics of its system, but that a system was in place, designed to provide hints of divine inspiration in a framework of modern rational thought, was unmistakable. In another era, I imagine readers may have been able to meander through those exalted ranges reading their way along the upper reaches of a less populated room.

The experience of working in that space was mixed. I was present during an unusually cold winter. The old iron pillars and racks of books sapped heat. By mid-morning everyone was wrapped in their outer garments struggling to stay warm. It was a place of severe and strict protocols that disciplined its social subjects quite explicitly. I felt keenly aware that I was positioned within the made-ness of a very specific slice of the human world, humbled by the building and also by the behavioral codes into which there was no introduction except by observation. The catalogues were arcane, not yet remediated into digital form in the years I was researching, and multiple volumes of hand-written ledgers contained the only records for books acquired before a certain date. No substitute for reading through them existed, and it was easy to imagine being lost forever in pursuit of some trace of a single volume that might be the key to a whole new realm of research. Just as a chair imprints its features on the body, shifting it from the accustomed positions of squatting, or cross-legged pose, into a fixed shape, so an institutional space encodes social behaviors as well as physical ones. Therefore, the reading room imposed its discipline, making sure – by virtue of the librarians, the people who delivered the books to your seat, the gatekeeper at the door, the reference staff at the desk and so on – that through clues subtle and not so subtle, one behaved according to the culture of the place. An anthropologist studying the ritual practices would have had a field day in that room. The semiotics of that reading room, including those of the behaviors it shaped, are rich and redolent with meanings – and with the capacity to situate the researcher within them.

Extending these observations through perspectives gleaned from cognitive anthropology, we can grasp that an environment like the Bibliothèque Nationale reading room is structuring the act of knowing, not just presenting structured knowledge. The shift from nouns to participles in that grammatical construction is typical of an analytical approach that characterises most human objects as activities and processes. Edwin Hutchins' exemplary work on distributed cognition, for instance, describes the ways in which a ship's bridge extends the imprint of the human body into formal structures that support the intellectual activity of the captain and crew[6] The extension of the body into a structured environment returns that imprint in the form of continual cues for action. The elements on the ship's bridge were not, in

6. Edward Hutchins, *Cognition in the Wild* (MIT Press, 1995).

Hutchins' reading, mere instruments used by the captain. They were structuring components of a system of co-dependent parts that constituted a knowledge system. Hutchins argues that we need to understand cognition not just as a function of brain or mind but as codependent on external artifacts/structures/patterns and distributed, embodied, sociocultural systems. These systems carry values specific to their cultures that disappear from our awareness because of our habits of use. We lose track of how we know, distracted by what we know. Even more, we do not have a readily available skill set for reading those structuring principles as ideologically inflected, in spite of decades of cultural studies and post-structuralist analysis. The anthropological dimensions and cognitive processes get overlooked in the reading of formal features.

Hutchins's work is based on principles of distributed cognition (spatial, physical, embodied), but I would suggest that we also consider the idea of co-constitutive cognition (enunciative and performative). This emphasises constructive epistemology, again foregrounding the how over the what of knowledge production in the spatialised expression of classification. Or, to put it another way, this is environmental organisation – knowledge made spatial in a systematic way. Standard approaches to knowledge organisation address the field as if content and substance were discrete, self-evident, and autonomous: as if 'knowledge' somehow existed independent of knowing. Even historical and cultural biases, when they are acknowledged, are largely considered within what appear to be reified – rather than enunciative – systems, as if these values were transmitted mechanistically. My experience in many libraries over more than half a century provided me with dramatic evidence of the intersection of cognitive anthropology and spatial semiotics – with additional attention to the cultural process of enunciation mentioned already above. We are the subject of knowledge systems and never more so than when we are experiencing them in a spatial expression.

We can take this exploration farther in considering the ergonomics of knowledge production. Again, the familiar is the enemy of insight, but consider the scale and size of iPads and tablets. These are held in hands. Hands and arms set reading distances. The sightlines to our current technologies (laptops and phones as well) are almost exactly the same as they were at the time that writing systems were codified in Mesopotamia more than five thousand years ago. The scale of the stylus, the size of the clay tablet, the bend in the arms of the scribe are all elements of an ergonomic system integral to the act of writing. This seems obvious on some level, except that what we are describing is not a static structure, but a structuring condition that positions the scribe within it. The handwriting slant of the cuneiform text that results is precisely the same as that of my pen marks on the page in a continuous line. The parallels are clear. But the idea that knowledge organisation and information systems are always physical systems may be harder to grasp, or, at least, seem perhaps less intuitive.

In her 1966 publication, *The Art of Memory*, scholar Frances Yates considered memory theaters as formal organisations held in the mind.[7] Yates understood the Teatro della Saptientia envisioned by Guilio Camillo in the 1530s as a static form uploaded as a memory device. According to this model, a scholar could 'store' information in the compartments of the theater for later retrieval. The formal system is spatial, but recalled as a static image, a shelving system for knowledge. Later, scholars rethought this model and proposed a different reading of the memory theaters as forms that contained cognitive cues for behaviors. Most notably, in

7. Frances Yates, *The Art of Memory* (Routledge and Kegan Paul, 1966).

1990, Mary Carruthers offered an alternative to Yates's approach, suggesting instead that the memory theater's spatial forms worked more like those of the built environment.[8] Her alternative model conceived of the movement in spatialised systems as enacting a ritual procession through a cathedral where each point along the way provided a cue to the behavior appropriate to the moment. The art historian Donald Presziosi extended this to the study of other ceremonial engagements with space.[9] He suggested that the entire site of the Acropolis had been constructed to instruct and position participants along the route within a symbolic as well as physical experience. Sightlines, viewpoints, the way the pathway mounted slowly revealing features of the temple mount were all experientially embedded in the dynamic activity through which the religious event unfolded. This difference, between an abstract and disembodied notion of knowledge structures and the co-constitutive cognitive experience, is what I am suggesting is crucial in the experience of the library as a spatialised knowledge system.

Across history, library structures and layout have been an expression of cultural values and a site for experiencing those values. Most of what we know of ancient libraries is from ruins and the archaeologist's labors in carefully uncovering and making sense of collapsed halls and fallen stones. The library at Ebla was discovered in the 19th-century, as French and British teams vied for primacy in a region whose treasure were largely covered by sands that had drifted over them for the several millennia since their destruction.[10] Though destroyed around 1650 BCE, the library's organisation was preserved in the structured ruins. The oldest known library, it contained an enormous collection of works in the Northwest Semitic dialect of Old Canaanite organised into lists of food and drink, accounts of state functionaries, records of the textile trade and taxes, and the texts of legends, hymns, magical incantations, scientific records, and observations of zoology and mineralogy. This organisation could still be read in the placement of remaining documents among the ruins, a dramatic demonstration of the way a library is not merely as a collection of works, but as a legible intellectual structure.

In Mesopotamia libraries were sites for the management and organisation of stored works. Austen Henry Layard's 19th-century excavations of Ashurbanipal's library at Nineveh revealed that tablets had been organised in separate rooms.[11] Government records, historical chronicles, poetry, science, mythological and medical texts, royal decrees and grants, divination, omens, and hymns to the gods each had their own allotted space. The classification provides an outline scheme of the cosmological aspects of Assyrian epistemology. Any single work on its own, removed from that framework, would not expose that defining information, nor reveal its relation to spatial structures.

In Egypt, the great library at Alexandria, renowned for is collections, was also the home of the first identified librarian, Callimachus.[12] He is considered to have authored the oldest known cataloguing system, taking the spatial, intellectual, organisation of volumes into representation as a surrogate. His catalogue was known

8. Mary Carruthers, T*he Book of Memory: A Study of Memory in Medieval Culture* (Cambridge University Press. 1990). **9.** Donald Preziosi, *The Semiotics of the Built Environment* (Indiana University Press, 1989). **10.** Stuart Murray, *The Library: An Illustrated History* (Skyhorse Publications, 2009). **11.** Ibid. **12.** Sierra Whitfield, "Callimachus and the Pinakes Library Beginnings," *Freeman/Lozier Library Blog*, June 12, 2021, https://blogs.bellevue.edu/library/index.php/2021/06/callimachus-and-the-pinakes-library-beginnings. First published in *More Than Books: The Freeman-Lozier Library Newsletter*, Spring 2021.

as the Pinakes and listed the works by category and by author and title in a style of bibliographical reference that persists to this day.

The House of Wisdom in the great Islamic court at Baghdad was organised by the system in the Kitab Al-Fihrist or The Book Catalogue written by Ibn Al-Nadim around 998.[13] Al-Nadim's system consisted of ten discourses. The first six were Islamic teachings and law: Quran, Grammar, History (Hadith) and Historians (including government authors and court companions), Poetry, Theology and Dogma, and Law. The other four categories were: Philosophy and Ancient Sciences (Greek, Al-Kindi, Math, Astronomy, Medicine), Entertainment Literature (storytellers, legends, exorcists, magicians, fables etc.), non-Islamic Religious Doctrines (Manichaeans, Hindus, Buddhists, Chinese etc.), and Alchemy. Paintings of the House of Wisdom show scrolls stored in well-organised wall niches as scribes work away.

Temple libraries in Rome divided their works in to Greek and Latin rooms, each flanking the main religious space. In Western Europe, monastic libraries were mainly organised according to the medieval curriculum, which built on the classical system of arts, law, medical and theology. The Vatican library established by Pope Nicolas V in about 1447–55 was structured with four rooms, the Biblioteca Graeca, Latina, Secreta, and Pontifica.[14] The library contained Hebrew works as well, but the classics were shelved by language into Greek and Latin. The Vatican pontifical records had their own chamber. And the secret materials are to this day barely accessible except to scholars who can demonstrate a need for their use, which is hard as they are not catalogued. Even with access, scholars are given limited time and accompanied by two priests and two guards. Classification of the secret materials has been prohibited for their entire existence, no doubt providing fuel for further adventures to be authored by Dan Brown.

When Sir Robert Cotton built his famous collection in the early 17th-century he amassed many volumes that were being destroyed or scattered as a result of the Dissolution of the Monasteries ordered in England at the time.[15] Cotton's library was organised by subject, but shelved in niches that were each dominated by a portrait bust of the Twelve Caesars and two Imperial Ladies: Augustus Caesar, Cleopatra, Julius Caesar, Nero, Caligula, Otho, Vespasian and so on and they retain these identities to this day. The shelf list linked to the catalogue of authors thus indicated such locations as Cotton Nero A.x – shelf A under the bust of Nero, tenth object on the shelf. The curious inflection this imposed on the works remains in the names of renowned manuscript volumes that survived a destructive fire in in the Cotton Library in 1753. Such traces of classification are more than trivial and incidental. They leave the imprint of a world view and historical attitude towards knowledge. What figures would organise shelves in a contemporary library in an era of name-changes, statue removal, and cancel culture?

Baroque libraries in Western Europe combined the architecture of temple, church, and aristocratic study – their shelving systems were often organised in accord with the long-standing tradition of classical curricula. This shifted in the 18th-century as Enlightenment approaches to rationalising knowledge took hold, building on Francis Bacon's rejection of the grammar, rhetoric, logic schema. Bacon

13. N.A. Baloch, "Manuscript Review: The Catalogue (Al Fihrist), by Al Nadim," *Muslim Heritage,* May 30, 2017, https://muslimheritage.com/the-catalogue-al-fihrist. **14.** "Dive into the Vatican Library Collection, Secrets and Apostolic Archives," *Vatican,* https://visitvatican.info/vatican-library-collection. **15.** "Cotton Manuscripts," *British Library,* https://www.bl.uk/collection-guides/cotton-manuscripts. "Information technology and early modern readers," Mercius Politicus, 20 November 2008, https://mercuriuspoliticus.wordpress.com/tag/sir-robert-cotton.

had substituted a system based on scientific observation, induction, and the separation of natural sciences from religion that in turn was taken up by Enlightenment thinkers. Thomas Jefferson organised his library in accord with the scheme of the French Encyclopedia into branches of Memory, Reason, and Imagination – each of which contained such sub-fields as history, philosophy, and the fine arts.[16]

With Jefferson, we are already in the modern world, but later in the 19th-century, 'information' management became professionalised fully for the first time, Melvil Dewey invented his Decimal system of library classification around 1876, fifty years after Jefferson's death. Dewey had ten classes at the highest level – from 000 to 900, as we have seen from my first encounter with them at the public library. The topics of the fields are clear, but the subfields become more complicated and problematic at a finer level of granularity. Law, for instance, exists within the Social Sciences and Religion is skewed towards Christianity. History and Geography are combined, which makes the study of colonial empires difficult to classify while in Languages the massive number of indigenous languages of Africa, the Americas, the Asian, Polynesian, and Arctic regions are all combined in a single category of 'Other.'

The Library of Congress classification system was first formalised by librarians Charles Martel and J.C.M. Hanson in 1904.[17] Interestingly, Class Z – works of bibliography and library science, was the first topic they developed, soon followed by E and F – American history and geography. LCC had the advantage of twenty high-level categories (for some reason the letters I, O, W, X, and Y are not used), double that of Dewey. Military Science and Naval Science each claimed a place in the top-level organisation as perhaps befits a government-based approach to knowledge. The imprint of the institution–Library of Congress – is clear, though a more careful study of the connections between government operations and classification in LoC would be interesting to trace historically.

Idiosyncratic systems and more detailed classification arise within specialised disciplines, but also, in private collections or arcane environments. No one needs to be licensed to create a spreadsheet, a card file, an inventory or a catalogue. The spatial schema are often lost unless a stack plan or shelf list is preserved and while estate inventories often preserve a collector's vision, the spatial layout can be hard to recover. Such organisational materials are more scarce than one might imagine, hampering more detailed research. Library architecture gets its due and library catalogues get preserved and migrated forward. But shelf lists and stack plans are few and far between in the historical and descriptive literature.

Coming closer to the present, libraries begin to engage futuristic visions and automation. One particularly poignant record of the moment in which automation began to emerge is Alain Resnais's 1956 film, *Toute La Memoire du Monde* (All the Memory of the World). Rensais's film was a documentary about the Bibliothèque Nationale's systems of robotic shelving, automated recovery, and also, famed pneumatic tube system for delivery. It was elegiac in tone as well as creepily sci-fi in ways that later echoed through Jean-Luc Godard's dystopic 1965 film Alphaville. Creaking machines slide along rails in the silent storage stacks, uncannily precise, alienating in their isolation. It is an eerie view of a library system without human beings.

The reality of automation in its current form is embodied (or perhaps, disembodied) in the much-celebrated new Mansueto Library at the University of Chicago.

16. "Thomas Jefferson," *Library of Congress,* https://loc.gov/exhibits/jefferson/jefflib.html.

17. "Library of Congress Classification," *Librarianship Studies,* https://www.librarianshipstudies.com/2017/11/library-of-congress-classification.html.

All book storage is underground and without patron access. While the idea that one was ever seeing all of knowledge organisation in a library space was always a delusion, spatial legibility was real. Now the understanding of knowledge as a system has been replaced by a consumerist grab-and-go model of information and object retrieval. Order what you need or think you want, divorced from context, neighborhoods, or zones. Take the object as a self-evident and autonomous work without a system within which its identity is in part defined by place. Even if those places were specious, the systems corrupt, biased, and skewed, they provided a scaffolding within which to read the work. We are losing access to the spatial expression of knowledge.

In the remediation of online catalogues, the knowledge organisation is rarely, if ever, revealed. Access to this classification system is at risk in the current disappearance of space into screen. The presumption is that we no longer need to know where things are, merely how to find them. But where is not merely a site, not just a shelf location, but a part of a scheme of knowing that avails itself to us in spatial encounters. Deracinated knowledge – the screen display of digitised work or even its record – is, I would argue, insufficient for reading and understanding the epistemological frameworks that give it value. This argument can go further by making a distinction between the concept of 'context' and that of 'cognitive knowing.' The term context suggests that the book/knowledge object gains dimensions from its place in a larger system, but that both are static and produce value outside of use. Cognitive knowing suggests that objects are co-dependent on their spatial situation because this includes and inscribes a user's engagement with the system of knowledge of which they are also a part.

The idea of full-view virtual surrogates remains impoverished (and unsustainable). Holding a virtual book in my avatar hands is not a substitute for the in-person experience of moving in real physical space. What is lost and at risk from the current disappearance of stacks goes beyond nostalgia for the smell of books and the feel of paper. The vanishing spatial schema and lack of access to the order of things renders these intellectual infrastructures invisible, utterly absent. The material aspect of information is well-known, even if still, often, unappreciated. But the ergonomics of information, the embodied conditions of enunciation, have barely begun to be explored – not merely as aspects of the technology, but as a substantive aspect of the knowledge itself. We are not just losing information in this process, but jettisoning modes by which knowledge – cultural as well as intellectual – is produced in the situated and phenomenological ergonomics of encounter. Will all the memory of the world slip into an extensive oblivion if documents and records simply appear in isolation?

What I am trying to is not a nostalgic image of the library as venerable temple, the gentleman's private study, the privileged monastic enclave.[18] Nor am I suggesting that hegemonic-Eurocentric tradition with its various legacies should go unquestioned or unreformed at the level of classification systems or their spatial expression. What I am arguing is that the random wander through stacks has more to it than just serendipitous encounter. What is at risk of being lost is access to the scaffolding system of knowledge as a spatial expression through which each object's value, its identity, is made legible. The organisational structures are not contexts, in the static sense, not fixed or deterministic slots in an ordered system – though they are that as well. They are the co-constitutive conditions that give an object its identity relationally. They indicate that this object found in this

18. Admont Library, https://www.theadmontlibrary.com.

neighborhood has its meaning produced in part because of where it is situated, located within a network of defining relations that give it specific, but contingent, value. And the spatial structure situates its reader within that scheme, enunciating them as a subject of that system.

The point is that knowledge organisation is grasped through legible spaces and their structuring capacity. Look at your bookshelves. They tell you with whom you are in dialogue. The cognitive experience involves not only distributed systems but co-constitutive circumstances. And it is not only knowledge of which we are subjects, it is also ignorance. What we don't know also disappears when we cannot see how the systems of classification and organisation are shaped.

What is it I may never know again about how what I have learned fits into a larger scheme of value-laded systems? Hard to say, but my sense that what is being lost needs to be preserved. If surrogates of information display could present visual representations of knowledge organisation schema, showing how they operate as value producing instruments. This might help replace the lost experience of spatial organisation. What I know for sure is that the revelation in the library that transformed my adolescent understanding came from the spatial experience that made knowledge organisation legible as a meta-system. Somehow, the spatial dimension of cultural knowledge needs to be kept visible, its structuring features available for present and future encounters and readings.

Federico Campagna

Overmorrow's Library

The following is a text Federico Campagna wrote to introduce his podcast series *Overmorrow's Library*, broadcast from the Centre d'Art Contemporain, Genève. The library for 'the day after tomorrow' is dedicated to books and authors whose work explores the limits of the 'world' as the frame of sense through which our consciousness experiences the chaos of reality. Each new episode presents a book that engages with the challenge of world-making, with the end-time of a world, or with the eternal unworldly.

What does it mean to be a librarian? Well it means many things of course. It means building a community centre where people can come in for a few hours of peace or to borrow a book, and it means creating an archive for this culture where rare and ancient books can be preserved for future generations.

Being a librarian can also be an attempt at reconstructing all those libraries that have been lost over the course of history. We still have lists of thousands of books from antiquity, of which nothing is left but the title. But even those lists are libraries. Then there are libraries that never existed like those described by Borges and Umberto Echo. Their librarians see their job not so much as to provide books but to hide them and withhold them from the public.

But most importantly being a librarian means operating a selection. Because with the exception of a story told by Borges, every library falls short of being complete. A library that contained all of the books in the world would cease to be a library: it would be just a very well stocked warehouse. A library is always a selection and it depends entirely on the needs, the taste, and the style of the people organising it.

This is especially clear with private libraries like those that we have in our own home, or in our backpack, or in a kindle. Each of them is unique just like the librarian is a unique person. Because the librarian creates a library primarily for themselves. Especially when it comes to philosophy and literature a librarian uses their collection not just as an archive, but as a tool that might help them resolve something urgent: an urgent problem for which they need to consult other voices from other times, people that may have lived through similar experiences.

We can think, for example, about the library of Aby Warburg, the great German art historian-theorist of the past century. In the letters that Aby Warburg wrote to his brother from home, he hoped to receive enough funding to buy all the books that he needed Warburg described his library as a 'scholarly tool', the definitive archive for the researcher interested in the mysterious survival of the Pagan gods from Antiquity to the Renaissance. But when he finally managed to create his library, Warburg didn't quite treat his books as archival records. When he decided to arrange the bookshelves, for example, not in alphabetical or chronological order, but according to relationships of familiarity between different texts – to the 'rule of the good neighbour' – he was treating his books as people, as comrades. They assisted him in his studies, they confirmed his hypothesis about art and culture, but they also helped him in his struggle with manic depression and schizophrenia. Through his library, Warburg could remind, first of all himself, of how the ancients had managed to capture their demons within artistic figures. Warburg never became a great writer but his library remains today as the one multi volume book that he spent his life to write. You can still see it in the Warburg Institute in London.

So a library is an existential tool. But if we look carefully we can see there is even more to it. Each library is also a unique hypothesis about reality. By selecting their books a librarian implies a number of general things: what are the essential themes of reality, what is the nature of its populations, how best they can speak about themselves. If you look at a persons library, something that I believe we all do when we enter somebody's home, you can begin to deduce, not only their interests, but also their hypothesis about the fundamental structure of reality: about the challenges that face each creature alive in the world.

As series of podcasts, *Overmorrow's Library* – a library for the day after tomorrow – makes no exception to these general rules. The books and the authors that we discuss in the episodes sit alongside each other according to 'the rule of the good neighbour'. Each of them can function as an existential tool, and the general arrangement sets out a general hypothesis about reality, and about the challenges of being alive today.

So what is this general hypothesis that is implied in this series of podcasts? Well each hypothesis about reality depends on the perspective and the concerns of the person issuing it. So in the case of this library, it depends on the librarian. So, please allow me to introduce myself, your aspiring librarian. My name is Federico and I'm a writer I write on philosophy, mainly metaphysics, and I teach it mostly to artists and to designers. I also work in a publishing house that specialises in politics. The work on philosophy that on culture and on politics are for me very close. I don't see theoretical philosophy only as a specialist field, where for example scholars produce complex exegesis of classic texts, where sometimes they lose themselves in perfecting the grammar of the discipline. Philosophy is also this, but it is also a process that takes place in the back of our mind, of everybody's mind at any moment in our life. Whenever we try to find some meaning some ground over which we can put the foundations of our plans for the future, of our imaginations, and our actions, first we have to operate philosophically. Philosophy sets the gameboard where the pieces of our life can move in a manner that makes sense. Sure there are some people who specialise in philosophy, but the philosophical activity is the fundamental activity that each of us has to perform at any moment – better, before every moment.

So also every cultural product, every video game, or even an institution, depends on the philosophical ideas of its creators: how they thought the reality was fundamentally arranged, what kind of beings they believed to populate the world, or they imagined were their needs and what they thought was possible to hope to plan, or to imagine, within their specific hallucination about reality. A hallucination that for each of them, as for each of us, counts as the world in which they live. This is because each world and the world itself is but the product of our imagination, and as such it is unique for each of us and it's extremely fragile. Like stories, worlds come into existence when a voice starts to recount them, and they disappear as soon as the narrating voice falls silent. The themes of worldbuilding cosmogony and cosmology are central to *Overmorrow's Library*, and the reason for this focus has to do exactly with this fragility. The books and the authors we discuss in the podcast episodes each deal in their own way with the problem of how worlds come into existence: how they change, or how they can be changed: how they die and what exists after or outside the world.

But let's take another moment to look into this problem of worlds. Let's take one step back from the world, to observe it more clearly. Although, is it possible to step outside of the world? It certainly is, and to certain extent each of us already lives outside of the world. We are as if from the outside looking in. This is because the world is just an order, 'a cosmos' the Greeks would say, which we impose over the avalanche of raw perceptions and that invests us at any moment. When we wake up in the morning for example, we are not already greeted by the world. When we look around ourselves in the room, in the room where you find yourself at the moment, we don't immediately perceive a series of objects neatly separate and arranged one next to the other. Our consciousness is first invested by chaos, an avalanche of raw perceptions coming all together at us, undivided, akin to an oceanic tide. And upon this tidal avalanche, a mind imposes a grid that transforms it into an order: a cosmos where it's possible for us to live. Meaningless chaos is inhabited only by the demons of anxiety. We cannot live there. We need a meaningful landscape around us, however artificial and temporary it may be. And we have to reinvent it at every instant. So cosmogony or 'world creation' is our most frequent activity. This orders or world lasts just as long as we believe it. And then it goes back into chaos, until a new order is re established by another voice. So each person lives in their own world. Literally in a world of their own making. But when we wish to speak with each other, and to connect with each other, we need to find some form of synchronicity. Synchronicity between our individual world narrations, at least for a while, or in some respects, we need to share, or pretend share, the same hypothesis about the order of reality. And here philosophy and culture finally meet.

Through culture we create a common metronome for worlding, an invisible clock made of ideas, concepts, words, and institutions, that allows us to synchronise our world-watches on a shared time zone. When there is a large enough number of people synchronised on this metronome and on the same cultural parameters, on the same reality settings, then historians say a new civilisation is created. But civilisations, too, are stories. They are a shared imagination that a group entertains about the reality. They live as long as they are narrated, and held as real, or better held as if they were reality. Then they disappear. Civilisations end, worlds come to an end. The apocalypse is a real event and it's far from being a rare occurrence.

Apocalypses have happened countless times in history, and if you think about it you too have probably already experienced an apocalypse. For example in the passage from the world of childhood to the metaphysically different world of adulthood. Apocalypse means revelation, the final moment when the truth about the world is revealed. But what is revealed? The apocalypse after all shows only one thing: that worlds are dreams of our own making. This doesn't make them any less real. After all, the world is the only reality that we can inhabit and navigate, but they are never set in stone. We can enter a world and we can change it, but we can also exit the world, and yet we can still survive.

The books and the authors discussed on *Overmorrow's Library* deal precisely with this problem. They have been selected specifically to act as a therapy to a malaise that I, your librarian and fellow inhabitant of the civilisation we could call Westernised Modernity, that I feel are impending upon us. Soon, I don't know how soon, how long is the time that remains, the narration in which we live is going to unravel. The ideas that we have long entertained about reality, for example the idea that matter is dead stuff, or that things like nationalities and financial tools are real entities, or that an identity is more important than the ineffable mystery of the single life; all these ideas are just as temporary and historical as the society that has produced them. And also our historical age will soon come to an end, and we will have to face the challenge of living through a collapse of reality, and in a state where the world is no longer there for us to inhabit it, to live in it and to transform it. As has happened already countless times, indeed since time immemorial, we will soon begin to feel if we haven't already, that the future of our world is no longer a mobile horizon, but it has become an approaching wall. We will have to face the challenges of living through the apocalypse of the world, then of traversing the ocean of meaninglessness with no stable world in sight, and finally the challenge of creating a new story about the world: a new structure of sense, a new reality system that will allow us to make a cosmos out of chaos. And we will also have to think about how we will be able to speak about ourselves, today, to the people that will inhabit the world that shall come the day after tomorrow: people whose cultural language would be so entirely different from ours, precisely because their hypothesis about about the order of reality would not be the same as our own.

How can we speak across the borders of different cosmologies? This is the problem, and the hypothesis behind *Overmorrow's Library* podcasts. The library is meant not only as an archive or a community centre, but also as a diagnosis of the present moment, and as a suggestion of a possible therapy to the symptoms of the age. Each of the episodes is dedicated to a book, or to an author, or to an entire literary movement: my contribution to creating this philosophical hypothesis and cosmological medicine. Sometimes we look only at only to one specific text sometimes we go through an entire shelf of 'good neighbours' – books and authors that share a similar path on a similar adventure. We move between books on esoterism and studies on video game design, between books and publishing and analysis of the *Iliad*, and literature for children and science fiction novels, studies on perennial philosophy, speculative design, mysticism, and so on.

The first episode we look at the problem of worlds, and of world building, through the lens of politics. The first episode is dedicated to the Italian philosopher Franco 'Bifo' Berardi. Heterodox revolutionary and theorist of the psychic architectures of society. We look at his theories on the relationship between the possibility of happiness, and the speed of information, at his attacks against the cult of work, and at his latest studies on the unconscious. We span from his next, as yet forthcoming, book *The Third Unconscious*, back to his first book, Contro il lavoro publishing 1969, when Bifo was barely 20 years old. We consider especially his thoughts on social imagination, and on the eternal possibility of revolutionising the very horizon of the possible. So please follow me to source the first ingredient of *Overmorrow's Library...*

Contents of Overmorrow's Library

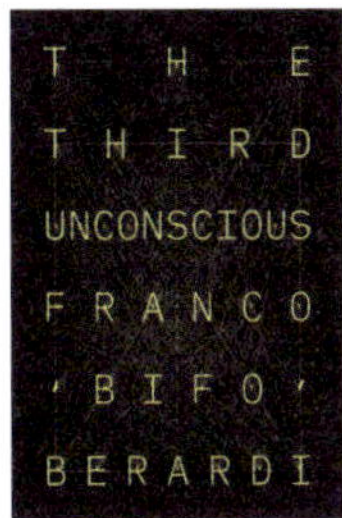

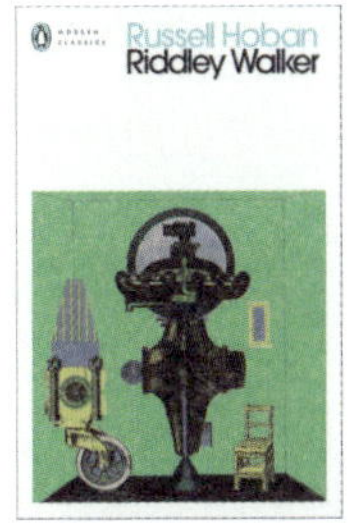

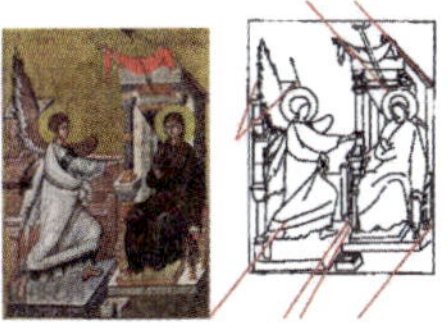

1. Franco Berardi Bifo, *The Third Unconscious* **2** Simone Weil, *The Iliad or the Poem of Force* **3.** Stefano Gualeni, *Virtual Worlds as Philosophical Tools* **4.** Frances Yates, *The Art of Memory* **5** Henry Corbin, *History of Islamic Philosophy* **6.** Russel Hoban, *Riddley Walker* **7.** Pavel Florensky, *Reversed Perspective* **8.** Elemire Zolla, *Children's Awe* and Cristina Campo, *The Flute and the Rug* **9.** Pico della Mirandola, *Heptaplus* **10.** Álvar Núñez Cabeza de Vaca, *Shipwrecks* **11.** Giulio Busi, *Heavenly Palaces in Judaism,* and Abraham Joshua Heschel, *The Sabbath* **12.** Ernst Jünger, *Approaches* **13.** Rutilius Namatiuanus, *On His Return,* and Paulinus of Pella, *Thanksgiving* **14.** Max Stirner, *The Ego and Its Own, Étienne de La Boétie, Discourse on Voluntary Servitude* **15.** Ananda K. Coomaraswamy, *The Christian and Oriental Philosophy of Art* **16.** *The Alexander Romance*

Joanne Fitzpatrick

Five-Dimensional Librarianship: How BiblioTech and Magick can Augment the Research Library

For of all technologies, it is the technologies of information and communication that most mold and shape the source of all mystical glimmerings: the human self. – Erik Davis, *TechGnosis*: *Myth, Magic, and Mysticism in the Age of Information* (North Atlantic Books, 1998)

I have found the pieces in the *BiblioTech* exhibition to be inspiring, recognising within them an expression and conjoining of many of the concepts I understand within my seemingly disparate areas of interest and operation: information, data, libraries; and magick and the performing arts. In this essay I will describe how Biblio-technics of the sort included in the exhibition can augment the work of libraries and librarians – and provide a route into cultural and mystical thought.

BiblioTech as augmentation of library work

In the case of data collections and research data creation [this] has also led to the rise of a new kind of library professional: the data librarian. But to what extent is this in fact a new role and in what ways does it differ from traditional librarianship? – Robin Rice & John Southall, *The Data Librarian's Handbook* (Facet, 2018)

As 'digital and data' take centre stage at the national strategic level of academic librarianship[1], my role in the library has become more strategically prominent: I am both my institution's data librarian and represent data-librarianship on Lancaster University library's 'digital transformation group'. Considering aspects of the increasingly data-needy environment, featuring such phenomena as data-driven decision-making and automation of processes, as part of librarianship and research

1. UK Government, *National Data Strategy* (2020) https://www.gov.uk/government/publications/uk-national-data-strategy/national-data-strategy.

culture, creates an incredibly complex environment with inherent conflict of interests, and multiple issues with no ready-made solutions or answers.

A seminal paper by Awre et al[2], authored when library research data management services were generally in their infancy, positions research data management as a 'wicked problem'. Describing a particular mapping exercise the authors comment, "Mapped out in this way, what was striking was a sense of the scale and reach of the problem. The overall map began to reveal a common landscape, if not, as participants commented, any common or complete solutions." Similarly, a miro board produced by Mounier in 2022[3] showcases a "Forest of Publications, Meadows of Data and Hills of Policies," in an interlinked landscape, clearly illustrating the complexities that exist in this space. My first impressions of the *BiblioTech* exhibition was that the pieces might inspire new routes through this landscape. Examining them in detail has provided a few.

Post Digital Research Data Management?

Firstly, considering the *BiblioTech* exhibition pieces themselves as a set of academic outputs, that clearly make use of data throughout the lifecycle of their production, brings us to the area of Research Data Management (RDM) for the Arts. Each work here functions as a problem of storage, containment and preservation with no easy solutions: raising questions around whether established RDM frameworks might be actively hindering the intellectual progress of the arts disciplines.

In "Archiving Brain Fruits",[4] I identify 5 areas where RDM interventions at the very least fail to provide any advantages to arts researchers. These are: the inability to translate advice on data to advice on immersive experiences, the reductive nature of capturing art pieces as an output, the importance of process and how this is not the same as methodology, the clear lack of benefit of any of this type of activity in a broad sense, and issues surrounding re-use including copyright.

These issues clearly play out within the pieces in the *BiblioTech* exhibition, though many of them involve data and code that can be published and archived in the usual way. For example, the *It's Not You, It's Me* piece has code associated with it that could be entered into a repository. However, the experience of interacting with the artificial intelligence is the crux of the artwork, and this cannot be captured. Publishing the associated code has the effect of elevating that above the true meaning of the piece, and is therefore detrimental to the research culture of arts disciplines. As a data librarian, I can not allow that to happen. But what to do? I am responsible for supporting research, even when it takes directions that place librarianship itself in odd, new territory. Relational and interactive art is one such example. I was inspired when learning that pieces in the exhibition take up collecting as a theme, as to whether the concepts expressed within them might steer me in the direction of what I can do for arts researchers and their outputs, rather than what I shouldn't do. Silvio Lorusso's *Post-Digital Publishing Archive*, is particularly enlightening in this area, especially the concept of, poor media,[5] where seemingly reductive

2. Chris Awre et al., "Research Data Management as a 'wicked problem'", *Library Review* Vol. 64 No. 4/5 (Emerald, 2015): 356–371. **3.** Mounier, Pierre, Connecting the Building Blocks of Open Science: an ecological approach, Miro (2002), accessed February 7, 2023, https://miro.com/app/board/uXjVP-zE1QU=/?moveToWidget=3458764540099894047&cot=14 (associated paper https://doi.org/10.7557/5.6772). **4.** Joanne Fitzpatrick (Apr 14 2023). Archiving Brain Fruits: Research Data Management for The Arts, UKSG Annual Conference 2023, Underline Science Inc. DOI: 10.48448/ynbg-2717. **5.** Silvio Lorusso et al, *Post Digital Publishing Archive,* accessed February 7, 2023, http://p-dpa.net.

formats, such as plain text, are positively described as better-supporting distribution, security, storage and usability than their rich media counterparts, which Lorusso characterises as being ornamental and serving only to justify the technology.

While given different emphasis and using different language, these are all already prized aspects of file formats in established research data management and digital preservation practices. Removing the proprietary nature of a file to allow for maximum opportunities for compatibility and migration, while retaining the usability and completeness of data, has the same effect of converting it into, poor media, and we are very much on the same page here.

I wonder if there are low-resolution solutions to RDM in rich media areas?
Similarly, the description of how the p-dpa supports experimental publishing is incredibly useful, and I found propositions for my own field in these aspects that underpin post-digital approaches:

> A practical, hands-on approach in which making produces meaning.
>
> An (inexorably impermanent) antagonism towards the mediating forces of the hegemonic discourse.[6]

Perhaps I could consider the decision making process that happens as a research project moves from the active data phase, to the phase that considers long term archiving of only some of that data, as a meaningful artistic process in itself. One where the shape of the output, i.e. the dataset, inspires rather than antagonises the creation of what will fill it. I can't imagine what a dataset like that would look like, but I do know that I will now recognise it when I see it.

Therefore, one wicked problem that *BiblioTech* has shed some light on for me is that when the 'reducing' happens, when preparing an arts research dataset for publication and archiving, then a conscious focussing on removal of ornamental 'nice to have' aspects and retaining the core meaning, might be a route to achieving a data output that is a true reflection of the artwork, and that the production of this output can be seen as an experience in itself.

Data as Information

Another area that I found the *BiblioTech* pieces to be supportive of my library work was in what I saw as a blurring of the lines between data and information. I often find that it's useful, although not entirely accurate, to think of a spectrum that consists of data, information, knowledge and wisdom, with librarians traditionally placed firmly in the area of information, or, 'data with meaning'. Therefore, as a data librarian, I am slightly misplaced.

Focussing on the *RNN Triptych*, particularly with regards to their focus on "the level of the letter, rather than the network of semantic relations,"[7] and then building this into a tool like *The Re-Reader*, has the effect of highlighting the limitations of the spectrum I described above, by redefining the relationship of data to information. Data can be thought of as a discrete form of information, the binary code behind forms of data that can be understood, and crucially, is used in the research project to underpin findings and academic arguments. However, in the *RNN Triptych*, the artificial intelligence has purposefully been built to be more error prone, highlighting

6. Ibid. **7.** Nathan Jones, Tom Schofield and Sam Skinner, *RNN Triptych*, accessed February 7, 2023, https://torquetorque.net/publications/rnn-triptych.

the concept that data is not infallible. In the pieces within the triptych, the discrete parts of the concepts – the individual letters or words considered without context – are only useful when transposed into being information. In the case of *The Re-Reader*, this happens when the user is able to read in a more efficient way, while in *It's Not You, It's Me*, this happens when new terms are encountered that aren't able to be defined.

I think approaching these concepts from the point of view of art, rather than technology and tools, has the effect of redefining the relationship of data and information. Rather than data being that which proves the information correct, its data-ness now becomes something that is used as a tool to generate or even inspire information-like encounters. The end user, who introduces the 'meaning' to the data that conceptually makes it information, has a different role here, not one of analysing data for its insights, but asking on presentation, "Is this data right?"

This feels like my 'in', as an information professional tasked with supporting work with data. Libraries lead in the area of information and media literacy, developing what are now essential skills, and they could also lead in data literacy, but not only that, in the link between all three. As RDM and library support for it develops, the emphasis will go from enabling researchers to publish data, to reaching a kind of data publishing 'critical mass' where the emphasis will tip towards re-using the large amounts of data outputs now available. Taking my cue from *BiblioTech*, I could emulate the artificial intelligence in these pieces, asking researchers looking for datasets, "Is this data right?"

Something else that is the concern of librarians, and the team I work on in particular, is the seeming divide between the digital and physical domains, and the loss of place, context and relevance that the advent of the digital library is said to preside over. Thomas Shaw articulates this in a piece for CILIP's Information Professional[8] "...we often think in terms of a digital-physical dichotomy, where these constitute separate pillars. I would argue this no longer reflects our reality. Digital-physical is a complex intersection, not two separate worlds."

This sentiment I saw reflected in the *BiblioTech* pieces, particularly the Library of Babel which theoretically contains every book that has and will ever be written, using an algorithm to generate them at the point of demand, rather than a physical space (as in it's fictional conception) to store them. The jump from physical to digital that has made this library possible highlights the power that lies with the digital domain, effectively flipping the physical/real and the digital/not real around, to show that here, it is the digital that is possible and the physical that remains impossible.

Similarly, the positive aspects of a physical library are retained: a sense of place through the links with the fictional Library of Babel, a method of orientation through the hexagonal chambers, a continuation of the use of serendipity and most importantly of all, the need for a person who has gone that way before to help you find the 'good stuff' amongst the 'nonsense'.

These are the useful applications of *BiblioTech* I see as a librarian within the exhibition pieces: a way to manage artistic data outputs, and support with blurring lines between both data and information, and the digital and physical domains. All of these are helpful with conceptualising the changes needed in order to support academia going forwards. But this is not the end of what I saw within the pieces and where I

8. Thomas Shaw, "No Separation Between Digital and Physical?," *CILIP Information Professional* (2022) https://content.yudu.com/web/43mce/0A43mcf/InfoPro41December22/html/index.html?page=16&origin=reader.

might be able to put the ideas within them to use: there is more that *BiblioTech* can offer digital and data librarianship – that is, if we look five-dimensionally.

BiblioTech as augmentation of magick and the occult

> Wisdom and knowledge can best be understood together. Knowledge is learning, the power of the mind to understand and describe the universe. Wisdom is knowing how to apply knowledge and how not to apply it. Knowledge is knowing what to say; wisdom is knowing whether or not to say it. – Starhawk, *The Spiral Dance* (Harper Collins, 1999)

While making use of artificial intelligence that uses errors within itself to speak in a charming fashion all of its own, and fictional infinite libraries that actually have been brought into existence, is wide enough thinking for a librarian, as a long term practicing occultist, I saw much material within *BiblioTech* that provoked me to think further.

When I say I am about to look five-dimensionally, I am referring to the concept within physics that concerns the next dimension beyond three-dimensional space and the fourth dimension of time. Out in the field and on the front lines of experimental occult practice, there is much excitement that quantum indeterminacy, discovered in physics, might act as a full explanation of why magick and spells work.

Founder of chaos magick, Peter J Carroll, places his current work in the emergent area of five-dimensional thought, advocating against the big bang theory, towards a theory that the universe in fact comprises a five-dimensional hypersphere.[9] In an earlier work *The Octavo*[10] where the beginnings of this work are discussed, he states, "Most magicians have an intuition that some sort of 'Astral' plane or 'Etheric' link between events must play a part in magic," and goes on to include the following in a Knight of Chaos invocation:

> Mathematical entrapment I abhor,
> The calculators they would imprison me,
> With numerous tricks and glamorous pics,
> But I get out of that with a quantum fix.

Articulating the modern magician's belief that magic is just a science that hasn't been discovered yet, and with scientific advances in this area suggesting links on a fifth dimension we can only perceive in part, we become ever closer to a full scientific explanation of magick.

This is the lens that I looked at *BiblioTech* through in the first instance, and this is perhaps why *The Blob of Impossible Images* became the piece that was most accessible to me in terms of concept. Very like Mournier's ecological mapping of Open Science, with it's Oceans of Platforms and Tools, the Blob features an, "Ecology of Compression Complexities"[11] to allow the images to be rendered, and also augments the possibilities and applications of physics research in a way I

9. Peter Carroll, *Hypersphere Cosmology,* (2017), working paper available at: https://www.researchgate.net/publication/32093. **10.** Peter Carroll, *The Octavo,* (Mandrake of Oxford, 2011). **11.** Rosa Menkman, *The BLOB of Im/Possible Images,* accessed March 4, 2023, https://newart.city/catalog/menkman-blob-of-im-possibilities. **12.** U.D. Frater, *Models of Magick,* (1991), accessed April 4, 2023, https://www.sacred-texts.com/bos/bos065.htm.

saw as very similar to Carroll's application.

This also brings me to a discussion of the, "Information Model," of magick, described in a frequently circulated Frater UD article[12] concerned with instantaneous, non-depleting information transfer through magickal techniques. I often wonder how information gained in this way, or through concepts such as unverified personal gnosis or divination or dreams, could ever be considered a source on a par with citable research. I identified 'Rationality vs Mysteries'[13] as a key concern of occultists interacting with information, where a reliance on this type of non-rational information was seen as an indicator of authenticity.

BiblioTech pieces, such as the *Blob of Impossible Images* and the Library of Babel, that both focus on rendering something imaginary (or without of the dimensions we can sense) to something real, I see as also building on the credibility and status of this type of information gathering, reinforcing the flow from inside to out that is at the core of magickal practice.

Intermission's *Negentropic Fields* contains many of these concepts, starting with it's construction within a hypercube, echoing the hypersphere above that allows magick to happen, and I also recognise within this piece chaos magick's focus on entropy, or as I usually describe it, creative disorder, as shown in this particular command, "Immanentise the Eschaton, any which way you can, shun entropy, but exploit chaos to the full."[14] I also thought of the section in TechGnosis that describes Philip K Dick's encounter with an entity called VALIS, described as a "spontaneous self-monitoring negentropic vortex"[15], later written into a novel of the same name.

Negentropic Fields I saw as not only mirroring many of these tropes, but again providing a practical application of them to information science, through a non-linear iterative cataloguing and preservation system that allows for serendipitous five dimensional wandering through its collection, and yet more methods of bringing the non-rational or non-tangible into being. The piece challenges me to return to the wicked problems of data librarianship, leave reality behind and think in the imaginary and non-rational realm first, and then look at what I can pull back into being with me. This is a magickal process that is very familiar to me, and Negentropic Fields provides me with some sense of a way to bring this to current information professional practices.

Further magickal practitioner's work that I recognised within the *BiblioTech* pieces was William S Burroughs and his cut-ups, and Austin Osman Spare's sigils, both incredibly popular techniques among magickal practitioners. Focussing on Burroughs, who used collages to achieve magickal aims that have the following effects, "With a cut-up you can break down the expected, inherited values and assumptions and retrain yourself to look at revealing possibilities, describing 'reality' more accurately than any linear system. Our languages are linear. Life is not."[16] The focus on non-linear reading chopped right down to its component parts of individual words and letters I saw reflected in both *The ReReader* and Anna Barham's *Poisonous Oysters* work.

13. Joanne Fitzpatrick, *If That Which Thou Seekest Thou Findest Not Within Thee, Thou Wilt Never Find It On The Internet: How Practitioner Contemporary Pagans and Ritual Magicians Access and Use Information.* Pomegranate, 23(1-2) (Equinox, 2022): 203–231. **14.** Peter Carroll, *PsyberMagick: Advanced Ideas in Chaos Magick* (New Falcon Publications, 1995). **15.** Erik Davis, *TechGnosis: Myth, Magic, and Mysticism in the Age of Information* (North Atlantic Books, 1998). **16.** Genesis P-Orridge, *Thee Psychick Bible* (Alecto Enterprises, 1994). **17.** Anna Barham, *Poisonous Oysters* (2019), accessed April 4, 2023, http://www.annabarham.net/images/poisonousoysters.html.

Within the process of making *Poisonous Oysters* which Barham summarises, "Passages from the texts... were read aloud by the participants and interpreted by speech recognition software over and over, creating a poly-vocal feedback loop with the machine,"[17] I can see magickal potential. Versions of this technique could be used to receive divinatory or precognitive messages contained within the words that the speech recognition software eventually picks out. This is similar to Burroughs most well described work, taking the audio of London's first coffee shop, and looping it on itself in a similar way using technology of the time. I am also drawn to the page that contains the black cut out shape that allows certain words to show through, which is close to techniques I would use for bibliomancy.

While I'm not sure that psychic librarianship will ever be professionalised, I do think that considering library collections and scholarly communications in this way might provide a strong solution to introducing serendipitous discovery into the digital space. While the sense of place is lost during retrieval processes searching for digital items, cut-ups offer a way of changing 'the place' so that it is suitable for the digital environment. This would create a digital environment that more closely reflects our minds than any physical space ever could, as cut-ups, "... probably more accurately mirror the way the world is experienced by most people in an increasingly accelerated, fragmentary, and seemingly random datascape."[18]

Moving onto Spare's sigils, I also saw the potential for meaningful sigils in the techniques presented by Erica Scourti's *Clean Sheets*, Mark Simmonds' *D-E-T-A-I-L* and Joe Devlin's *Marginalia Drawings*. "Sigils are monograms of thought... a mathematical means of symbolising desire and giving it form that has the virtue of preventing any thought and association on that particular desire, escaping the detection of the Ego"[19] and they can be created in any way the magician deems suitable, the most common method being to reduce the component letters of a statement into one form, drawn on top of each other.

This is the technique I recognised within *Clean Sheets*. In Scourti's poem, "Lost to the Phosphorus,"[20] I see hints at this influence too, "How to write an apotropaic visual device?" could be interpreted as a sigil, and, "I've always felt alienated from my own voice," describes some of the mental processes that sigilisation causes to happen. The sheets themselves I saw as an example of a hyper-sigil, a technique attributed to Grant Morrison where, "The 'hypersigil' or 'supersigil' develops the sigil concept beyond the static image and incorporates elements such as characterisation, drama and plot. The hypersigil is a sigil extended through the fourth dimension."[21] *Clean Sheets* showed a clear period of time, the national lockdowns, represented in these extended hypersigils.

D-E-T-A-I-L and *Marginalia Drawings* I saw as inspiring me in the same area, with the former making me consider using the negative rather than positive shapes of letters in sigils which I have never seen done, and the latter again showing superimposed writing, but having the effect of showing the spaces or negative parts of a book page, and with the intention of causing linking between the readers. This linking is a key addition in *Marginalia Drawings* to this area of exploration for me, and part of traditional witchcraft practices of course make use of touch in order to

18. Matthew Levi Stevens, *The Magical Universe of William S Burroughs* (Mandrake of Oxford, 2014). **19.** Austin Osman Spare, *The Book of Pleasure* (Co-operative Printing Society, 1913). **20.** Erica Scourti, "Lost to the Phosphorus" in *Spells: 21st Century Occult Poetry*, eds. Sarah Shin and Rebecca Tamas (Ignota Press, 2019). **21.** Grant Morrison, "Pop Magick" in *Book of Lies: The Disinformation Guide to Magick and the Occult*, ed. Metzger (Disinformation Books, 2003).

receive divinatory information on a subject, or obtaining personal items in order to perform spells, and thinking of locks of hair in this way will give you an idea of the kinds of links I am referring to. Handwriting is a less than optimal, but not unusable object to form magickal links with, and I can now go back to the opening statements on quantum indeterminacy. Although it seems in our three-and-a-bit dimensional world that disparate people's handwriting is not linked by the magickal act of superimposing them on top of each other, if the universe really is a hypersphere, then this act most definitely does link them on this fifth dimension.

Presented within the context of the *BiblioTech* exhibition, and being encouraged to consider these methods used as a form of writing and publishing, rather than a method of magick, was an additional grid I could look through to reframe the skills and knowledge I have developed in sigil craft. Initially, this view has the effect of shifting focus again from the output and onto the method, something I identified earlier as being key to effective RDM for the arts. But not only this, it presents a clear use case for the concept of the 'micro-publication', as reflected in innovative platforms such as Jisc's Octopus[22], where methodology becomes a type of publication that can be cited in its own right.

However, I also consider that what the addition of a magickal viewpoint to these works offers, is a focus not on the method, but on the experience of going through the method. Elevating experience is something I identified within my 'Principles of Open Source Witchcraft'[23] where I advocated that embodied experiences within a set time and space were not something that could ever be effected by sharing secret oath-bound knowledge, the nature of our being means they remain yours and remain hidden to others.

For this reason, I cannot imagine 'experience' ever appearing as a form of micro-publication, and I think this is where *BiblioTech* really has reached the limits of what is possible, yet I find myself finishing this essay with a hope that further developments in all the areas presented in the exhibition might just find a way.

BiblioTech as a binding of libraries and magick that shows the way

> Pure information, in the mathematical sense, does not require energy;
> it is that which orders energy. It is the negative of entropy, that which
> brings disorder to energy systems... The meta-physiological circuit, then,
> is this cosmic Information System... It is hard to avoid hyperbole when
> talking of such matters, but everything one can associate with
> the idea of Oneness With God – or Oneness with 'Everything' –
> is part of what is experienced in the vistas, beyond space-time,
> of this meta-physiological circuit.
> — Wilson, *Prometheus Rising* (Falcon Press, 1986)

The *BiblioTech* pieces offered me a lot, not just in considering how I would manage them as research outputs, and helping me to position myself within a fast developing landscape, but in other, less tangible and hard to describe ways.

Knowledge obtained in a non-rational way is often hard to accept within increasingly STEM focussed academia, but it is often the place where the inspiration

22. "Octopus: Creating a new primary research record for science," accessed April 4, 2023, https://www.jisc.ac.uk/rd/projects/octopus-creating-a-new-primary-research-record-for-science.

23. Joanne Fitzpatrick, *Open Source Witchcraft* (Magickal Women Conference 2022).

and the breakthroughs seep in, and I found *BiblioTech* emphasised and elevated this, on occasion providing the beginnings of practical methods of handling this type of knowledge.

Another key take away I discovered was an approach regarding one of the libraries' best loved aspects – the sense of place, and particularly moving this from the physical to the digital. *BiblioTech* offered a way of changing the place to be suitable for digital spaces, rather than scrapping the place altogether, and the result was an environment that was more like our minds than our bodies.

Although in their infancy and with much development left to do, the potential for micro publications was something I saw within *BiblioTech*, and I would like to see arts research outputs supported with innovative infrastructure such as these, as well as increasingly sophisticated digital preservation systems. The pieces have influenced me to further advocate within this area.

Finally, I saw the importance of experience within *BiblioTech*, something that I already believed in. I am left feeling optimistic that at the very least experience will increase in value, to match that of quantifiable data outputs and visible changes, and at the best continued developments in *BiblioTech* might find a way of documenting, sharing and reproducing experiences of art, and the occult alike.

What would the implications of all this wide thinking, development work and binding of disparate influences be for the field of data librarianship? Returning to the Rice and Southall quote that described this as a new role just 5 years ago, there are still clear opportunities to shape a definition of the responsibilities. However, given that there are many unanswered questions and intangible concepts to deal with in this discipline, fraught with wicked challenges and landscapes with no map, after this examination of the *BiblioTech* pieces, I think this process of defining and 'territory claiming' that comes from a maturing field is something we should avoid, as it would prevent much of the learning and development from augmenting what is possible.

The role of the data librarian has potential to expand, into arts and magick and experiences as outputs, but if I become more specific with that – it has the potential to become not just a role concerned with research data outputs, but with all 'alternative' outputs. Research datasets are often seen in broad terms within RDM, encompassing anything that is required in order to prove that arguments within traditional research outputs, such as journal articles and monographs, are based in fact. Expanding what is included within this definition is required to expand the disciplines data librarians are able to support, which in turn moves further away from data and further away from that being a useful description of the remit of this type of librarian.

BiblioTech has shown that the best way of supporting the arts is not to find the data output, snapshot it and preserve it, but to tread much more carefully, changing ourselves so as to avoid changing, or even erasing, a whole discipline in an increasingly data hungry world. To me, this more fits what librarians are trying to do than could ever be achieved by seeking to data-fy outputs in order to provide evidence.

Similarly, datasets are already seen as a type of grey literature, but the relationship between data and grey literature is also evolving, so that on occasion, I am given grey literature in the form of posters, presentations and reports to preserve as if they are datasets, because that is indeed what they increasingly contain. Almost a synonym for 'alternative' research outputs, but not quite, grey literature is also an emerging output type of importance that has the potential to show a more accurate picture of a researcher's strengths and impact, again something that more closely fits the values of librarianship than providing increased access to data does. Many of the *BiblioTech* pieces could be considered as grey literature, further emphasising the importance of bringing this into the role.

If the blurring of concepts that *BiblioTech* has helped me to explore can be brought back into my field, then I foresee a blurring of the role of data librarian and digital archivist, into a discipline that advocates for the merits of an incredibly wide range of available research outputs, keeps those outputs preserved and accessible, and works to establish them all as having equal status and value.

The emphasis of data librarianship today is very much on publishing, sharing and archiving research datasets. As the availability of published datasets reaches critical mass, also in acceleration is the support needed for finding, re-using and citing datasets, and the accompanying grey literature and alternative outputs that I am expecting. In future, subject librarians that focus on a particular discipline will not only focus on navigating traditional content and resources, but will provide the access, platforms and literacy skills to make best use of everything. The lot. Even the impossible things.

Because, as DuQuette[24] explains, "God can only realise Itself by becoming Many, and then experiencing all possibilities through the adventures of Its many parts," and when we publish, share, archive, and subsequently find, re-use, cite and link all of these outputs, we are linking all of experience, and linking God back to Itself. This is the 'Supreme Enlightenment' that DuQuette describes, and the 'Oneness with God' that Wilson describes, and I would describe it as just a day at work.

24. Lon Milo DuQuette, *The Chicken Qabalah* (Red Wheel/Weiser, 2001).

A Bridge Made of Books – An Interview with Wafaa Bilal

Sam Skinner

This interview explores *168:01*, an artwork by Wafaa Bilal which was first shown at Art Gallery of Windsor, Canada, in 2016 and has since gone on to be presented at numerous galleries worldwide. The project seeks to rebuild the library of the College of Fine Arts at the University of Baghdad, which was destroyed during the invasion of Iraq in 2003. The installation comprises a library of blank books, which can be purchased and money raised is used to buy books on an online 'wishlist' compiled by staff and students at the college. As blank books are bought they are replaced by books from the wishlist in the gallery, before being sent to Iraq. Since its inception the project has expanded to receive donations from The Metropolitan Museum of Art in New York and add to the collections of libraries at the University of Baghdad, University of Mosul, University of Babylon, and the Iraqi National Museum. This interview took place online in April, 2023, between Wafaa in New York, USA and Sam in Oxford, UK.

Sam Skinner: Thanks so much for taking the time Wafaa to meet today. It's great to reconnect following your participation in *The New Observatory* exhibition at FACT in Liverpool.[1] That exhibition sought to manifest a peculiar type of observatory; one run by artists and composed of various weird and wonderful instruments and artworks, which engaged with the how knowledge is produced and what is put into motion through observational practices. I had been studying floorplans of different historic observatories, and alongside laboratories, computer rooms, and telescope chambers, I found that there were often libraries and reading rooms in observatories. We wanted to represent these different facets of the observatory within the exhibition, and make them functioning, participatory, and live, to be able to really bring an observatory to life. I was aware of your *168:01* project and it felt like it could resonate beautifully within the project. I loved the way the artwork was a real functioning library, but one which existed in multiple spaces at the same time and echoed how early scientific and scholarly

1. *The New Observatory*, FACT, Liverpool, 22.06.17–01.10.17. Group exhibition co-curated by Sam Skinner and Hannah Redler-Hawes, accessed August 1, 2023, https:www.fact.co.uk/event/the-new-observatory.

networks were defined by exchange and connection between different people and places, via the mediums of observation, inscription, and resultant media. Gianni Pomata writes about observational notebooks being passed between early scientists in the 15th-century on horseback, which is a wonderful image of a kind of packhorse powered BiblioTech!

Your project *168:01* although echoing these early systems of exchange is stridently contemporary in how it addresses the rebuilding of Iraq and uses modern systems of book distribution, in particular Amazon 'wishlists'. There have been multiple iterations of the project. Perhaps speaking about the genesis of the project is a good place to start?

Wafaa Bilal: The project's objective was an attempt to understand and engage with two places: a place of conflict and a place of comfort. The site of conflict being Iraq, and the place of comfort, the relative safety of the USA and Canada, and other western countries where the work was exhibited in its 'blank book' form. And I have these two places in mind since I have existed and lived in both.

What I wanted to do is use the library as an open space and take the politics out of the conflict, to enable a conversation between an individual and another individual, a group and another a group, with a clear objective; to reward everybody. But the mechanism was difficult to come up with. What happened with the exchange? You purchase a book based on a list from the Baghdad College of Fine Art, then in return for your donation, you get a blank white book. And that blank book reminds you of your contribution and also reminds you of how access to education is privileged in some places and how it has been affected by conflict. But most of all, it reminds you of what that book, and others, stands for and what its effect may be on future generations.

SS: It is interesting to think how your white book, however blank, remains a book. I remember during conversations for the *The New Observatory*, you were explicit that they should be properly bound books, made to a certain specification, not just readymade sketch books. The bookmaker we used had never received such a commission! The point being you're not denying people a book who purchase one. The content is missing, in one sense, but not in another. It's not a simple negation.

WB: Yes, it's really not. And in order, I think to deeply contemplate this project, we just have to go a little bit back in time and understand how it operates as a kind of trigger device. I think it was 2010. I was in Canada for the *Images Festival* and I met Srimoyee Mitra, who was an independent curator at the time. We began a conversation about the destruction that took place in Iraq, specifically to libraries, and these conversations turned into a proposal for an installation, but nothing participatory, at the Art Gallery of Windsor, in Canada, where Srimoyee was working.

I visited the gallery and was planning an installation concerned with raising awareness of what had happened in Iraq. Then with not long to go before the exhibition was due to open, I called and said I have an idea, a different one. What I want to do is connect these two places, build a participatory project where both sides get rewarded, but there is a tangible result on the ground. Sadly, when the dust settles in the conflict zone, everybody packs and leaves. Perhaps too in an exhibition, when an installation is taken down or thrown out, something similar happens. *168:01* is a project about this moment *after* destruction, about processes of rebuilding, and forging longer-term, deeper connections.

LANDON MACKENZIE
Design
FLORENCE

Left: Wafaa Bilal, *168:01*, Art Gallery of Windsor, Canada, 2016. Photos: Frank Piccolo and John Dean

As a child, I was told a story that the Mongols in the 13th-century threw all the books from Baghdad's Bayt al-Hikma library into the Tigris River to create a bridge to cross to the other side. And the crucial moment came when, people tell us, the water ran blue for seven days. Washing all the knowledge and the ink into that river. I began to imagine what happened to these books after the knowledge was washed away. They become white, right? Let's imagine that. And let's imagine that moment. As a trigger to reverse the destruction. The title comes specifically from the seven days. If you count the hours in seven days it's 168 hours. Then I added the minute, the 0:1 after that. This is the moment to reverse the clock by participation.

Alongside this I was thinking about the library in the Baghdad College of Fine Art, which I used to visit, where 70,000 titles were lost during the 2003 invasion in a fire. I called Srimoyee and I explained what the new idea was, what the centrepiece would be and I think it went silent on the other side of the phone. And I thought either this is a great idea or Srimoyee is freaking out about it. I said I want 1000 pristine white books with nothing printed on them.

I had a very specific vision for the book; how they were bound, hardback, dust-jacket, etc. The feel of the book was important. At the beginning we went through multiple printers checking lots of samples before we settled on which type to make. I also didn't want the influence of an individual or particular institution on the project via funding. I wanted to take the politics out of this exchange, partly because I was anticipating what would happen when the books arrived in Iraq. Officials would be asking where does this donation come from. So, for me it was clear that I had to go to individuals and use Kickstarter to enable the purchase of the blank books and those on the College wishlist. It was surprising; we were aiming for $10,000, but within 30 days we had collected $56,000.

> **SS:** The project clearly caught people's imagination and resonated with the gallery's community in Canada and beyond. I wonder if you could say something about those that donated and received white books in Canada. Alongside that, it would be interesting to hear about the development of the wishlist of books that individual's at Baghdad College of Fine Art collated and their experience of the project. Also, relations between these sites, communities, and individuals, and how the project developed more broadly, for example I know it took a long time for the books to arrive in Baghdad.

WB: It did take time for Iraqi government permissions to be granted for the delivery of books, but I'll come back to that. It's important to say that a principal question was: What kinds of books would it be and how would they be chosen? We can't enforce particular titles on people, hence the college collating the wishlist. But initially we were faced with scepticism, which is logical when it comes to Iraqis on the ground. This has everything to do with how many people promise, and sadly, no one delivers. So, we focused on being very transparent, connecting with people, communicating what agency means in the project and how exchange occurs.

Within the project one objective was to place a book in the library in the Baghdad College of Fine Art, and the second was to break the isolation of the Iraqi intellect. Years of war and embargos left Iraqis isolated from the rest of the world. With this project connections made are more important than the books themselves. *168:01* connected students and their faculties to the world outside in order to complete the exchange.

Right above: Wafaa Bilal, *168:01*, Art Gallery of Windsor, Canada, 2016. Photo: Nadja Pelkey.
Right Below: Wafaa Bilal, *House of Wisdom*, Sharjah, 2021 – ongoing. Photo: Bernard Jouaret.

SS: So, the books acted as connecting devices to something larger, stitching together and catalysing a network of relations, but the journey of books to Iraq was not an easy one as I understand?

WB: One of the biggest problems we faced is a global one: bureaucracy. In Iraq, the government has a system to address or mask unemployment – they hire more people than needed for government jobs. But this creates a bloated, ineffective bureaucracy, an ineffective system with so much redundancy. Whether this is intentional or not who knows, but they make it really hard to achieve anything. Then there was the problem of who is in charge and who wants these books to be in Iraq or not? And that problem didn't go away to this day. Some don't like the idea of books coming from outside, because I think some in power would love to exist in darkness. The expansion of knowledge does not help politicians and the books were a threat. Let's put it that way. It took me two years to get the first books there. So, on one side, the project was successful, but on the other, in Iraq, there were entities preventing this exchange. Acting in fear to control knowledge.

SS: In this way the project echoes how historically books and libraries have been targets for violence or censorship. It's interesting that *168:01* was in part inspired by the Mongol's supposed desecration of the library in Bagdad, whereby it is the outsider who commits an act of violence upon knowledge, that you seek to reverse. But your act is met with resistance as it is perceived as a kind of Western imperialism. So, there is a kind of diffraction occurring in *168:01* between differing spatial, political and temporal forces.

WB: Well, it should be noted that they were mainly Western books written in English, with the exception of course, of when we did the project in Taiwan and Sharjah. But this notion of foreign books, we don't know what they bring, and the idea of keeping control of the individual, are both at play in this project. Historically, it was easier for the regime when the place was locked. Before the Internet, before satellites, nothing except the power of the government. Today, if you want to make things work in Iraq, if you can, you go to the highest authority in the land and it happens right away. I refuse to do that. And the reason for that? I didn't want the project to be enforced on anybody. This is why the slow careful process of participation is not a problem and where the strength of the project lies.

SS: Yes, if you were to ask permission from the top, you are subjugating yourself to that hierarchy. Giving it life and perpetuating it in the act of recognising it.

WB: Exactly, but the situation is also more complex than that because as one cedes power to authority, you also diminish the power of the individual. Because it's not coming from the ground up, but top down. And I felt that if this idea, this project, is not rooted in the belief system of the individual and does not build from the ground up, it's not going to work.

From, the beginning there was rejection of the project from within the college itself by the dean. I was told we don't accept charity. The battle took two years. We began to make progress when we put conversations with the university's

168:01
168:01
168:01
النقد الفني
دراسة في المفاهيم والتطبيقات

administrative forces to one side and began working with Zaid Luqman from the faculty of ceramics and more directly with the students at the college. What also helped was a chance meeting with Iraq's previous minister of culture when I was in Abu Dhabi and gave a talk there. I told him about the project and he loved it. By that time it had been two years with nothing moving, books in storage, costs mounting and frustration increasing. The ex-minister put me in touch with those in the cultural ministry and the next thing we know the dean accepted the gift and the first shipment of the books could be sent. I didn't go looking for this help, but when it came, at the right time and after a long wait, it was too fortuitous to refuse. However, we had another problem, because when the library was burnt down it wasn't just the books that were lost but the library itself, so although they had rebuilt the building there was no designated library space or shelving for the books to go. And we had to begin to think about this.

> **SS:** I would describe the project and your practice as an act of *library-making*, which hybridises practices of printmaking and bookmaking with elements of participatory art and institutional critique. Your project really demonstrates that a library is not simply a collection of books, but also architectural space, storage and information systems, and the community that maintains and uses the library itself.

WB: Yes, and in the case of *168:01* how are these things brought forth from a place of historic destruction and in the face of the continued resistance we faced. So, I really got to explore in the project the question of: What is a library? And to me the library is a place for contemplation, thinking and interacting, and of course, on top of that knowledge, right? But that notion of the library got disrupted by the digital age.

I know the effect of libraries. As a child growing up in a home with seven kids, every morning I would wake up, my mum would make me my tea, put it in a thermos and I would go to the library. I was there from early morning until midday, before returning home and then going to school. In libraries there is a kind of unsigned contract saying: Hey, when you come to this place, you suspend everything else in your life. This is why they have always been important, but also in the digital age why they begin to take on a new and increasing relevance. In this space of suspension, after perhaps browsing shelves or searching something out, I focus on one thing – a book in front of me. It is a place to acquire knowledge. To be quiet and then to contemplate, undisturbed. That quiet space is as important as the book itself, particularly now as we deal with the distractions of digital media. And distractions are not the only issue, because the computer and digital media challenges the book and the library as the primary source of knowledge. Individuals have started to think if knowledge is widely available through devices and the Internet what's the need for the library. But I think that's a big mistake because we are beginning to understand now that the digital is not a simple replacement, it comes with a host of issues and there is a degree of loss at play.

> **SS:** I like how you spoke about the unsigned contract of the library. How do they differ to the unwritten rules or intrinsic effects of less embodied digitised architectures of, and interfaces to, information. All the small gestures that occur when visiting a library, like the thermos your mother packed for you, your journey to and from the library. The physical book and the library still compares well in technical terms to digital formats and platforms, for example the ability to fan through bound pages beats most scroll bars, or lithographic

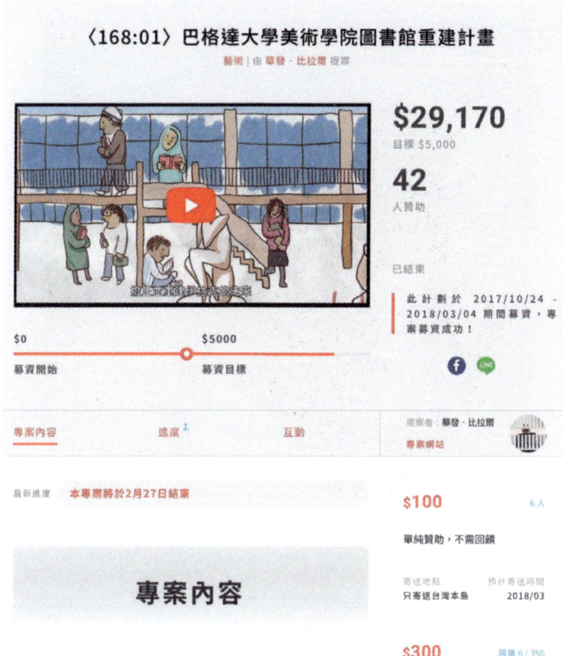

Screenshot from Kickstarter for *168:01* for the 2017 Asian Art Biennial

printing is in many ways higher resolution than most screens, paperbacks are lighter than tablets and don't need charging, etc.[2] But of course the beauty and dynamic potential of the situation is that there doesn't need to be a binary between print and digital, online and public library, one better or worse than the other. But in a culture where we are being pushed subsidised devices or there is the herding effect of algorithmic curation, it's difficult to read and use libraries in different post-digital hybrid ways that is equitable, creative and possesses a degree of autonomy. It does feel that public libraries and printed media have a special relevance as the experience of, and access to, online media is so controlled by a small number of platforms. You explore relationships between digital and print via the wishlist and the purchase of printed books in the project, for example, but did this surface in other ways?

WB: One of the early criticisms of the project was people saying why would you undertake this when you have digital access, right? Well, let's break that down. At the beginning of the project, we are talking about Iraq in 2016. Where electricity comes two hours a day. So right away digital access is affected. Let's say denied, right? Then we come to a greater problem, which is that access to knowledge when it comes to the digital is restricted by an institution's access rights and costs. Then it goes deeper than that because if you prioritise the digital over physical artefacts and space, you loose access to everything that comes with that.

Sometimes I spend hours on one sentence to decode it, to contemplate it, to relate it to others. I believe we are losing that ability because of how digital media is changing the very function of our brain. Digital culture is defined by and promotes

2. See Alessandro Ludovico's *Post-Digital Print – The Mutation of Publishing Since 1894* (Onomatopee, 2012) for a deeper articulation of this.

Wafaa Bilal in New York with books purchased from the *168:01* Wishlist, 2018

instant access and ever-present distraction, at the expense of the time we need to observe, to contemplate, and to reflect. Our attention span is becoming shorter and shorter. So, alongside this context and understanding, what Iraqis were going through at the time, the rebuilding of the library itself became very important.

In this regard, the creative idea was simple. If you have classes at the college where their focus is interior design, why don't you give this project to the class. We ran another Kickstarter campaign and raised the required funds that were used for rebuilding the library to house the books. That group of students supported by Zaid Luqman and others made it happen and did something remarkable.

> **SS:** The photos of the new library are wonderful. You really sense the student's excitement. It's rare for something very ground up, student-led, and experimental to happen in universities. Also, it's a unique moment for the library, any library, to be made anew.

WB: Yeah, it was very joyous. Also, kind of shocking because they didn't wait for any permission. They went into the space. They planned for the remodel. They ripped it apart. And they did it within one semester. And not only did they make and design the space, but it was then filled with the books they wanted.

The delivery of the books took much longer than the remodeling of the library because they had to travel through more bureaucratic and global systems. You have to walk it slowly and acknowledge people within that system in order to get something done. I've never talked about the politics of that project until now. But things change in Iraq now, things are moving forward much faster. And having completed this process it has enabled other articulations of the project to follow.

> **SS:** Can you say something about the broader achievements of the project and how it has grown?

WB: The project has begun to grow in terms of different sites, types of donations and communities involved and inspired by it. For example, I was working with the Metropolitan Museum of Art on a different project, but they know about *168:01* and

Delivery of books from the *168:01* exhibition at Aga Khan Museum, Toronto, Ontario, arrive in Baghdad, 2019.

they donated 2000 books on archaeology in Iraq. The museum had two libraries, which they merged together, and the result was 2000 duplicates. Some of them had never even been opened. The Met were trying for years to get these books to Iraq, but they didn't have the infrastructure, or they didn't have any partner in on the ground. And so, *168:01* offered some kind of gateway. We were given advice that these books should go somewhere central to support access to them. So, they were sent to the National Museum of Iraq and I worked with them to create a space for the books. We have also sent books to libraries at the University of Babylon and University of Mosul. In total it is now 10,000 books we have sent. And remember every book has been listed, and there are multiple stages of verification before permission to ship.

SS: I suppose all the books at the Met were at one point requested by researchers in the US for the Met library, a little like the wishlist made by those at the Baghdad College of Fine Arts, and then years later those books find their way to Iraq. It would be fascinating to map the movement of all the books and relationships in the project. To date I believe you have presented *168:01* at: Windsor Gallery (Ontario, Canada) 2016; FACT, (Liverpool, UK) 2017; Asian Art Biennial at the Taiwan Museum of Fine Arts, 2017–18; Aga Khan Museum (Toronto, Canada) 2018; Confederation Centre for the Arts (Charlottetown, Canada) 2018–19; Wiseman Art Museum (Minneapolis, USA, date TBD), 2019; New Orleans Museum of Art, 2019; National Veterans Art Museum Triennial at the Chicago Cultural Center, 2019; and House of Wisdom (Sharjah, UAE), 2020–ongoing.

This most recent incarnation of the project is interesting, as it is the first time the 'blank books' installation element of the project has been hosted in the Arab world and it is also I believe a permanent installation. Will the project ever end and where might it go next?

WB: It's interesting how at the beginning the focus was on the books but through the project the place that houses the books has become more important. Also, the encounter with the College of Fine Arts, the library's destruction and rebuilding, started to multiply in my head. And crucially combines with a very different kind of destruction and revisioning – the dramatic shift in how we consume information. Now, I'm exploring the question: can a place, which functions as a public monument, a public sculpture, become its own entity. Could it not only house books, but also give access to other activities and I think this is where the library, can become another space, or provide access to other spaces, both architectural, but also of thought and being. In particular, in relation to the post-digital. How can libraries be a place of social interaction and a space of contemplation.

SS: So, if it's not too much to put it this way, would you say the project has reached a kind of meeting point between the post-digital and post-war conditions, how we rebuild, rethink, refunction architectures and communities of knowledge production?

WB: I'm not sure if I would put it that way, but it's an interesting observation. I'm certainly interested in ways that the digital age has destroyed or at least radically transformed aspects of human behaviour. And what kind of places can we create that might be at least resistant to hierarchical power structures *and* the pervasive connectivity of our digital devices. Have you ever been on a digital detox?

SS: No, not specifically, but it sounds good!

WB: I did and it was remarkable. You go to a place where there is no connection at all. The only connection you have is a phone in the office of the retreat. Now I'm not saying all digital is bad rather that we need means to rebalance. How can the library function in relation to the distractions of the digital? How can the library be a social sculpture of place, not only to acquire knowledge, but to relax, to interact with ourselves and other humans? I'm currently working towards a social sculpture in central Baghdad that brings the physical library together with the connectivity and experimental character of social sculpture.

SS: Wow, a very exciting and ambitious project to bring to fruition! It's interesting to think about the degree to which what you describe will

Above and following pages: Images from the new library being rebuilt, launched and new books from the wishlist being received, College of Fine Arts Baghdad, 2018.

still be a library. Libraries have of course changed with the times and still fundamentally today even when you walk into a library thick with computers and few books in sight, to me it's still unmistakeably a library. This chameleon like character is fascinating. Could one say that the essence of a library has changed, whilst still remaining a library? What does this say about libraries and more broadly institutions?

WB: Well, I believe the library has changed, or perhaps should change, from a space of isolation to a space of connection *and* isolation.

SS: This idea of 'andness' is really interesting and something we come back to within the Torque project and that *BiblioTech* explores. How can we learn to read in different ways, learn new methods like speed reading, but not at the expense of more traditional methods such as so-called close reading. Katherine Hayles articulates this in her text Deep vs Hyper reading.[3]

WB: Yes, I suppose we might think also about hearing versus deep listening, right? Deep listening is a kind of power afforded through isolating and connecting oneself. And that's what the library provides, perhaps, because sometimes you need distraction and a place to get away from yourself. But other times, other people, need to be around others to focus, like how working in a café has become popular. Seattle Library Public Library is interesting as a good example of this. It brings different things together. There is a children's centre, café, shop, meeting rooms, and access to printed books are really celebrated in the building, alongside stacks of public computers. If someone wants to check their email there is space for it. If somebody wants to read in silence, there is a space for it.

So when I think about social sculpture and libraries I'm thinking about making space, but also of making value, not simply assigning value to an object. For a long

3. N. Katherine Hayles, "How We Read: Close, Hyper, Machine," *ADE Bulletin,* No. 150, (2010): 62–79.

time, I was occupied by the issue of Iraq and trying to activate participants to engage with the issues through various projects, from *Domestic Tension* to *Virtual Jihadi*, to many other projects. It was a practice of reflecting the times. And I always said OK, well, I'm an artist, I'm a member of a social and political system, right? I'm reflecting. I'm a mirror. That took place for a very long time since I left Iraq in 1991 until recent times. But, I think *168:01* ushered in a new direction in my work. And the way I look at it is we're post-conflict now, right? And this necessitates a completely different art making. *168:01* opens up the participatory to include very tangible results. I think in a post-conflict context, I'm looking at the reality on the ground from a different perspective. And that perspective is informed by what do we need most. I've done a lot of engaging. Letting people know what is happening, but time has shifted in Iraq, on the ground, and now it's time to rethink. With *168:01* it's time to connect, to heal and to move forward. And the poetic gesture in the art, gives you a licence to be creative and the creativity enables connections to form.

> **SS:** If you look at the history of art and the range of different things that artists have done and how transdisciplinary art practise has become, artists have a unique freedom now to collaborate and move and work in different ways. That other fields can't so easily. It feels like your practice and work is really embracing these pluralities and everything you've learnt, and is putting them to work in very situated ways.

WB: Exactly. Look, I don't pay attention how value is assigned to the work, because that is irrelevant. What is relevant is how the project is effective. You call it activism, somebody calls it art charity. It doesn't really matter. What's the objective? What's the creative method? How to trigger a platform for your participant? *168:01* was launched with an animation on the Kickstarter page that was accessible to a child or adult. It makes clear what happened, what needs to happen, and that you have the power to participate.

The last thing we want as artists is to impose our ideas on others. But as I said earlier, the project operates in the duality between the conflict and comfort zone. When one plays with aesthetic pleasure and aesthetic pain, it's not tricky to inspire

you. To make you stop and think, but it's really up to you if that encounter activates you or not. It doesn't activate everybody. *168:01* resonates with people, right? The idea of the loss and the gain, rebuilding and participating. The artist is a trigger, an agent of change, but it only works if everything is carefully connected, you have an objective, and it leads to a tangible result on the ground.

> **SS:** So, thinking how the project might evolve in the future, can we expect to be stood on a street in Baghdad looking at 'your' library, your social sculpture? Not a library within a gallery or possessing the nomadic decentralised character of the kind that *168:01* has manifest, but something that we can walk into and find a space for contemplation and connection?

WB: Well, what I learnt from *168:01* was that things take time and that is part of it, don't rush it because interactions with people, building things slowly from the ground up, is absolutely vital and the most rewarding thing. I have conducted research into the historic Grand Library of Baghdad, also known as the House of Wisdom, and been researching social sculpture, but we need funding. However, something else I've learnt is that I think when there is intent you establish a trust. And with trust you can build a system of exchange because you and others are deeply invested in it. I'm not like an artist who's walking and thinking of hierarchy. No, it's not the way. To me the asset that is rarely utilised when it comes to art making is the other. Right? How to work with others to create every project. Have intent, but keep it open. It's like Walter Benjamin talking about the task of the translator, the storyteller. If you do it in a concrete open way, there is no you in the story. The storyteller is in characters, in the story, and with others' participation they are included in the story, and they gain a story too. When we believe in that notion, then we believe in the notion of the work. Work which is not created individually, but created collectively. I mean if you think about how many people collaborated in order to move 10,000 books to the different sites, plus all the blank books and different processes involved, it's a process of persistence in the face of resistance. It's a project that seeks to make a point, a difference, and the point, the difference, cannot be made unless it's collective.

Mahdy Abo Bahat

Fizzles From the Bleed Marks

1.

I sat in the library admissions office close to a quiet American and far, the furthest I could sit, from a loud French couple. It was pretty empty. But that typical waiting-room-ambience thrilled the air, where slight glances were heard, and others' sighs felt intimately deep and wet. We sat on leather seats designated for waiting while the Library system processed each and every one of us in the order of our arrival. With our forms in our hands, we were all facing the secretary sitting behind the desk guarded with sheets of perspex glass.

Everyone except me was glued to their screens, yet present with a 'hybrid' type of attention. All very aware of the secretary's presence behind the glass. As they scrolled, they sensed her *(there)*, her departures from the desk zone and disappearances behind the staff door *(gone!)* and her returns *(there!)*. Administrative peekaboo. Perhaps we could even smell whiffs of Freud's *Fort/da* game here, but one devoid of the pleasures in repetition and desires of mastery.[1] Just analogue notifications experienced by the user-viewer-consumer-neo-liberal subject through pixelated and over-compressed signals. Glances were launched briefly from phone screens to the admission desk's screen – reflections eternal. The secretary placed something on the horizontal glass and slammed shut the photocopying machine. Eyes returned to thumb joints, and heads turned towards the ground. Who can blame them? Who hasn't learned to mistrust 'mother bureaucracy'? – unless she is to attend to her maternal duties through the communication powers of an app.

I was a 'subject' – I think – about to be further 'subjected' or even interpolated by an arm of the state in the utmost mundane, passive, casual and boring way. But nonetheless, I felt lucid. I was after all there as a reader, in waiting. I watched everything with the suspicion of a cat. I had learned the art of lingering from great pioneers, big schools and fatal smells, and possessed a personal archive of cunning schemes for exhibiting 'good-boy' behaviour at crossings. So I waited – in my own way – for my turn to be 'admitted'.

The value of the Bodleian Reader Card is pedestaled by many, most notably by the establishment itself and its subjects. It's a key that gives the holder bespoke dual access to the local and the global. To be more precise, the world – seen through its vast collection of books – and a cluster of historic buildings in Oxford's urban centre. The card possesses intrinsic, fetishistic qualities. The lucky cardholder

1. Sigmund Freud, *Beyond the Pleasure Principle* (Penguin Modern Classics, 2003): 15.

has instant access to discover the uncharted 'other', the outside – mapped by previous lucky cardholders – and all-inclusively experienced within the comfort of a Mediaeval-themed Academic-Disneyland compound, which is one of the oldest still beating epicentres of power and monopolies of knowledge operating today.

Additionally, the lucky cardholder is blessed with new powers of orientation and epistemological dwelling, the beginnings of a spatial grasp of the city's coded urban topography. Suddenly the mediaeval skylines composed of quads, churches and colleges (that once merely functioned as fast-consumed backdrops for day trip tourists) become not just sites that are inwardly accessible but, as a whole, digestible and comprehensible. It is as if the idolatry nature of the city's facade, conjured by tourism's market forces, could finally be deciphered, explained away, decoded into units, functional buildings, or even spaces of extreme 'textolatry'[2] practice, where texts are preserved, generated and protected from the malignant forces of discontinuity.

The Bodleian Reader Card is something of a divine permission ossified into a thin, fast-printed, plastic card. If the cardholder was to see beyond the mundane nature of its production in the dreary Admissions Office and its cheap plastic composition, sooner or later, climes of data would descend onto the cardholder's consciousness. There will be lines upon lines of texts, meta codes generating the very realms we breathe and see. Permissions to baptise in waterfalls of pure linearity, to revere in the endless orders of 'beginnings' – as we are all told to this day – was the word.

I didn't care. Deeply absorbed in the slumber of waiting, none of this could rouse me nor move me an inch. I have always reminded myself that my relationship with the academic world is parasitical. The same could be said for other worlds that I've been lured into: Literature, Politics, Poetry, Family, 'Community' (its many, many flavours) and Homeland, such as Art. Even my very own social and individual determinants – that identify me to others – are, in fact, truths I feed on by solely leaching onto their surfaces. The experience of the crossing concerns me more than the endless data that waits beyond the Bodleian 'border'. No doubt, the wealth and abundance behind the door would tempt most thinkers to go – 'open sesame' – and enter. But can illuminations not come to those standing still with the dignity of a cobweb, in the opening of the threshold, in the space of the door?

2.

A strange banality is often felt and shared between those who have just crossed a hard border, boundary, test, or social landmark. It's common that after working hard to attain the capacity – or will – to cross, a feeling of anti-climax soon begins to sink in. In more extreme contexts, similar feelings can even be associated with surviving trauma. The paradox of survival is that wounds from the central violent event don't dwell in the psyche alone, but must share a nest with other separate wounds caused by the violence of surviving the event itself. The trauma of waking up.

Redwan, a fellow conspirator, good friend, poet, writer and recent refugee from Yemen, once tried to express something like this to me. It was a feeling of frustration and a taste of disappointment he felt after surviving a crossing. We were walking up the high street in Oxford's city centre, not far from the Bodleian, heading eastwards, past all the iconic and historic facades, blistered with stone-carved miniature nightmares. Redwan consumed his share of Oxford's tourist spectacle very quickly as we crossed the road opposite All Souls College Library and then moved on to disclosing the important and good news he had received that morning.

2. Vilém Flusser, *Towards A Philosophy of Photography* (Reaktion Books, 2000): 12.

Despite the monumental nature of his accomplishment – the good news – he expressed it with a banal expression, bare of any excitement. We walked and talked, circling around the kernel of what was unsettling him. Finally, we climbed to the top of Divinity Lane and the mediaeval valley harbouring demons made of sandstone. Paper and ink was now far behind us, fringed by the non-event of East-Southern-English residential urbanity. After catching his breath, he concluded: *"Why does life, after all the blood, tears and drama, finally discharge us our well-earned shares of its sweetness in the most banal of gestures and most passive ways?"*

He was a writer, and an essential part of our friendship was subconsciously founded on our shared inability to tell our painful pasts. The inability to tell one's trauma is one of the oldest universal conundrums and now the largest of markets and economies. But maybe what bonds Redwan and me are the imaginative strategies we deploy to recount the past and return. Firstly as conspirators, renegades. Then as storytellers or writers. And perhaps finally as comrades and friends. Setting our eyes aside we traverse blindly, lost, led by the memory of sounds, tastes and smells – without a particular enemy in mind or in sight – regardless, we both have faith to avenge the past.

One of the pains in Redwan's past, particularly his journey and migration to the UK, sits at a particular border and crossing. A legal Greek-Turkish border, a part of a long translucent steady line drawn on trembling waves of the Mediterranean Sea. In his own words, Redwan believed he was fortunate. His migration route couldn't compare with what he heard at all the deportation units and centres he was held in. In fact, he believes his journey was relatively smooth. It's just "what happened at the Greek crossing" and the towering waves of the Mediterranean Sea, which need a *modus operandi*, along with a band of co-conspirators, such as myself. Despite surviving the crossing, and apart from being contingent on his current presence, its wounds have no tangible trace on him or his life. Except sounds he sometimes hears in his head. Even his own 'country friends' – who were with him on the boat – survived. He didn't lose anything or anyone except for a new friend. A 22-year-old young man named Akram who he first met whilst being smuggled in some forests outside Izmir less than twenty-four hours before the boat capsized, and Akram drowned and took to his death. Redwan later discerned to me that sound he often hears in his head. A voice that he usually hears on the threshold of waking up. Redwan is certain that it's not his own voice but a memory, a sound bite, of someone with a higher-pitched voice, Akram, and it cries *La Tofalitonee*, which is parochial Yemeni and classical Arabic for: *Don't let go of me. Don't leave me behind.*

The good news that Redwan revealed on his visit to Oxford was delivered to him earlier that morning in the form of a letter. It was from the Home Office. He had finally been awarded legal status and residency. He had waited two years for it. One year longer than his country friends who survived the sinking and arrived with him. The process consumed him for months and days, deepening his already legal, economic and spiritual state of limbo. Now that he was legally free – by the book, by the letters and the word – to go wherever he pleased on this island, the sudden passivity of the world that was once set against him now sat in his mouth with a bitter taste.

And who wouldn't agree more? Don't we all trust the primal senses of our tongues and noses before the mirrored images in our eyes? What would rouse the body and spirit, four letters reading fire, an image of flames mirrored through a camera obscura? Or the smell of smoke? (And isn't it all some sort of conspiracy, anyway?).

3.

It was my turn. I communicated with the secretary through the screen. Another translucent border, but made of perspex, dividing service providers from users, workers from consumers, virus from host, and institutions from their subjects. I handed her my proof of identification: my passport. And eventually, I peered into their camera for my photograph to be taken. Soon, I was to be finally admitted into their system – one probably in parallel, but incomparable in age and size, to the mighty archival order that subjugates their books. But the system lagged, glitched, and it/I could not be progressed.

As things slowed down, I started to notice things differently. Perhaps a different view is granted to those who are in closer physical proximity to the admission process, similar to looking down from a theatre's stage for the first time after spending most of your life looking at it from below. I couldn't help but notice the material uniformity of the admissions desk. Particularly the dominant tone of beige, blaring through the synthetic marble that covers the walls and floors, continuing throughout the rest of this newly renovated part of the building. However, the secretary, the workers, and all the institution's operators wore casual clothes and were only defined by lanyards hanging from their necks. If it wasn't for the absence of a uniform and the grand hall upon arrival – or the looming threat of state violence that levitates above particular subjects as they cross particular nation-state borders – it wouldn't be far-fetched to think that I'd been waiting in some sub-bureaucratic arm of a shitty police station or immigration processing centre. Perhaps what saves the Admissions Office from it being a decent hallucination of a border checkpoint is the visual scarcity of uniforms and the sonic absence of announcements, points of order, sirens, grunts, crying, gunshots, and the promise of books.

I guess there are no dangers, no stakes, at least not for me. The silence of waiting at 'Bodleian Border Control' can be easily confused with the protocol of silence mandated within the walls of its libraries. The system was still lagging and it began to feel dreary. I tried to ground my brain into lucid thoughts. I thought of the biodiversity in the Bodleian's library spaces and whether solidarity could be extended to rats, moths, and all conspiring beings crawling for the right to access, to feed, to dwell. But my mind flickered aimlessly like a video machine failing to catch the tape. However, in my counting of animals and insects I was reminded that my immediate existence within this place, along with my relation to it, is parasitical. I was brought here by invitation – to contribute to the library, so something more mutualistic or perhaps predatory also lurked on the horizon.

4.

It was too late. Symptoms had crossed the screen, and the lethargy had now reached the secretary. I made sure not to give away any signs of my awareness. But it was hard to ignore. The keyboard was redundant. Her shoulders drooped. And contact with the computer had receded to the point of abjection. She had no hope but to stare into the monitor with verbal interjections of sighs and grunts. No signal. No progress. No acceleration. A time for curse words and prayers. To a place where linear desires for causal processes were now futile, repressed, and prohibited. So long as we were all waiting, quarantined within the walls of a 'liminal time' induced by the malfunction of a bureaucratic computational apparatus – and even if it was for a brief window in time – we were all in the same boat.

However, my mind began to feel immune to it all. Hanging from the container of some heavenly binary, swinging between a 'zero' and a 'one' (without touching or landing on either), I was somehow at home. Interestingly, some experiences that have resisted categorisation in the library of one's 'lived experience' suddenly emerge into the light in these moments. Classed in a pile of the 'painful, fatal and unnecessary', they assume a cognitive quality, they become writable, readable. Briefly, they even mould to linearity when one recounts their history – from that moment – with a prism that accepts 'waiting', akin to dreaming perhaps, as a worthy category and a critical human act. Like an illuminating cross-section or an informative catalogue, one can't help but compare when one is given the chance. The Bodleian Libraries' Admission system is incomparable. But it does bring to mind other waiting games I've played.

Such as the wait on the phone to 'Student Finance England', where hopes of receiving a maintenance loan (and ending the homeless but-grateful-Greater-London-couch-surfing-city-tour) trembles on the line under multi-groans of exploited northern Irish call-centre workers and floods of soul-breaking 'music on hold'. Or the security check of 'HM's Passport Office' on re-issuing a passport with a Muslim name, flagged for frequently travelling to a terror-listed country. Or waiting for an 'interior' security check when passing in or out of the Egyptian border. Or the wait for an exemption order from the Egyptian military conscription authority. Or the wait to be discharged by Military Intelligence in a makeshift court erected in a bunker's corridor because the army has taken the role of the recently dissolved police force and has run out of space; hundreds sit crouched on marble floors, blind-folded, waiting in unison to be issued back to their families or shelved.

Regardless of the stakes, all is waiting. But a waiting that happens in certain instances where a particular innocence needs proving. An innocence that sits outside one's agency, out of reach, and quantified through a 'processing' of one's individual determinants of identity.

However, as much as hanging in limbo can provoke one to look inwardly to private suppressed histories, it points to a far greater – and a less neurotic – truth of the 'world and self'. Entire worlds are born and expired in these sorts of cusps. Millions grow and fall in the shade of binaries without knowing their interior nature. Unprocessed. Not individually innocent, but deemed guilty by existing within drawn enclaves on maps. Unprocessable for the crossing. Unnameable for the word and sentence. Millions, and Akram.

5.

At midnight on the 22nd of January 2020, Redwan and his fellow companions blew up the boat to its full-size on the coast of Izmir Province in Turkey. It was big enough to carry all the Yemeni people in the group: Redwan, his two friends he made during his stay in Istanbul, a family of four, a young college student, and his classmate, Akram. The group, however, was thirty-five in total, including two women, three children and a baby. Their nationalities included Iranians, Sudanese, Syrians, and one Palestinian. Set to cross the waters for the Greek island of Chios, they were all told by their smugglers that it was in theory a 45-minute journey. The crossing took them roughly two hours until the boat hit rocks in Greek waters and capsized.

Redwan sensed the crossing was doomed from the get-go. And once the engine was attached, he was sure of it. He shrugged his shoulders – we were in my studio – *"But what can you do? Even if you had learnt the truth of what was to come and knew it like your name. There's no going back."* Weirdly, even if Redwan were to follow his gut at that moment and not board the boat, he would have been far too deep beyond his 'Rubicon'– his point of safe return. Even though his conundrum on the Izmir coast would have matched the very outset and beginning of every idiom and saying that addressed states of no returns (the water would have still literally been facing him and not yet behind him), it would still have been far too late. Redwan and the 45 others had already burnt their bridges, broken their kettles, and sunk their boats in a flat in Izmir twenty-four hours before they even set their eyes on the sea. It was just a part of a two-fold economic transaction. First, they paid the smugglers; then, they – *crossed* – handed over all their passports, legal documents, and papers proving the individual determinants of their identities. By that point, all directions were reckless, uncertain, and more or less the same; what slightly differed was the medium of travel, land or sea, and the violence of their gatekeepers, Turkish or Greek.

The smugglers had promised that the boat would be steered by a professional. Someone with experience. But once the vessel was assembled and ready to go, the smuggler who escorted the group through the forest demonstrated to one of the young Yemeni men how to operate the outboard motor: *"Push right, is left. Pull left, is right."* He left them a jerry can of fuel and then quickly disappeared. The young Yemini did have experience. But not in operating power boats. Apparently, he had tried this same crossing fourteen times before. Each time he was caught and deported back to Turkey. It took him nearly an hour to get a basic grip on the steering. The waves were high. Redwan pointed to the studio roof behind a wooden joist, indicating the distance to where he saw the boat's engine hover above him when they hit the most towering wave he had ever seen. *"I can't paint the picture,"* he smiled. It was too foggy and dark. But he tried to describe the sound. Between the fat growl of the petrol-burning engine and the high sustained roars of the Mediterranean Sea, Redwan was hearing a third sound; a thin hiss fluttering above his shoulders, piercing through and sitting unnaturally in amongst the overwhelming cacophony he was already submerged in. It disturbed him. It wasn't until he caught someone's lips shuttering fast in the dark he realised what he thought he was hallucinating. They were fizzles of everyone's prayers and frenzied utterings whispering behind his ears. Redwan smiled. He recounted lightly: *"Poor souls, you realise later that we were sailing on that blow-up boat with nothing but heaps of innocence."*

As they zig-zagged towards the Greek border, the sea eventually calmed. The person in charge of the GPS machine announced they had crossed the maritime border between Turkey and Greece. The news brought relief to everyone onboard, but due to the fog, the achievement felt still conceptual. Nothing could prove their crossing except for a screen with flashing dots. According to Redwan, the virtual nature of the official crossing drove most of the group impatient. They needed a visual marker on the horizon to compensate, a witness from the other side of the threshold. Sadly, it was when they saw the town lights on the Greek coast, that they hit the fatal rocks. Redwan shook his head and stated one of the first – and for some the last – tragic and eerie lessons of the migration praxis: *A ~~border.~~*

Crossing a border demarcated on a map isn't the same as crossing one in real life, the lines and zones are much thicker, stickier and nebulous. And crossing a border in real life has nothing to do with crossing it legally in *their* words, in *their* sentences and on *their* paper. There are different borders within the same crossing. To cross, one must carry oneself in shards across fragmented lands. Fragmented by systems created and managed by writers of history, those who have won. Systems that shed their skin and finally rest in the royal necropolises, the well-preserved graveyards, the libraries.

6.

In the stillness of the admission office, a slither of motion suddenly shook the fatigued ambience. One person had nearly stormed out, dropping a loud, quasi-aggressive grunt just as they disappeared behind the door and stamped their way down the beige corridor. He had arrived shortly after me and obviously couldn't take the wait. The secretary completely ignored his exit. It was as if it had never happened, and the impatient applicant had never waited. Unlike him, I sat with complete comfort and patience. And unlike him, who anxiously fled back to check on his boats, my application was already on her desk; my name was half-punched into their system; I was drowning my boats in litres of white spirit and gasoline, ready to strike the match; I was crossing my Bodleian Rubicon. By this time, the secretary had vanished several times behind the staff door, complaining to her co-workers about the inefficiency of the Library's admission system. I frowned politely whenever her eyes turned to me, and I tried my best not to show too many signs of comfort.

7.

Alas, the system was back. Our time had finally ended. The joys of the messianic return were short-lived, expressed through a brief interaction of smiles and a sigh of relief from the secretary. The banality and mundaneness of labour, applications, and admission processes quickly sunk in. As if the absence had never happened. The secretary picked up and peered at my admissions form.I had already printed the form, filled it out, and signed it before my arrival. It had three pages. And as I remember clearly, each page performed one of the three-fold functions of a border.[3]

The first page is the 'Personal Details' section. It starts with the basics. Name, date of birth, and details of a permanent address, ending at the bottom of the page, with a box regarding 'academic affiliation', asking for the 'institution' and 'end date of status'. The secretary, however, was concerned with her section on the page. At the top sits a grey box 'For staff use only'. It has tick boxes for a list of all the possible means of identification; passport, identity card, driving licence, bank statement, or bill. And three spaces for the secretary to state; name, number, and 'admitted by'.

For some, it is the familiar and the mundane. It's the typical protocol and procedure. It's the habitual smell of home. For others, it is the foremost encounter of the outer wall, a first wall of defence, and the familiar (and particular) sight of the border's exteriority. It is the aroma that turns stomachs and gags throats. It is the nausea of grave danger. The scent of the predator's nest. The smell of shit. And it's that crossing that requires that innocence. One whereby its criteria are the official measurements of identity. Its role is not to grant access to those who respond correctly through numbers, letters or transactions. But to determine who is worthy, innocent enough and with the correct measurements, to ask for entry at the door before it is even granted or refused. To distinguish those with the language to pronounce the question, the 'open sesame', from those unable, who utter sounds with their split tongue. To invite some and repel others. To govern the passage. ~~*(To forbid)*~~

The second page is the door. Its header reads 'STATEMENT OF RESEARCH NEED'. Right in its centre there was a large daunting white box for the applicant to fill. At the foot of the page was a declaration and a space to sign. It asked to state the reasons for using the Bodleian Libraries' resources. This statement is the key to the applicant's 'new powers of orientation and epistemological dwelling' mentioned before. Here is where the plea for entrance and further forgiveness is formulated. A request that attains an innocence beyond the one assigned at birth. It's on this page where ideas of one's subjectivity become tricky, and things get messy. The shitty smells of the outer border fuse with the musky scents of comfort and

3. Michel Serres, *Malfeasance: Appropriation Through Pollution?* (Stanford University Press, 2010): 43.

stability from the inside, reeking through doorways, pores, and portals. Here, the bureaucracy has to be less automated and violent, more passive and bureaucratic. To have the bare minimum of capacity to think. To read and to question. To process and admit. *~~(To exclude)~~*

The third and last page is titled 'DATA PROTECTION'. The page lists answered questions regarding how the library's admission office manages and uses applicants' data. In one of the columns, a section reads 'your rights'. Prosaic, uninspiring, but necessary, it is a pitch and contractual statement. Its role is to solely inform without receiving. To be understood by only those who are inside. To guarantee efficiency and ensure comfort. To promise wilful acts. To pledge order. It is though perhaps the closest one gets to an acknowledgment of power by the institution. *~~(To protect)~~*

Interestingly, the three layers of the border reflect the generic concept of the three characteristics that define humans from animals and plants (or parasites). According to Aristotle's scheme, plants have life. Animals have life and perception. And humans have both, along with rationality. If we were to employ this on the three pages of the Bodleian Readers Admission Form and ask for the library itself to complete it: The Data Protection Page might detail how it manages the 'life' within its walls; The Personal Details Page would perhaps describe the institution's means to operate its organ of 'perception'; and the Statement of Research Need would be the governing rationale to conserve and make accessible its paper empire. Furthermore, suppose we employ our human rationale on the three pages and imagine the bureaucracy of the admissions office as a passive old hunchback, who can only use the brute force of the word. For the old gatekeeper to *forbid* the visitor, he must ask *What?* To *protect* those who have entered, he would be obliged to demonstrate to them how. And to exclude those who have passed the *what,* now modified and humanised to *who,* the gatekeeper must ask the visitor *why?*

Apparently, parasites could be plants or animals, but according to Aristotle's theory neither can be rational. When I wrote in the Statement of Research Need box – my why – it had little trace of my capacity for discursive language, reason or even other abilities of imagination. I wrote no more than a sentence. My entrance was contingent on disclosing them a code.

> "I'm undertaking research for a commissioned artwork to go into a Bodleian exhibition, in autumn 2022, and will need access to the artefact that I'm responding to, shelfmark: (RHO) 535.12 r. 28."[4]

8.

After four hours of suspension in the sea, holding onto the sharp edge of severe indeterminacy, grasping the capsized boat, and clutching onto parts of the fatal rocks' constellation, the Greek coastguards finally received Redwan and his group on board. Two were missing: the unnamed Palestinian and Akram. The group had different theories regarding their fate and whereabouts.

One was hopeful. An Iranian on the boat had spotted the Palestinian after the boat capsized, hiding further away in between the rocks. Everyone knew his plan

4. "The Demerara Rebellion of 1823: An Official Account of Military Operations" is a document that was issued by the Governor of Demerara and Essequebo, Major-General John Murray, in which he describes the military operations of his forces against the enslaved rebels in the colony of Demerara. A copy of the document is not available online via the Bodleian, but a Library of Congress version is available here: https://tile.loc.gov/storage-services/public/gdcmassbookdig/accountofinsurre00brya/accountofinsurre00brya.pdf.

was different. He couldn't afford to get caught by the Greek border control due to strategic reasons regarding his larger migration route. Unlike others, his plan was to cross, and once landing, not to be witnessed and or get caught. If he was to be processed and his biometric measurements and fingerprints were taken, he could, being Palestinian, risk being stuck in Greece. Redwan explained to me how people have different strategies, depending on their nationality and desired destination. But he and the rest of the Yemeni group knew Akram wouldn't follow or accompany the Palestinian. Akram's college friend and companion was sure of it. Redwan remembers him shaking his head, uttering: *it isn't like him.*

A few weeks after arrival on Chios they learned the truth. Redwan and the rest of the Yemeni group were called to the local police station. They stood outside a foreboding room. Redwan stood at the doorway with no desire to enter. They were asked to identify a body. Redwan remarked he only knew Akram for one day and wasn't the best candidate to identify him. *But who was?* Redwan asked. According to Akram's college friend, when he entered to identify the body, he couldn't see Akram. The corpse had been in the sea for more than a month. Now it lay still on an examination table in a police station. It had no looks; *it wasn't like him.* Of all the intangible measurements and determinants that we attempt to associate with the essence of the self, two traces confirmed Akram's identity.Two shards of him survived. His pair of trainers and a folded-up document that was found tucked in his sock. The laminated paper was Akram's official residency documents issued by the Turkish authorities on the basis of his educational studies. He preserved it in his sock against the orders of his smuggler in Izmir. A memorial to that first border he refused to cross.

9.

I was handed more documents to sign. They were, more or less, duplicate copies of what I initially signed on the form. I was nearly there, but receiving my freshly printed Bodleian Reader Card depended on a twofold transaction. Firstly, I had to pay a fee for a three-year membership with my debit card. Secondly, I was directed by the Secretary to look at an old wooden sign hanging behind her on the wall and read it aloud. She stated in a bored manner, *"It's the Bodleian Libraries' Declaration."* I tried to follow the words and sentences of the declaration. It read like an old oath. She interrupted me politely and whispered off the record, *"You can read it later, as long as you know it's there."* The payment went through. And the Secretary handed the card along with another document. It folded out into three small pages. Most of it was maps and details of all the different libraries' locations, restrictions, and opening times. On the first inner page was the declaration in a dark blue font, in a white translucent box, over a generic photo of students in a library bleeding to the edges. It read:

> "I hereby undertake not to remove from the Library, or to mark, deface, or injure in any way, any volume, document, or other object belonging to it or in its custody; not to bring into the Library or kindle therein any fire or flame, and not to smoke in the Library; and I promise to obey all rules of the Library."

To exit the admissions office, I had to enter the Weston Library's public foyer. The space was massive, with an aura that wavered between an airport terminal and an old temple. I looked back at the doorway, from which I had emerged. It was a 15th-century gateway from Ascott Park, which was conserved and reused for the

Weston Library's recent renovations. Its sandstone harmonised with the beige tones of the synthetic marble dominating the entire library. At the head of the portal's arch, it stated in Latin: *'SI BONUS ES INTRES, SI NEQUAM NEQUAQUAM'*, which translates as *"If good come in, if wicked, by no means"*.

Images on the following pages were specially made in 2023 to accompany the above essay. They rework images of artwork produced by the author for the exhibition: *These Things Matter: Empire, Exploitation and Everyday-Racism*, held at the Weston Library, Bodleian Libraries, November 2022 – February 2023.

WELCOME TO THE
BODLEIAN LIBRARIES

In this leaflet you will find handy informat

ONDITIONS OF ACCESS

valid Bodleian Reader C
leian Libraries

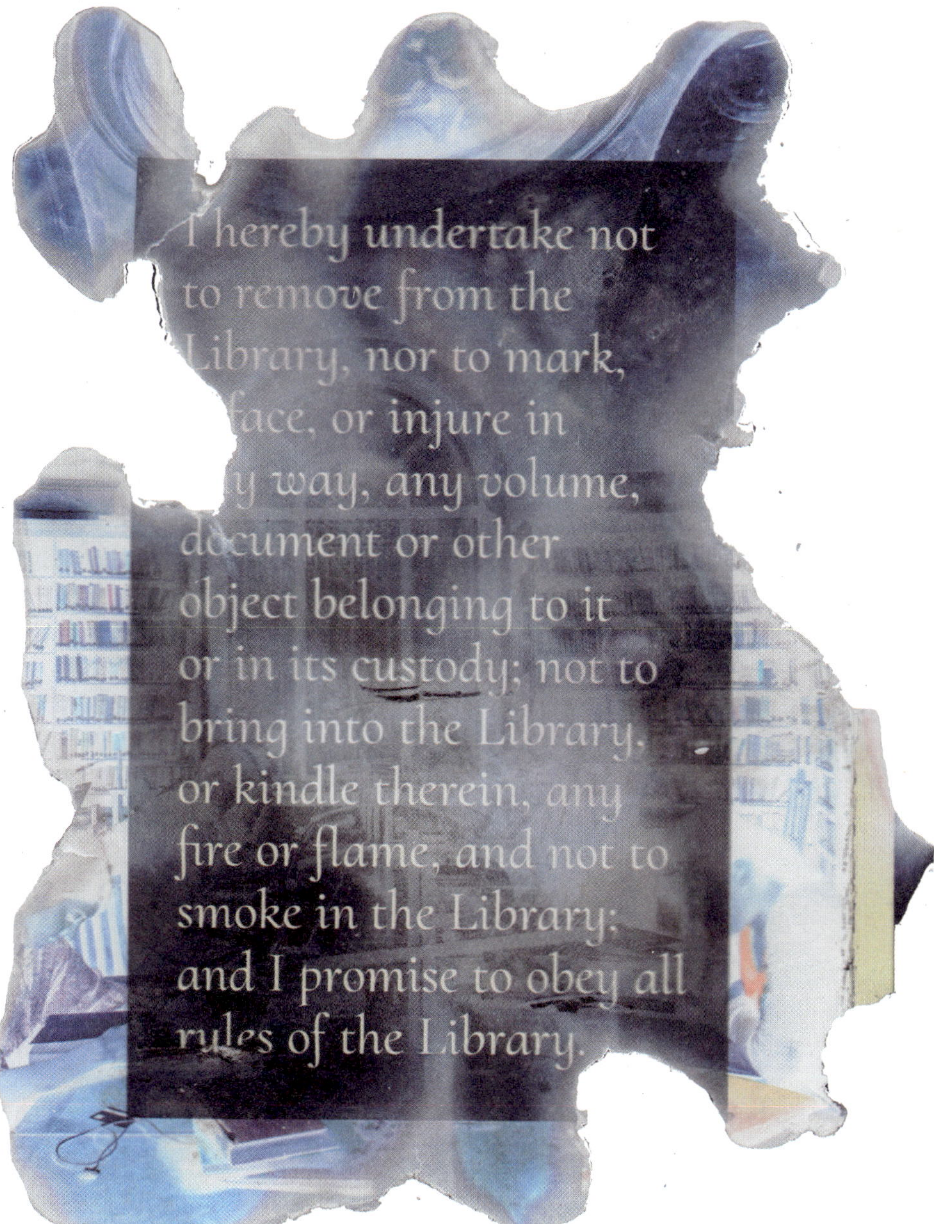
I hereby undertake not
to remove from the
Library, nor to mark,
face, or injure in
y way, any volume,
document or other
object belonging to it
or in its custody; not to
bring into the Library,
or kindle therein, any
fire or flame, and not to
smoke in the Library;
and I promise to obey all
rules of the Library.

Rosa Menkman

A Collection of Collections

1. A Collection of Collections Folded into the Prelinger Library

In 2004, Megan and Rick Prelinger founded the Prelinger library, a privately funded public library situated in San Francisco. The Prelinger library is not a typical library, as it holds many special collections of not just books and zines, but also buttons, maps, license plates, scrapbooks and so forth. The library is essentially a collection of collections, or as they refer to it, "a library of serendipity." Last year, in 2022, I had the opportunity to visit the unique space. Because the space resonated with me deeply, I decided to scan the library and use it as a vehicle to categorise and talk through my own collections. What follows is a selection of my collections. It should be noted that these categories are not cleanly delineated as some objects (such as rocks and shells) fit in multiple collections.

2. Traditional Collections of Finite Sets

A category that includes objects such as stamps, coins and panini stickers. These collections involve objects that are well-defined and have clear limits.

3. Traditional Collections of Non-Finite or Permutating Artifacts

This category includes my collection of seashells and rocks. These collections are not limited in number and may change over time. They also stem from my childhood and as such are more focused on the process of collecting rather than on the specific objects collected.

4. Naive or Sentimental Collections

These naive collections consist of objects I cannot seem to throw away, but also don't seem to use. They include: casts of my teeth, my old stuffed animals and the sock and bone collection of kraker (dog). These are collections of sentimental value: souvenirs and knick-knacks that hold personal value.

5. *Collections that Function as Abstract or Essence of a Space*

These collections could include objects that represent a place or a memory: they are the random objects I found at different locations and are kept to capture the essence of a particular experience or location.

Australia: Corals. A ponytail of an actual pony. Shells. Part of a clock.

USA: A dried salamander, 4 butterfly wings, a bug. Some precious notes by my mom including a list of names of the friends she met and some notes on how to enjoy each others company (be happy, share, do things together).

Russia: A floater, a spring, some old barbed wire.

Japan: A leave, some strings, 3 bugs, dried grass. About 100¥ (0.73 cents) saved in a side view car mirror cover.

6. *Objects that are More than just an Object*

This category includes objects that hold cultural or symbolic significance beyond their physical attributes. Pictured here are a collection of wishbones that still have a wish inside of them and a few dried frogs (that will never be kissed).

7. *Unclaimed Objects (collected for someone else)*

Sugar bags saved for the sugar bag museum of my childhood best friend. These bags never made it to his museum because his mother found out he secretly ate the sugar in bed at night, after which the museum got suspended.

8. *A Collection of Collections*

My collections often stem from a desire to capture something, to pin it down and to make it tangible. It's impossible to fully capture what these objects represent, because as I collect these objects, the sum that represents the collection has become more than just the individual items themselves. The objects have become a conduit for imagination, forming a cosmos in their own right.

The rise of digital assets such as NFTs has made owning digital art more accessible. McKenzie Wark suggests that the future of collecting may not be about owning something unique, but about owning something that everyone else has. Yet the act of collecting still holds a powerful allure, connecting us to our past, present, and future selves. This is why to me, collecting still remains a deeply personal pursuit.

https://newart.city/show/a-collection-folded-into-a-library

VOID VOID VOID

THE VOID

VOID VOID VOID

SENTIMENTAL OR
NAIVE COLLECTIONS

A Collection of Collections

Folded into the Prelinger Library

GLITCH COLLECTION
OBJECTS THAT ARE
MORE THAN AN OBJECT

raditional Collections of Finite Sets

Carl Upmann
Utrecht
Holland
My Wish

Traditional Collections of Non-Finite or Permutating Artifacts

Naive or Sentimental Collections

Collections that Function as an Abstract or Essence of a Space or Place

Objects that are More
than just an Object

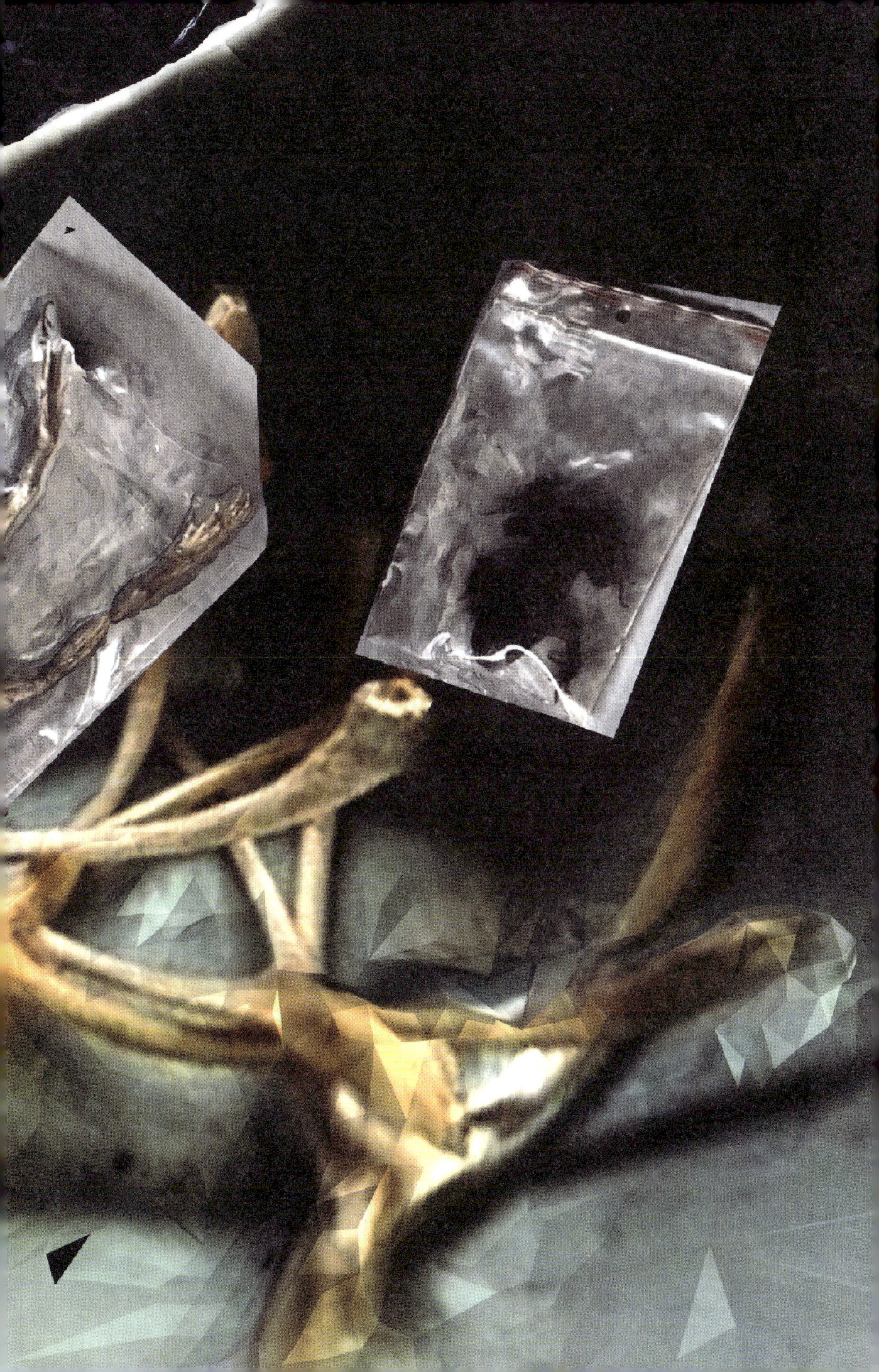

SUCRE
SUIKER
cafesrichard.fr

Unclaimed Objects (collected for someone else)

A Collection of Collections

Technolgies of Reading Writing and Writing Reading

Joe Devlin

Marginalia Drawings & Dog-Ear Compositions

In Joe Devlin's *Marginalia Drawings* (2004–ongoing), the marks, writing, highlights, drolleries, and doodles made in the margins of library books by readers are carefully collated, copied, and compressed onto single sheets of paper by the artist. Devlin's act of redrawing and rewriting notations like a post-digital monk copying the wrong part of manuscripts brings readers of different books into dialogue with one another and connects historic practices of annotation with newer digital contexts of scanning and reproduction. Crucially, the original printed text has been removed within the drawings, pushed out of sight, shifting the peripheral into frenzied focus to become the central 'body text' itself. The inscriptions contain hints of their origin but have broken free, only to be caught in a web of other kindred notes from the margins. In so doing, the series highlights how acts of stabilisation that printed and digital media perform, compel acts of destabilisation and rewriting, ad infinitum. Equally, they demonstrate how the act of reading turns to, and is co-constituted with, the act of writing. As we read, thoughts, ideas, and words are inscribed in the mind, reprogramming us. We execute these codes, inscribing, affecting, and making public (publishing) further acts and texts for others to read and write in the margins of. Imagined zoomed out, en masse, marginalia is a counter practice, and produces a counter image, of a more decentralised, deterritorialised, 'out to sea' sense of author/reader-ship and accompanying textual worlding.

Devlin's *Dog-Ear Compositions* (2023–ongoing) are paper constructions based on dog ears, the folded down corner of a book used as a bookmark, which Devlin unearths in the pages of library books. These works are bibliophilic siblings to the *Marginalia Drawings*, where again the book and the body text is nowhere to be found, instead we find a marker of the marker, a reading of the reader, the need to remember, your place in it – the book. It should be noted that Devlin's work is in part a response to, and an archaeology of, his work as a librarian at the University of Manchester. Thus, these works are produced from the hybrid modalities of artist, librarian, reader, and attend to, on the one hand, the peculiar creative interventions that readers perform through their own inscriptive and sculptural meshings with the materialities of paginated media and, on the other, the counter-role of the librarian responsible for the care, conservation, and accessibility of such media. The librarian and the reader meet in these works, on the corner, two converging book-wormholes. After all, the act of dog earing relies upon the corner of the page to enable a tender, discreet, almost unthinking fold to occur. A fold we make in a twisted echo of, and camaraderie with, the folds at the centre of the book, the moment before we close it and move on, only to return to again until it is read or reread. – *Sam Skinner*

An
GROUNDED

ARTS
BUSINESS

Moral courage

e talks in concrete, non-
the observer
Culture
we in Stories
Responsibility
Religion
sensibility
Artist
Attitude to
Politics

characters
— Are really Sensitive
tied together — want to get away
can't tied by religion, family

05-96
beginning & end
PATTERN = PATTERN
FORM

CF "ARTIST"

97_98
no one

NB → in the past perfect tense

Joyce's attitude to

WORLD

IMP.

General

IMP.

BEST CHOICE OF NIGHTMARES

FASCINATION OF THE ABOMINATION

Pink

BIT

FATHER

monstrous

reflects

which is

social issues

example

Bibliographical

Victor

Thunder

Fanny

Erica Scourti

Clean Sheets 2020–2021

Clean Sheets is a series of 7 hand-written sheets, begun in September 2020 when the artist arrived in Athens, and continued throughout lockdown into the summer of 2021. Scourti states: "During lockdown, as part of my morning routine, I wrote my journal on the sheets with marker pens, creating a layered patchwork of text, a record of a daily practice and a mass of now unreadable language." Scourti's confessional writing extending onto sheets is representative of a larger shift of how writing, different modes of publishing and the nature of the library itself has become distributed, decentred and spread into all corners of our lives.

Images on the following pages show *Clean Sheets* installed at *BiblioTech* in Liverpool, 2022.

Silvio Lorusso

Post-Digital Publishing Archive 101: Pamphlet Describing the Post-Digital Publishing Archive

A Broad Notion of Digital Publishing

Much of the discussion around publishing is informed by a model of interpretation in which digital technology acts as the natural successor of printed matter. This model fosters a narrative of linear progress among media, according to which screen will eventually take over paper. As a consequence, the relationship between the two is read as a form of rivalry and thus produces endless, often unconstructive, lists of pros and cons, improvements or worsenings.

This perspective doesn't take into account the dynamics of mutual arrangement and negotiation among media, including the various 'backward' influences, so to say from screen back to paper. At the same time, it often tends not to dwell upon the specificities of the various typologies of artifacts that define the publishing field. Lastly, it is driven by an obsessive quest for future models, therefore the space where innovation is sought frequently corresponds to the narrow ecosystem of the newest device or platform, often transitional, that does not reflect the slower, less flashy, but deeper mutations. In doing so, the universe of commonly used digital tools is often omitted from the discussion along with the analog, traditional, even retro technologies and the role they currently play. In order to accurately define the current condition of digital publishing and to deeply comprehend its broader scope, wondering what is the best device for e-reading or what is the fate of paperbacks could be reductive. The discourse on digital publishing should broaden its own horizons, asking whether the book itself can be considered a medium, investigating the existing relationships between the 'closed' form of the printed book and the ever-changing landscape of the Internet. It should find out what print has to say to digital media besides skeuomorphism, without considering digital tools as means to merely consume content. It should question how knowledge and access are affected by mass digitisation initiatives.

Actually, such questions aren't new, but they are rarely addressed by designers, developers and publishers through critical designs or theoretical reflection. On the contrary, new technologies are often blindly embraced, as the capabilities of the devices are explored with the aim of developing commercially successful products. For instance, while countless design programs are devoted to the development of iPad apps, only a few involve design and artistic strategies to analyse and communicate the implications of iTunes and its distribution model.

Whether independently or within institutional contexts, some artists and designers (a good number, but still a few in comparison to the creative industry of publishing) have grown a practice-based, speculative and often critical attitude toward publishing, whether digital or not. It's neither a self-aware current nor an avant-garde, since those people work in distinct disciplinary areas and with different aims. Sometimes their practice only accidentally deals with publishing. But their work deserves attention because it could be able to anticipate, comment and interpret the various issues that emerge at the intersection of publishing and digital technology. P-DPA aims to bring together those experiences.

Post-Digital Publishing

The term post-digital was coined by composer Kim Cascone in his essay *The Aesthetics of Failure: 'Post-digital' Tendencies in Contemporary Computer Music.* According to Cascone,[1] "the revolutionary period of the digital information age has surely passed. The tendrils of digital technology have in some way touched everyone". At least in the First World, digital technology is an integral part of our everyday life, and it is consequently taken for granted. In this sense the very attribute digital becomes meaningless, as almost every artifact we deal with is produced, distributed, mediated or at least affected by digital means.

The notion of post-digital was borrowed by Alessandro Ludovico[2] and Florian Cramer[3] to be specifically applied to publishing. While this field hasn't yet profoundly undergone the radical mutations implied by digital technology, neo-analog means of production, such as the risograph or letterpress printing (and the style that characterises them) are restored both by independents artists or designers and big publishers because "they compensate for deficiencies of digital files – deficiencies that are both aesthetic and social, since tangible media are means of face-to-face interpersonal exchange".[4] Frequently the resultant artifacts are deeply informed by digitality anyway, either as a source of content or as a reference model. When digital is the default, analog becomes a firm choice that, while is not necessarily a form of opposition, often derives from the awareness of the specificities of both possibilities.

The 'post-digital mindset' allows a more inclusive research framework of the publishing field, in which e-books and book-apps aren't the only object of study and where 'old' and 'new' media are not in a natural opposition. In the field of post-digital publishing, printed matter doesn't belong to the past and digital tools are not inherently innovative. Artists and designers seamlessly shift between blogs and stapled zines. The digital environment is at the same time a source of inspiration, a repository of raw data to filter and organise, a channel for collaboration or dissemination, a space for exposure, a mix of communication modes to exploit, a set of tools to tweak or to autonomously build. It is not an easy task to identify and analyse the various aspects of such a broad context. Likewise, it takes a big effort to trace

1. Kim Cascone, "The Aesthetics of Failure: 'Post-Digital' Tendencies in Contemporary Computer Music," Computer *Music Journal* 24 (4), 2002: 392–98. **2.** Alessandro Ludovico, *Post-Digital Print: The Mutation of Publishing since 1894* (Onomatopee, 2012). **3.** Florian Cramer, "Post-Digital Aesthetics," *Jeu De Paume*, May 1, 2013, http://lemagazine.jeudepaume.org/2013/05/florian-cramer-post-digital-aesthetics. **4.** Ibid.

back the many ways in which digital technology addresses the specificities of traditional media and processes of publishing. Through a thematic approach to collection and archiving, P-DPA investigates experimental publishing in order to highlight aspects that specifically deal with digital technology and analog means, especially when they're not blatantly apparent.

The Archive

The aim of P-DPA is to systematically collect, organise and keep trace of experiences in the fields of art and design that explore the relationships between publishing and digital technology. The archive acts as a space in which the collected projects are confronted and juxtaposed in order to highlight relevant paths, mutual themes, common perspectives, interrelations, but also oppositions and idiosyncrasies. Among the main questions posed by P-DPA, there are:

> How do artists and designers articulate the relationships between publishing and digital technology? In which ways the role of printed matter is redefined by digital technology and what kind of negotiation takes place between the two? In the post-digital era, where does publishing cease to be publishing? What boundaries need to be drawn in terms of media, ecosystems and practices? Are artists and designers able to identify issues that are not covered in the debate on the future of publishing, generally led by a straightforward, normative and often commercially-driven notion of innovation? Which strategies are they introducing to address those issues? What kind of impact do experimental modes of production, intervention and dissemination of content have on publishing?
>
> What sort of meaning do traditional forms of printed publishing (such as the book or the magazine) assume when immersed in a context characterised by the pervasiveness of digital technology? P-DPA is a curated archive but it's open to submissions. It allows users with backgrounds in various disciplines to develop their own paths and interact in a specific way with its contents. For instance, the archive could be useful to interface designers, literature historians, publishers, media theorists and art critics. Furthermore, P-DPA houses critical reflection and commentary on the projects and their context. In this perspective, general overviews, critical analyses, articles and interviews are hosted. While the main form of the archive is as online platform, works that have a physical existence are collected through a donation model and through fundings. Each item included in P-DPA is defined by a comprehensive set of information that, if the creator agrees, is made available for download.
>
> General description of the (art)work- Bibliographic data (e.g. ISBN, page number, size, publisher)- Photo/video documentation (e.g. screenshots)- Source code and digital versions (e.g. EPUB, PDF, EXE)- Contextual data (e.g. artist's statement, press coverage, critical reviews)- Technologies employed both in the production and the fruition of the work (e.g. InDesign or Scribus, Chrome or Firefox)- License (e.g. creative commons, public domain)- Aesthetic profile (e.g. movement, subject, community)- Location (e.g. institution, collection, archive code)

The development of P-DPA, which is currently not publicly accessible, is documented on p-dpa.tumblr.com. The archive also acts as a thematic aggregator of materials found in various other archives and sources (such as the *Library of the Printed Web* or Rhizome's *ArtBase*).

Preservation, Connections, and Networks

Within the instability and forgetfulness that are typical of the information age, P-DPA acts as a mean of preservation, not only storing the digital versions of the single work, but also investigating and philologically addressing the context, the ecosystems and the cultural conditions in which those experiments exist. As net art, and contemporary art in general, has shown, preservation becomes a particularly urgent and tricky issue when it's aimed at natively digital works (e.g. software, websites, devices): the obsolescence of devices and platforms often tangles a genuine reproduction of the experience provided by the piece. Sometimes even the specific aspects addressed by the artwork (e.g. interface designs, a function of a software, production and conversion systems) quickly disappear from the records, complicating the interpretation of its scope.

Printed matter in turn results often volatile: for instance, as several collected items are books available only in print on demand, some of them even play with the impossibility of being purchased and thus becoming physical objects (e.g. selling the book for an extremely heavy price). And even when a certain amount of physical copies do exist, it could be difficult to interpret the book's context because of the absence, so to say, of author name, publication date, etc.

Finally, while the inclusion criteria are primarily thematic, the artist's or designer's reputation is not relevant. Therefore, the archive comprehends several works by students, amateurs, and outsiders of the arts and design world. In doing so, P-DPA deals with the widespread empowerment provided by 'universal' access to digital tools.

The thematic focus of P-DPA aims at revealing unnoticed relationships and connections between experiences belonging to different fields. Those relationships and connections represent the starting point for a conscious critique and a history of post-digital publishing employing artworks as landmarks and critical statements. The archive is also an opportunity to create a space for dialogue and exchange between artists and designers.

Inclusion Criteria

The (art)works should inherently address or anticipate one or more aspects of publishing and one or more aspects of digital technology according to the following categories. - Tools, modes of production, design (e.g. DTP, crowdsourcing, print on demand);- Digital features (e.g. DRM, Internet, database);- Devices (e.g. computer, e-reader);- Distribution, dissemination, appropriation, intervention (e.g. remix, plagiarism, download);- Categorisation, archiviation, organisation, structure (e.g. ISBN, tags, metadata, index);- Bookness, bookform, book as object (e.g. skeuomorphism, binding, book as prop);- Spaces and rituals related to books and publishing (e.g. online store, bookshop, library);- Book typologies (encyclopedia, catalog, magazine). Inherence Not every printed book designed through digital tools or distributed via online platforms should be included in P-DPA. Here's where the 'inherence' of the single project becomes crucial: in order to be included in the archive, a work, through its own nature, should actively question, highlight or reframe constitutive aspects of publishing in the post-digital age. Of course, this perspective on the works holds a level of ambiguity that is the result of the unique identity of the archive, which point of view is ultimately subjective. Inherence is a fluid criterion in a dialectic relationship with the digital environment. For instance, nowadays we consider copy-paste an inherently digital function, but it has not always been so. Anticipation An experimental project that predates the universal spread of digital technology shouldn't be excluded from the archive a priori. P-DPA applies a 'post-digital gaze' to experiences that, more or less consciously, anticipate modalities of the digital age. As an example, several 'network-enabling' counterculture magazines could be considered as tangible expressions of what would later become known as the blogosphere. It is no coincidence that Steve Jobs described the Whole Earth Catalog as a sort of "Google in paperback form, 35 years before Google came along".

Main Fields of Inquiry

In order to guide the research of the projects to include in the archive, three main fields of inquiry are defined:– Critical design: the space in which graphic and interaction design intersect and act as critical tools;– The field of artists' books and bookworks;- The area of new media art. In those areas, several perspectives on publishing and experimental forms of dialogue between digital and analog are embedded into more extensive inquiries regarding the impact of technology on behavior, on the dissemination of knowledge and on the very definition of culture. The confrontation with these issues often requires the development of operative strategies that allow to test the limits and potential outcomes of technologies. In doing so, artists and designers outline parallel universes in which the extreme consequences of progress are highlighted and therefore opposed to the status quo.

In *Critical Design,* Anthony Dunne writes that the work of the designer can lead to "conceptual design proposals offering a critique of the present through the material embodiment of functions derived from alternative value systems".[5] The 'critical designer' develops artifacts, prototypes or even concepts, the purpose of which is to raise questions on the implications of design itself on society. Those experimental designs are often able to provide direct and effective arguments against or in favor of a certain issue and exploit the possibilities of dissemination of new technologies.

Artists' Books and Bookworks Johanna Drucker (2004), book artist and historian of artists' books, states that "artists' books are almost always self-conscious about the structure and meaning of the book as a form".[6] In this sense artists' books are useful analytical tools of the current condition of the book as a designed artifact, as a cultural object and as a commodity. Furthermore, they provide alternative reading models, often anti-functionalist, as they are "books in which the book form, a coherent sequence of pages, determines conditions of reading that are intrinsic to the work".[7] The proposed models, more or less viable, often represent a radicalisation of the technical aspects that affect the act of reading.

New Media Art 'New media art' could be a misleading term because it seems to refer only to new media, and so to artworks that include digital technology to be developed or displayed. Frequently new media art takes into account digital tools as a cultural reference, therefore it's not unusual to encounter projects employing traditional techniques and media such as painting or printed books. The notion of

5. Anthony Dunne, *Hertzian Tales: Electronic Products, Aesthetic Experience, and Critical Design* (MIT Press, 2005). **6.** Johanna Drucker, *The Century of Artists' Books* (Granary Books, 2004). **7.** Ulises Carrión, "Bookworks Revisited," in *Quant aux livres/ On books* (Héros-Limite,1997).

'newmedia' itself is problematic and, in the context of this research, it will be interpreted both as digital technology and as emergent media opposed to settled ones.

Related Archives

Library of the Printed Web, Rhizome, Artbase, UbuWeb, Monoskop Log, AAAAARG.ORG, Artists' Books Online.

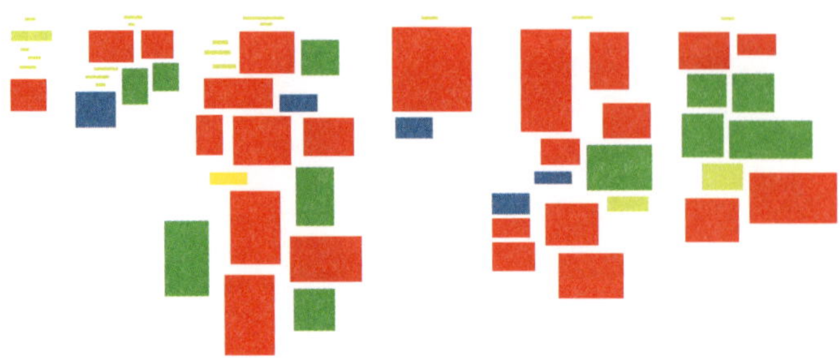

PREMISE

"There is no Telos"
– F. Kitten

Oral History

Ideas > Projects

A "deluge" of names

ORIGIN STORY

2011

Maria Minaya

Yung Silvio Lorusso

Margreet Riphagen (camera)

Institute of Network Cultures

Geert Lovink

'Generally, INC's publications can be read online, downloaded, and even ordered as physical books for free. As a consequence, it sometimes happens that these free books are then sold for a price elsewhere. However, people at the INC do not complain. What they care about is the dissemination and circulation of ideas, so they are enthralled by the unexpected ways in which content is redistributed and reframed.'

–Silvio Lorusso

http://p-dpa.net/networked-standardisation/

Theory on Demand Series

Espresso Book Machine

Lulu (Pod Service)

Print on Demand

Rhode

Experimental publishing can be positioned as an i mode of critique, and a tool of speculation. It is a about writing and publishing today that has at its commitment to questioning and breaking down di between practice and theory, criticality and creati between the scholarly and the artistic.

In this series of events we propose to explore cont approaches to experimental publishing as:

- an ongoing critique of our current publishing sy practices, deconstructing existing hegemonies an the fixtures in publishing to which we have grown from the book as a stable object to single authors copyright.

- an affirmative practice which offers means to re- existing writerly, research, and publishing institut practices through publishing experiments.

- a speculative practice that makes possible an ex different futures for writing and research, and the new, potentially more inclusive forms, genres, an publishing, open to ambivalence and failure.

– Janneke Adema, https://openreflections.wordpress.com/2022/02/2. publishing-vi-critique-intervention-and-speculat

"EXPERIMENTAL" PUBLISHING

2013 - Present

presso Book Machine

Lulu (Pod Service)

Print on Demand

Paul Soulellis

Rhode Island School of Design

Willem De Kooning Academie

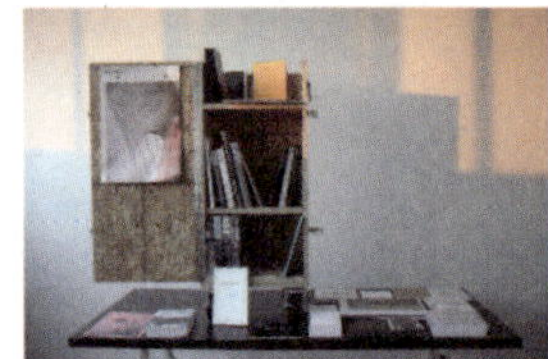

Library of the Printed Web

Publishing has never been a fixed notion. "What i relevant inquiry, but with an increasingly expand response, as platforms, channels and modes of p Let's begin with the post, exposing its origins as a note publicly nailed to a piece of wood. Its descen visible on the wall, in the feed and in the stream a deeper history of documents — the scriptural eco publishing?

– Paul Soulellis, RISD Experimental Publishing St

https://web.archive.org/web/20180209081633/ht eps15

POST— DIGITAL PUBLISHING ARCHIVE

Experimental Publishing Informed By Digital Technology

Post-Digital Publishing Archive

The simplest definition of 'post-digital' describes a media aesthetics which opposes such digital high-tech and high-fidelity cleanness.
– Florian Cramer, 'What is 'Post-Digital'? (2014)

http://lab404.com/142/cramer.pdf

Florian Cramer

Alessandro Ludovico

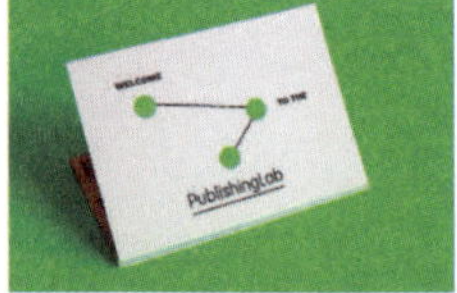

PublishingLab

Very few terms have been used so habitually and carelessly as the word 'experiment'.

– Peter Bilak (2005)

My impression is that in the field of publishing the goal of experimental projects has mostly been to overcome the financial and identity crisis of the sector.

In my perspective, experimental publishing is something different. I'd say it resonates with avantgardistic attempts to push the boundaries of their medium of choice. The problem is that nowadays pushing the medium's boundaries is the very dominant attitude.

So, in my opinion, a genuinely experimental practice requires:

a practical, hands-on approach in which making produces meaning;
an (inexorably impermanent) antagonism towards the mediating forces of the hegemonic discourse.

– Silvio Lorusso, FAQs, 2016

http://p-dpa.net/faqs/

Required Reading: Paul Soulellis on Experimental Publishing

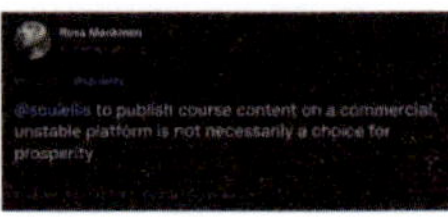

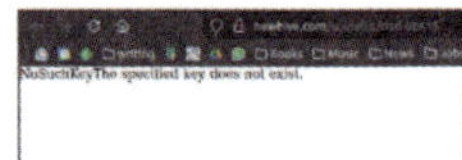

Experimental publishing can be positioned as an i mode of critique, and a tool of speculation. It is a about writing and publishing today that has at its commitment to questioning and breaking down d between practice and theory, criticality and creat between the scholarly and the artistic.

In this series of events we propose to explore cont approaches to experimental publishing as:

- an ongoing critique of our current publishing sy practices, deconstructing existing hegemonies an the fixtures in publishing to which we have grown from the book as a stable object to single authors copyright.

- an affirmative practice which offers means to re- existing writerly, research, and publishing institut practices through publishing experiments.

- a speculative practice that makes possible an ex different futures for writing and research, and the new, potentially more inclusive forms, genres, an publishing, open to ambivalence and failure.

– Janneke Adema, https://openreflections.wordpress.com/2022/02/2 publishing-vi-critique-intervention-and-speculat

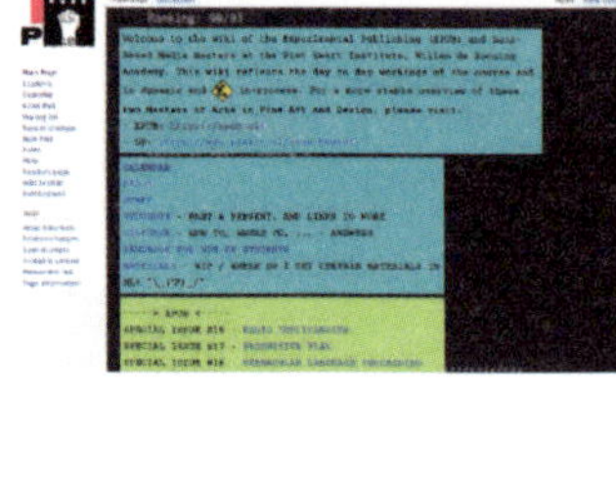

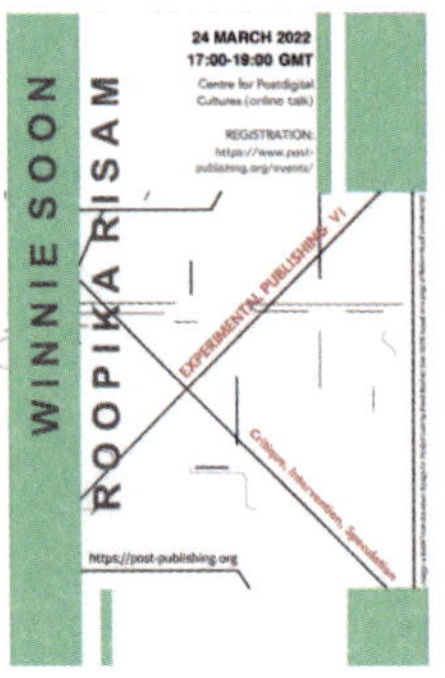

Janneke Adema

XPUB's interests in publishing are twofold:

first, publishing as the ***inquiry*** *and* ***participation*** *into the technological frameworks, political context and cultural processes through which things are made public;*

and second, publishing as the desire to expand the means of discourse circulation beyond print media and its direct digital translation, so as to create public in the age of post-digital networks.

– XPUB description

https://www.wdka.nl/programmes/master-media-design-experimental-publishing

Mitch Goldstein

Panthology (noun): a pathology that consists in seeing everything through the lens of one's own discipline or practice. Panthology can be understood as a particular form of apophenia. Notable examples: 'everything is architecture', 'everyone is a designer', 'my dog's poop is information', 'making a sandwich is a form of publishing'.

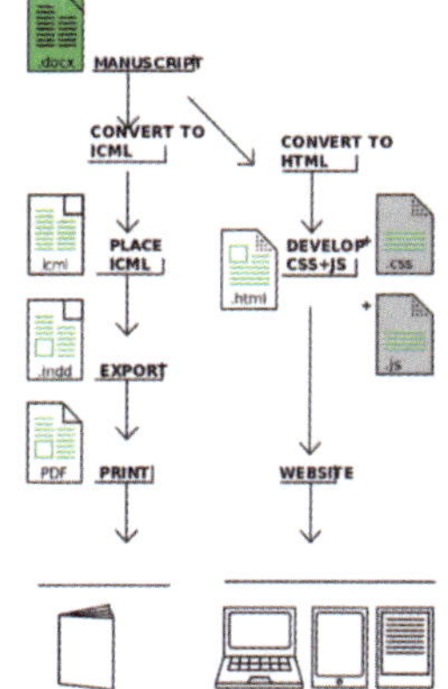

EPUB Trailers

At the same time, a celebration of materiality (as it becomes apparent) and its negation (as it can be trascended).

flip flop (n.) 1. the process of pushing a work of art or craft from the physical world to the digital world and back, usually more than once; 2. a work of art or craft produced this way

– Robin Sloan, 2014

Robin Stam

ReFlow

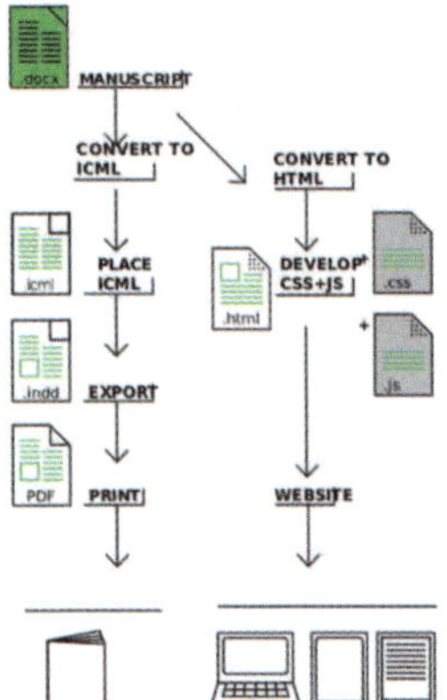

FROM PRINT TO EBOOKS A HYBRID PUBLISHING TOOLKIT FOR THE ARTS

FROM PRINT TO EBOOKS A HYBRID PUBLISHING TOOLKIT

EPUB Trailers

EDWIN ABBOTT ABBOTT

Michael Murtaugh

Traumawien

At the same time, a celebration of materiality (as it becomes apparent) and its negation (as it can be trascended).

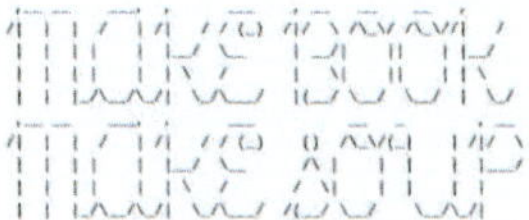

flip flop (n.) 1. the process of pushing a work of art or craft from the physical world to the digital world and back, usually more than once; 2. a work of art or craft produced this way

– Robin Sloan, 2014

The goal is to approach the workflow from a more imaginative and speculative perspective. The participants are therefore asked to create new automatic "recipes" that are then included in a growing "cookbook".

ReFlow, Martin Wecke, 2013

Robin Stam

Varia

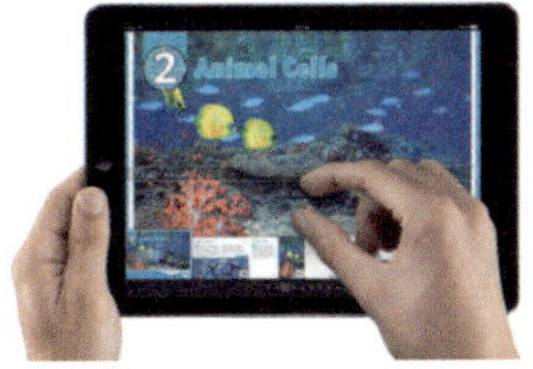

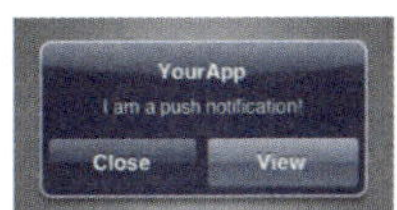

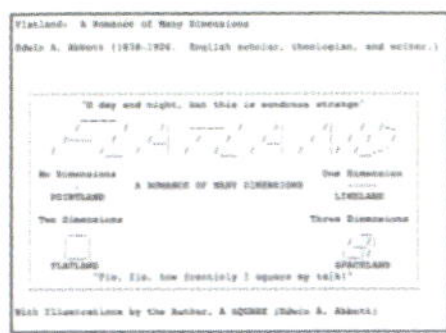

Flatland on Project Gutenberg

Poor media foster duplication and boost circulation. They are lightweight. Poor media suggest an active use: frequently they can be converted, dissected, remixed, reorganized, updated. The modest simplicity of poor media doesn't contradict the possibility to preserve them. The duplicating aura they carry amplifies their resilience: "lots of copies keep stuff safe," archivists say. The poverty of poor media should be better called frugality, since it's characterized by the conscious, serene renunciation of embellishments in favor of accessibility and spread. The spartan look of poor media might not be beautiful, but it's undoubtedly charming.

– In Defense of Poor Media, 2015

This is a motherfucking website.

Seriously, what the fuck else do you want?

Well guess what, motherfucker:

It's fucking lightweight

Rich media reflect the privileges of rich countries. Several enhanced publications are developed without considering hardware and network conditions on a global scale. In 2012, among the first eight textbooks available through iBooks, the smallest was more than 700Mb big. Some of them were bigger than 2Gb (Brownlee 2012). Such files require lot of available space and a very fast connection.

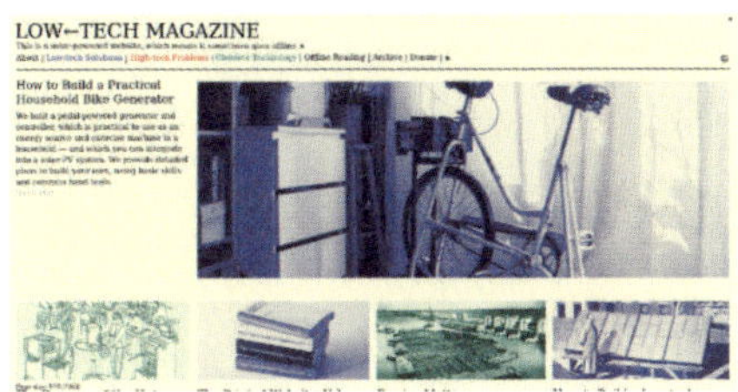

Roel Roscam Abbing Kris De Decker Marie Otsuka

Ebook Backup, Jesse England, 2012

Jake Reber

PODematerialisation of the Book Art Object

Print-on-demand book technology has radically changed the publishing industry, allowing for much smaller print runs and no upfront cost to artists and writers. This shift has produced new possibilities for what the book can be and who has access to creating book objects. Printed books of screenshots, text dumps, and other digital ephemera can be collected and produced, revealing the points of contact and ruptures between digital and print aesthetics.

The critical use and misuse of these technologies has been described by Andreas Bülhoff and Annette Gilbert as artistic print-on-demand.[1] They describe artistic print-on-demand as "a critical media practice that continues avant-garde, underground, and counterculture traditions and also responds to our post-digital age in compelling us to re-conceptualise our understanding of the book and publishing." These are publishing projects that engage with various formats and mediations in and around book objects. These artistic print-on-demand (or POD) projects are grappling with post-digital aesthetics, automation, economic precarity, distribution/ circulation challenges of scale, library acquisition, waste, etc. This produces a printed form of content that operates according to the logics of digital production, while still interrogating the materiality of the book.

Echoing the approach of Lucy Lippard's *Six Years*,[2] I intend to frame the practice of artistic print-on-demand through materials and fragments from others: interviews, images, book descriptions, archives, and commentary. This method also mimics the practices of collating, scrapping, reconfiguring material across the internet as seen in many POD projects. My essay will contend with the concerns outlined above and also collect images and examples of projects that are representative of artistic print-on-demand. The essay will also engage with and implement some of the techniques and practices outlined in Paul Soulellis' essential essay on web-to-print practices. The essay will document and practice the techniques that define the post-digital publishing practices of artistic print-on-demand.

1. Andreas Bülhoff and Gilbert Annette, "Collection and Research," *Library of Artistic Print On Demand,* May 16, 2021, https://apod.li/about. **2.** Lucy Lippard, *Six Years: The Dematerialization of the Art Object from 1966 to 1972* (University of California Press, 1997).

Dematerialisation of the book

In Lucy Lippard's introduction to her book, *Six Years: The Dematerialization of the Art Object from 1966 to 1972*, she discusses the process of dematerialising art through the formation of conceptual art. She writes, "Conceptual art, for me, means work in which the idea is paramount and the material form is secondary, lightweight, ephemeral, cheap, unpretentious and/or 'dematerialised.'" The strand of conceptualism that she focuses on comes out of minimalism. With minimalism, there was an emphasis on only including what was essential, an art without excess. She writes, "if Minimalism formally expressed 'less is more,' Conceptual art was about saying more with less." She discusses this as a process of dematerialisation, where "the idea is paramount and the material form is secondary, lightweight, ephemeral, cheap, unpretentious and/or 'dematerialised.'" The format and object status of the book follows a similar trajectory with the rise of the digital age. The arrival of POD could be called a dematerialisation in the sense Lippard refers to, where the book is "lightweight, ephemeral, cheap, unpretentious."

Throughout the text, Lippard identifies primary examples and fragments that help to articulate the formation of this new movement. In some ways this is essay intended to do a similar sort of task. While Lippard had a difficult to task in documenting and referencing the ephemeral practices of the artists she collected, the documents, paratexts and institutions that exhibited the work are in many instances tended to have a physical presence that could be traced in the world, some of which remain present to the contemporary moment.

The POD projects in this essay are dealing with a digital landscape that is intensifying the process of dematerialisation. Websites, digital archives, online magazines that host POD work are already deadlinks. Error messages and 404 pages proliferate. Not only the works, but even their context is evaporating. Much like Lippard's attempts to document art practices before they disappear forever, I hope to provide a documentation of some of these tendencies, techniques, and approaches to thinking the book through PODematerialisation.

I intend to examine the disappearance of the book and the emergence of the POD book art object.This is not to say that other art-book tendencies have completely evaporated, but it is to highlight a new tradition or movement that's emerging. Many of these projects are also available as PDFs and circulate in this other mode, completely stripping off the physical markings of the book. And yet, these files still resemble a certain bookishness in their layout and formatting. PDFs POD books often still have page numbers, title pages, and even some sort of copyright or publisher page. There's a certain sort of pressure placed on the book in these works.

Mimeo and Rapid Publishing

An important connective thread between the conceptual work Lippard discusses and the contemporary practice of POD is the print publications produced by these conceptual artists. The use of rapid production and distribution has accompanied material print culture, only shifting forms with the arrival of the internet.

During the 1970s, small presses and artists used mimeographs to duplicate and produce cheap publications. Vito Acconci and Bernadette Mayer, two figures that loom large in the realm of experimental small press poetry, ran the magazine, 0 to 9, using mimeo. They also are intertwined with the network of artists and events collected in Lippard's text. Inexpensive, fast, lofi publishing emerges on the edges, evading certain types of attention, while still cultivating an aesthetic lineage and history. And just as mimeo carried traces of the information technology of the time, the aesthetic POD works carry the markings of contemporary information technology.

The markings of technology and the materialisation of language are entangled in this movement towards art and aesthetic practices related to information and grounded in conceptual art. In his introduction to the online addition of conceptual writing anthology, *Against Expression*, Craig Dworkin draws on conceptual art to frame and contextualise writing practices that come after the apparent 'dematerialisation' process. He writes, "the supposed dematerialisation of the art object was bought at the cost of the rematerialisation of language."[3] Language is no longer just framing or supporting, but instead, it becomes an object. The spaces between words can be entered into, they can be processed and opened up. The rematerialisation of language described by Dworkin as a component of conceptual art is something that also resonates with the tactics of POD publishing. It is a mode of "assembling, rearranging, and displaying information; or sorting and selecting from files of accumulated language pursuant to a certain algorithm – rather than producing new material from scratch."[4]

Search compile publish

In his essay, "Search, Compile, Publish," Paul Soulellis describes POD objects as "web culture articulated as printed artifact[s]."[5] The works collected in Soulellis' essay range in their construction methodologies, and Soulellis attempts to articulate a few of the approaches seen in POD publishing practices.

Techniques: Grabbing, Scraping, Hunting, Performing

Soulellis' categories are particularly useful in trying to establish a categorical method for examining the various works of POD. *Grabbing* is a process of using search engines to collect and organise text and/or images. The materials are recontextualised, shifting and reconfiguring the authorial function. As Soulellis writes, "The grabbing and re-presenting under a different context (the context of the artist's work) make these almost like readymades – appropriated material that asks us to confront the nature of meaning and value behind an image that's been stripped of origin, function and intent."[6] *Scraping* is essential more extensive versions of grabbing that often require additional forms of automated methods or scripts to deal with information in bulk. *Hunting* often requires wandering through the internet, sifting through digital space. Instead of relying on the methods of the grabbers and scrapers, "these artists target scenes that show a certain condition – something unusual or particularly satisfying."[7] The last method is *performing*. This approach "involves the acting out of a procedure, in a narrative fashion, from A to B. The procedure is a way to interact with data and a kind of performance between web and print."[8]

I would like to add another category which emphasises the material constraints of the POD object. I referred to this as an extension of dematerialisation, or more precisely, the PODematerialisation, of the book.

So we have print-on-demand as a common production technique.
But what about the actual work? What concepts on view here might
suggest what it means to be an artist who cultivates a web-to-print
practice? And how is print changing because of the web? Are there
clues here? / We could say that these are artists who work as archivists,

3. Craig Dworkin, "Fate of the Echo," in *Against Expression: An Anthology of Conceptual Writing* (Northwestern University Press, 2011): xxiii–liv. **4.** Ibid. **5–9.** Paul Soulellis, "Search, Compile, Publish," *Soulellis*, May 23, 2013, https://soulellis.com/2013/05/search-compile-publish.

or artists who work with new kinds of archives. Or perhaps these are artists who simply work with an archivist's sensibility – an approach that uses the dynamic, temporal database as a platform for gleaning narrative. – Paul Soulellis[9]

Poor publishing

Using Tumblr to host our PDFs and Lulu to print books with no upfront costs, means we didn't have to waste money on staples, paper, or xeroxing. In effect, Print-on-Demand and PDFs are what poor publishing looks like. – Joey Yearous-Algozin[10]

In 2016, Troll Thread published Joey Yearous-Algozin's *how to stop worrying abt the state of publishing when the world's burning and everybody's broke anyways and all you really care abt is if anyone is even reading yr work*. It's a 3-page PDF and POD book that provides instructions to publishing and running a press through Lulu, even taking advantage of the hosting abilities provided by Lulu's ebook upload process. This brief document beautifully encapsulates the particularities and peculiarities of POD publishing. Yearous-Algozin's book exists in a potential state, as an ebook, as a PDF all at once. It also circulates as a 'how to' guide, spreading and expanding the possibilities of this practice and communicating the specifics of actually doing this work. Troll Thread is one of the more prominent small presses producing POD books, and they articulate the values and desires seen across POD publishing projects.

Hito Steyerl writes on the capacities of digital distribution and rapid circulation in her essay "In Defense of the Poor Image." While her writing is primarily focused on the status of the image and cinema across digital networks, Steyerl's comments provide a way to begin thinking about the potential of post-digital publishing. She writes that the low-resolution 'poor image' can be "distributed for free, squeezed through slow digital connections, compressed, reproduced, ripped, remixed, as well as copied and pasted into other channels of distribution."[11] It provides a more open experience, with greater distribution, but one that is degraded: "Its genealogy is dubious. Its filenames are deliberately misspelled. It often defies patrimony, national culture, or indeed copyright. It is passed on as a lure, a decoy, an index, or as a reminder of its former visual self. It mocks the promises of digital technology."

Apart from resolution and exchange value, one might imagine another form of value defined by velocity, intensity, and spread. Poor images are poor because they are heavily compressed and travel quickly. They lose matter and gain speed.

Drawing on Hito Steyerl's work on the "poor image", Silvio Lorusso writes about POD publishing through the concept of "poor media," describing a book format that "foster[s] duplication and boost[s] circulation.... they can be converted, dissected, remixed, reorganised, updated."[12] These publications allow for critical attention to the physical qualities of the book, working with and against the material substrate that underlies the book object.

10. Joey Yearous-Algozin, *how to stop worrying abt the state of publishing when the world's burning and everybody's broke anyways and all you really care abt is if anyone is even reading yr work*, Troll Thread, 2016. **11.** Hito Steyerl, "In Defense of the Poor Image," *e-flux journal* 10 (2009), https://www.e-flux.com/journal/10/61362/in-defense-of-the-poor-image. **12.** Silvio Lorusso, "In Defense of Poor Media," *Printed_Web_3. pdf* (2015): 35–90.

Library of the Printed Web

Alongside the production of POD books has come a rather idiosyncratic collecting and archiving practices. The decisions around collecting and curating specific physical objects and different file types is handled differently by the various small archives, some of which are also the publishers and artists.

Paul Soulellis started *Library of the Printed Web* as an "archive devoted to archives. It's an accumulation of accumulations, a collection that's tightly curated by me, to frame a particular view of culture as it exists right now on the web, through print publishing. That documents it, articulates it."[13]

Library of the Printed Web is "a way for us to monitor the artist's relationship to the screen, the database and the printed page as it evolves over time."[14]

I could see this entire collection becoming a dated account of a very specific moment in the history of art and technology, perhaps spanning only a decade. And that's how I intend to work with this collection – as an archive that's alive and actively absorbing something of the moment, as it's happening, and evolving as new narratives develop.

Gauss PDF

Gauss PDF is another example of this sort of urgent publishing practice that uses POD, among other methods. Started in 2010 by J. Gordon Faylor, *Gauss PDF* publishes and distributes completed projects that move between different filetypes, genres, and aesthetic forms.

As Faylor describes it, "GPDF's inaugural release came about in November 2010. By that point, I'd made a good number of friends/acquaintances in both the NYC and Philadelphia experimental poetry scenes (and elsewhere, naturally) who I thought were producing very engaging work, and wanted to present a platform through which they could publish their strange projects in toto, quickly and easily."[15]

It became an environment of "aesthetic instability," really exploring the friction between files, formats, and POD objects. The POD book emerges, in this context, out of the instability of digital materials and the ways they can slip between filetypes, carrying traces of transfer and transcoding.

> I am specifically interested in how you see the relation between digital works and print publication – in terms of how works are commissioned, how they are distributed, and how they are consumed. – Tan Lin[16]

> The goal is to make GPDF releases as available as possible. The best physical equivalent for this is print-on-demand, and the most user-friendly POD marketplace I've found belongs to Lulu. It's not ideal (e.g. they charge way too much for S&H and the paper stock isn't so hot), but it's the most efficacious way to manage hasty production at a relatively low cost... – J. Gordon Faylor

13. Paul Soulellis, "Search, Compile, Publish". **14.** Ibid. **15.** Tan Lin, "Gauss PDF Interview with J. Gordon Faylor," Harriet: *A Poetry Blog,* May 4, 2014, https://www.poetryfoundation.org/harriet-books/2014/05/gauss-pdf-interview-with-j-gordon-faylor. **16.** Tan Lin, "Troll Thread Interview," *Harriet: A Poetry Blog.* May 4, 2014, https://www.poetryfoundation.org/harriet-books/2014/05/troll-thread-interview.

Edit Publications

The possibilities for rapid publishing and collaboration are clearly seen through the Edit Publication event that produced a series of texts responding to and extending the work of Tan Lin.

On July 29th, Edit Publications launches eleven books expanding Tan Lin's Seven Controlled Vocabularies and Obiturary 2004. The Joy of Cooking (Wesleyan Poetry Series, 2010). These printed editions derive from an event at the Kelly Writers House at the University of Pennsylvania on April 12th, 2010 titled "Handmade book, PDF, lulu, Appendix, Powerpoint, Kanban Board/Post-Its, Blurb, Dual Language (Chinese/ English) Edition, micro lecture, Selectric II interview, wine/cheese reception, Q&A (xerox), film.[17] From a Critical Reader that functions as a full-text digital library to an exquisitely unsettling Google English-Chinese-English translation exactly reproducing Lin's Seven Controlled Vocabularies (7CV), these gorgeous books have been painstakingly edited and carefully designed for (entirely) free download or (mostly) at-cost print-on-demand. Please feel free to download the entire set or the individual books listed below – then, if you like, reupload to lulu for your own republication – while PDFs are wonderful, you just might want to read these things on the page. As Benjamin Disraeli once said: "the best way to become acquainted with a subject is to publish a book about it."

The POD book publication event turns the book into an immediate process of documentation and networked entanglement. It is a generative process that continues to proliferate the life of Tan Lin's book, continually rewriting and extending itself, materialising the book through more books. PODematerialisation is a process of extending the material possibilities of the book, making books out of any sort of material.

PODEMATERIALISATION

While there are many different artists that have used this form of print production to create their work, I want to highlight the works that are actually considering the material constraints of POD publishing. The approaches and techniques highlighted by Paul Soulellis are useful ways into the web to print publishing practices, and they provide a framework that cuts across the type of works I want to highlight. I use the phrase "PODematerialisation" to capture the strange status of materiality of the works I intend to offer as a particular subset within post-digital publishing.

These works draw on the history of conceptual art, experimental small press poetry, lofi digital media, and post-digital art. The status of their materiality is always in questions, existing in a state of potential and challenging the actual process and production of the printed page.

They operate through a form of what Vito Acconci called 'dumb literalism,' taking seriously the way in which language materialises and sets the terms for the material object. The process of PODematerialisation does not necessarily require the books to be printed, and some of the examples have never existed in a print form. However, these texts all take seriously the technical constraints and possibilities of POD, embedding the weird status of transfer and remediation required to move from web to print.

17. Danny Snelson, "Edit Publications, 2010 Series, 11 Books Expanding Tan Lin's Seven Controlled Vocabularies and Obituary 2004. The Joy of Cooking, YouTube Readings, Postcard, &MediaWiki," accessed January 10, 2023, https://aphasic-letters.com/edit/publications.html.

HOW TO SEE THINGS CLOSE UP

Details

Publication Date	Apr 21, 2012
Language	English
Category	Fiction
Copyright	All Rights Reserved - Standard Copyright L
Contributors	By (author) Joey Yearous-Algozin

Keywords

9/11 911 Joey Yearous-Algozin

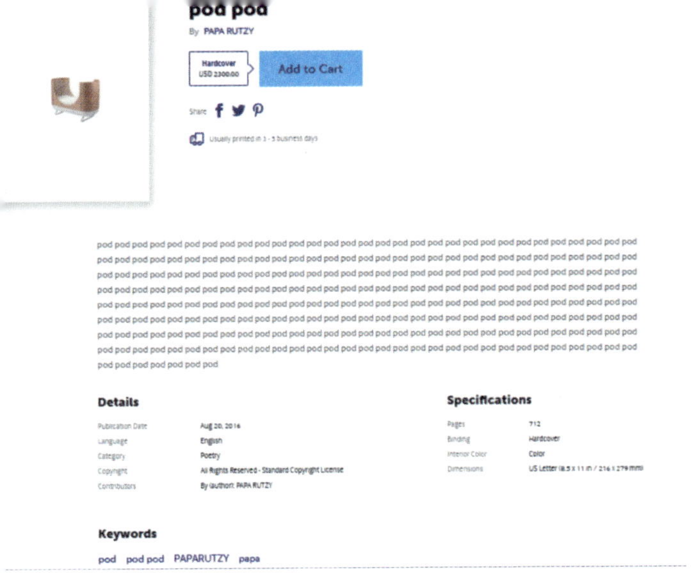

pod pod

Details

Publication Date	Aug 20, 2016
Language	English
Category	Poetry
Copyright	All Rights Reserved - Standard Copyright License
Contributors	By (author): PAPA RUTZY

Specifications

Pages	712
Binding	Hardcover
Interior Color	Color
Dimensions	US Letter (8.5 x 11 in / 216 x 279 mm)

Keywords

pod pod pod PAPARUTZY papa

JEAN KELLER

PAPER PASSION

Paper P

By Jean Keller

Paperback
USD 14.00

Share

Usually printed

The book you are looking at is the largest Anthology of Concrete

A Scanthology of Concrete Poetry

Williams, one of the founders of the movement, and with the over 200 ...

... poetry movements and in introducing so many major writers from so many countries between covers for the first time to the American reading public.

Poetry will be made by all!

Search

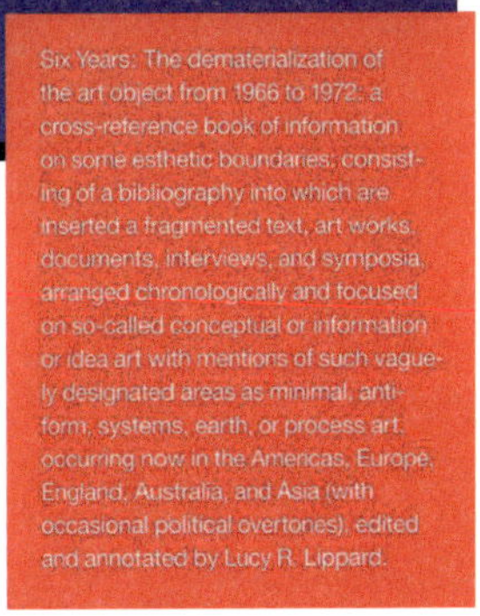

On the Road Gregor Weichbrodt	Fargone Nicole Razlys Fong	Space Administration Ken Hunt	Do palpável... Hugo Crema	El sacrificio... Sandra Martinez	The Current Cheryl Hoffmann
Reflections Maddy Aby	DI$H Emma Ramadan	Suspended (of)... Kieran Daly	Spiritual Education Carolyn Nicole Daussin	Apartment Complex Laura V Rivera	TXT Michael Vallnsky
art&education Rachel Valinsky	HARD HELL Dylan Hansen-Fliedner	om dig har alla... Elis Burrau	NOT TO DISCOU[RAGE] YOU Faye Green	Added Powers,... Jake Samuels	Al envés de la voz Cristian Pino

Six Years: The dematerialization of the art object from 1966 to 1972: a cross-reference book of information on some esthetic boundaries: consisting of a bibliography into which are inserted a fragmented text, art works, documents, interviews, and symposia, arranged chronologically and focused on so-called conceptual or information or idea art with mentions of such vaguely designated areas as minimal, anti-form, systems, earth, or process art, occurring now in the Americas, Europe, England, Australia, and Asia (with occasional political overtones), edited and annotated by Lucy R. Lippard.

JEAN KELLER

PAPER PASSION

"With Vilém Flusser, one could call the post-digital object an Unding – an object suspended between ontological states. A book produced by POD technology has the potential to be a post-digital Unding. Its vacillating states are usually described as 'analog' and 'digital,' its forms of presence as material and immaterial. The most notable way in which it embodies its ontological ambiguity is in the relation between file and product." – Hannes Bajohr[18]

Tactical Media

One notable example is Holly Melgard's *Black Friday*. This book is composed of all black pages, set for the maximum size that Lulu allows, attempting to break the printer by placing such a high demand on the actual material production. As the publisher, Troll Thread, commented in an interview, *Black Friday* was "originally designed with the hopes of breaking an industrial printer." Attempts to order and print the book resulted in errors, failing to print or produced sloppy prints, highlighting the shortcomings of this rapid printing process. This type of project is, in many ways, a tactical form of media. It becomes an active aggression towards the production process in the service of the artwork.

Joey Yearous-Algozin's *911 9/11 CALLS IN 911PT. FONT* explores the material constraints through a form of dumb literalism, taking the repetition of 911 to determine the size of the book and font. The text runs off the page, just revealing these obscured bits of letters and words around the edges of the page. The book becomes both too much and not enough to actually read – just a material document of the act of calls that refuse an outside listener (or reader). The materiality of the language and it's failure to fully materialise is all we are left with.

ON TROLL THREAD:
"It's a place where we can put all our poetry that no one else wants."
– Holly Melgard

PAPARUTZY

Another artist that engages quite directly with the constraints of the publishing apparatus is paparazzi. All of paparazzi's books use pricing as a central feature of the books physical constraints.

One particularly noteworthy example is his book, *800k Val#ue*. In the title, there is the immediately apparent 'dumb literalist' punning: 800k = BOOK

There is a profusely layered form of isomorphic gesturing here, the book is being sold for 800,000: the price is determined through its own linguistic/numeric isomorphism. The interior contains 800 pages, each with the letter of letter 'K', made out of 800. Each K contains 1,000 repeated 800s which again totals to 800000. The layered literalism and sculptural familiarity is part of the isomorphic movement that configures this project. Additionally, the cover and all the text are in red, which has a hex value of 800000, and the price is set at $800,000. The various forms of value, including price, become formal aspects of the art object – possibly the most materialised manifestation of his conceptual project. Each aspect further solidifies and thickens, but it doesn't actually reach out – everything closes in on itself.

Even with this tight literalism, there is always the wager of exchange – will you pay $800k for 800ks made of 80000 in the color code 80000? Paparutzy has

18. Hannes Bajohr, "Experimental Writing in its Moment of Digital Technization: Post-Digital Literature and Print-on-Demand Publishing," *Research Quarterly* 22, no. 3 (2006): 3–16.

found a way to establish value without exchange. It is determined isomorphically – concrete poetry fully realised. And still, the 'book' is still in the virtual, not quite actualised, only formed through relations or in the interface, before relationality is fully established.

Papa Rutzy's *Million Dollar Million Dollar Baby Script Script* is another POD book formed through an isomorphic gesture. The book is the javascript from the webpage hosting the script for *Million Dollar Baby*, and it's being sold for one million dollars. Again, we have the book functioning in this space of potential exchange, gamifying the fetishisation of the book art object. You get exactly what you pay for.

Paper Passion

Jean Keller's *Paper Passion* is a POD book that refers to a perfume of the same name, "[d]esigned by Geza Schoen in close consultation with Gerhard Steidl and in collaboration with Wallpaper* magazine."[19]

The perfume was released by the publisher, Steidl. On their website, a brief description is provided: "the perfume expresses that peculiar mix of paper and ink which gives a book its unmistakable aroma, along with the fresh scent which a book opened for the first time releases." The fragrance was released in a limited edition packaging, a cut out book. It is "an homage to the luxurious sensuality of books." It fetishises the book object's sight, and smell, while disengaging the particular material reality of the book object. The limited edition, the high price, and the emphasis on high quality are all subverted by the POD book. Keller's book is not an abandonment of materiality, but a hypertrophic attention to material constraint. Instead of expensive and limited, Keller's *Paper Passion* is cheap and endlessly available. The material book is brought back to its materiality as matter, emphasising its facility as a distributive and circulating technology, not getting tangled up in the immaterial and abstract notions of the book, a vulgar materiality.

From the Library of Artistic Print on Demand

The implied advertising promise, in Jean Keller's words, is: "With Paper Passion you get the smell of the intellectual world without reading a book." Jean Keller then makes a point for the intellectual value of content, and for the book as a medium for structuring thoughts. Such a book can even be as cheap as a 40-page print-on-demand paperback—in contrast to its fetishisation as a container for a perfume. This ultimately brings him to the final statement: "ART IS ART / AND / A FART IS A FART."

Grey Libraries & Glitchy Books

Danny Snelson has been working on producing books in collaborative classroom environments, blurring the process of reading, writing, and publishing. He refers to these books as a grey library, where the projects remain

> "open to formal invention and pedagogical play, these books are free of the demands placed on traditional publishers and publication genres. The grey library can be as carefree as an idle doodle or as focused as a precise laboratory experiment. When learning about the poetics, aesthetics, politics, and practices of publishing is the goal, the aims of publishing shift their coordinates accordingly."

19. "Paper Passion Perfume," *Steidl Verlag*, accessed January 10, 2023, https://steidl.de/Books/Paper-Passion-Perfume-0008152458.html.

These books include various forms of grabbing, glitching, scanning, collecting, and other techniques of collaborative bookmaking. The books in the grey library challenge the authorship function through the strange parameters of collaboration and the pedagogical environment. They challenges the materiality and reproducability of the book through the concrete reanimation and glitching.

Emerging out of the work in the grey library, Luca Messera's *Poetry of America: A Revised Anthology* uses tactical glitching and transcoding in the context of POD.

Messera writes,

> "This edition of William James Linton's *Poetry of America*; selections from one hundred American poets from 1776 to 1876 was scanned and uploaded by Google Books, edited in a bootlegged version of Adobe Acrobat Pro, has been run through google translation services in the order of historical colonisation of the New World (Spanish : Portuguese : French : Dutch : English) in order to do away with the Anglo-standardisation of both language and continent."[20]

Messera then replaced Linton's book in the library stacks with the glitched out version. Messera's process of replicating and replacing the original takes the POD book towards new possibilities, allowing for the individualised publication that can be modified and adjusted to exist in a singular context.

PODematerialisation makes these interventions possible, allowing the perfect-bound mass-produced book to be made singular, and rapidly producing books that may never go out of print. It allows for the endless making and modifying of books, printing materials that may never have been considered for the printed page.

These new materials entering into distribution also slip by the economic burdens placed on book publishers. In an interview with Tan Lin, the publishing collective Troll Thread discussed the ways financial constraints and dismal market conditions shifted their attention to digital publishing platforms. Holly Melgard writes, "No need to wait, depend on, or appeal to outside interests to put out the shit we want = More time spent getting basic needs met and less time worrying about someone else's curatorial vision." She goes on to describe POD as "a technocratic shortcut across what has otherwise been an overpriced and time consuming pageantry constipating the release of poetry into this shit world we've inherited."

The book can be produced rapidly, short circuiting the procedures and strictures of more formal printing practices. POD allows for a text to exist in a perpetual state as a potential physical book, ready to be printed when called upon, but only existing as a set of print-ready files on a POD platform. In folding in the platform itself, the PODematerialised book art object considers the distribution, pricing, printing, and text to be entangled in the material reality of the book. These are not dematerialised object, but objects that are hyperaware of their materialising as it occurs, as the works move from digital files to printed pages.

To return to the dematerialised artworks that Lucy Lippard writes on and through, there is a similar sort of consideration of this slippery sense of physicality and materiality. The works of conceptual artists were frequently described as immaterial, but this only captures a singular view of this process of dematerialising. Alongside this absence of material was a stark visibility of the materiality as matter, seen in something like Robert Smithson's *Asphalt Rundown*.

20. Luca Messera, "Poetry of America – A revised Anthology," *Undocumented Press*, October 8, 2019, https://undocumentedpr.es/publications/f/poetry-of-america---a-revised-anthology.

The dematerialisation is also marked by a rematerialisation, allowing a consideration of way art moves through material forms, tracing the shifts in medium, tracing the points of contact and networks of movement. Similarly, the PODematerialised book makes the material conditions of the book more visible. It results in a reconceptualisation of the book when it slips between these material forms. The spine might be slightly askew, the edges might not be cut perfectly, and the printing might show some glitch artifacts. These sorts of 'errors' are not uncommon with POD printing, and further enhance the presence of the materials themselves.

The PODematerialisation of the book might be most obvious when looking at these texts produced in these environments, but like the dematerialisation of the work of art, the consideration of these concerns bleeds outward, reconfiguring the way you interact with the book, a shift in attention that opens up new readings and then fades again.

Malthe Stavning Erslev & Søren Bro Pold

Post-digital Electronic Literature, Libraries, and Literacy: A Retrospective View to the Future of Post-Digital Libraries

The post-digital library is a thing for the future – something soon to come – right? Not quite; as we discuss in this article, we have been experimenting with post-digital installations, in collaboration with Danish public libraries since 2010.[1] This ongoing practice has helped broadening the scope of what digitisation means in a library context in Denmark, enabling librarians and citizens to engage with electronic literature, and thus helped spread awareness an emergent and (still) relatively marginal genre of digital art.[2] Moreover, the experiments have sustained insights of a more conceptual kind: the post-digital library emerges as a distinctly contemporary and dynamic situation for literature and its presentation. Our experiments, presented below, will be discussed as explorations of the changing manifestations of the post-digital library.[3]

1. Since 2010 we have been continually collaborating with public libraries in Denmark and internationally with Roskilde Libraries as an ongoing partner joined by others including Aarhus, Herning, Silkeborg, and Elsinore Libraries as well as the online library magazine, Litteratursiden.dk. For a more detailed overview of these projects, see: https://stars.library.ucf.edu/elo2020/asynchronous/proceedingspapers/7. **2.** *By electronic literature* we mean works with important literary aspects that are developed for, presented through or otherwise heavily dependent on digital computers. Electronic literature integrates computation as a central part of the literary quality of the work and not just as its medium of distribution, meaning that a work of electronic literature could not meaningfully exist without computation, in contrast to e-books and other document types that merely use computers as media of distribution and are thus not classified as electronic literature, but as digitised literature (cf. Rettberg; cf. Hayles). **3.** This text is a development of a manuscript previously presented at the 2020 ELO Conference and Media Arts Festival (virtual edition). Available online: https://stars.library.ucf.edu/elo2020/asynchronous/proceedingspapers/7/. Some parts of this text are further developed from previously published work, cf. Erslev, Malthe Stavning. "Contemporary Posterity: A Helpful Oxymoron." *Electronic Book Review,* 2021, https://doi.org/10.7273/gzy8-m368.

The notion of post-digital is itself getting quite old – at least in a context in which obsolescence sets in after only months rather than years or decades. The term was coined in 2000 by computer musician Kim Cascone as a specific conception of a broader realisation that "the revolutionary period of the digital information age [had] surely passed".[4] Although the notion did get some traction in the early noughties, it was not until the 2010s that it began to exert greater influence on discourses of digital culture. In 2014, in what is today the most influential definition of the post-digital, Florian Cramer argued that the concept should be understood as "the messy state of media, arts and design *after* their digitisation" (Cramer 17, original emphasis).[5] The post-diagital was first and foremost identified in cases where oft-assumed distinctions between digital and analog modes of expressions were broken down. In this way, the post-digital was observed to be connected to a tendency for artist and designers to "choose media for their own material aesthetic qualities... regardless of whether these are a result of analog material properties or of digital processing".[6]

In a library context, the integration of digital and analog materialities means that instead of perpetuating a dichotomous separation of digital e-books from analog paper books, a post-digital library should integrate digital contents in a way that sustains "both a break and continuity between contemporary literary practices in digital media and hundreds of years of literary tradition".[7] As argued here by Scott Rettberg in his general introduction to electronic literature, we also consider such post-digital literary experimentation to belong to, and thrive in, the context of digital (or electronic) literature. Electronic Literature was developed as an art form along with the computer and born out of some of the first experiments like Christopher Stratchey's *Loveletters* generator in 1952 and it has been defined as 'born digital' in opposition to printed literature.[8] However, with the increasing digitisation of all forms of literature, this distinction between digital and analog media has gradually become fuzzy, and today electronic literature refers not only to literature that integrates computation, but more specifically to literature that critically reflects on (its own ongoing) digitisation in artistic, literary ways. Hence, electronic literature shares and often includes neighbouring practices such as artists books and experimental publishing.

The circumstance that mass digitisation had broken down distinctions between digital and analog media does not, however, mean that we should consider digitisation to be finished or static. In this sense, it is important to be aware of the post-digital's somewhat problematic potential to lend itself to simplification and, perhaps, even bastardisation with regard to temporality. As Geoff Cox argues, the prefix of post – and the centrality of the *after* in Cramer's definition – risks sustaining a harmful periodisation of "simply declaring something as being 'post' something else".[9] At its worst, such periodisation perpetuates a "wider cynicism towards the possibility of social transformation [...] rendering us unable to participate in or even recognise the transformative potential of historical processes".[10] In other words,

4. Kim Cascone, "The Aesthetics of Failure: 'Post-Digital' Tendencies in Contemporary Computer Music," *Computer Music Journal,* 24, no. 4, (Winter 2000): 12. **5.** Florian Cramer, "What Is 'Post-Digital'?" *A Peer-Reviewed Journal About,* 3, no. 1, (June 2014): 17. **6.** Ibid.: 18. **7.** Scott Rettberg, *Electronic Literature,* (Polity Press, 2019): 4. **8.** Katherine N. Hayles, "Electronic Literature: What Is It?" *The Electronic Literature Organization,* January 2, 2007, https://eliterature.org/pad/elp.html. **9.** Geoff Cox, "Postscript on the Post-Digital and the Problem of Temporality," in *Postdigital Aesthetics: Art, Computation and Design,* edited by David M. Berry and Michael Dieter, (Palgrave Macmillan, 2015): 161. **10.** Ibid.: 15

unless we understand that even the post-digital condition continuously changes, we risk losing sight of new concerns and particularities in society and in effect become unable to navigate it. Things are not just digitised once and then, as if by the stroke of an algorithm, become passively post-digital for posterity. Rather, digitisation is an ongoing process that continues to happen to materials as they emerge, already-digital and otherwise. To take a particularly recent example, the Covid-19 lockdowns, in which societal, cultural, and professional activities depended intimately on digital platforms, showed us that things we thought were already digitised became re-digitised in ever more intensive ways. After the lockdowns, society has returned to normal, somewhat; but still, platformisation continues to penetrate all aspects of our lives and culture to a much greater extent than before the pandemic. What we learned from the pandemic, then, was that the current configuration of digitisation has not reached a status quo. The notion of a post-digital library must be understood in this light, also.

Our approach moves through a case study of a longitudinal experimentation with post-digital configurations in Danish public libraries, which has been ongoing since 2010. In reviewing our experiences, we note a series of shifts in terms of the focus of the experiments: from early projects focused on the possibility of even doing post-digital exhibitions in a public library space to later projects focusing more on creative possibilities of disseminating and teaching electronic literature in post-digital situations. Ultimately, we argue that the post-digital situation warrants the development of certain kinds of literacies that allow us to navigate the messiness of a post-digital world. To that end, we propose a notion of *post-digital literacy*. Before doing so, however, we orient our focus to the series of projects that have, for more than a decade, sustained our ongoing inquiries into the post-digital condition of (public) libraries.

Electronic literature and the Poetry Machine

The experimentation began in 2010 with a ripening project at Roskilde Libraries intended to seek out and establish a framework for incorporating electronic literature in Danish public libraries. The project laid the groundwork for the following experiments by choosing to investigate how to exhibit electronic literature in the *physical space* of libraries rather than focusing on web-based services (Pold).[11] In this sense the projects were from the start conceptualised as post-digital, in the sense that they were born-digital materials designed to be integrated into the library as a pre-digital institution and physical space, leaning on the library's centennial tradition of focusing on printed literature, and capitalising on the network of library departments spread out across the country.

The following project (2011–2013) continued developing physical installations exhibited at libraries and Roskilde Festival in 2012. One of the installations exhibited in the Roskilde Library "Poetry Hall" was a *Poetry Machine* ("About The Poetry Machine").[12] It is an installation that produces combinatory poems, based on collaborative interactions between up to three simultaneous users/readers. These users interact also with the author of an original text, and the machine's own agency

11. Søren Pold 'Digital litteratur og bibliotekernes nye roller' (Aarhus: Center for Digital Æstetikforskning, 2010),https://darc.au.dk/fileadmin/DARC/workingpapers/16_pold_reduced.pdf: 1–14. **12.** "About The Poetry Machine | The Poetry Machine – Collaboratively Generated Literary Interface," *Ink After Print,* http://www.inkafterprint.dk/?page_id=45. Accessed November 3, 2022. See also: "Litteratur i Digital Transformation," *Roskilde Bibliotekerne,* accessed: November 3, 2022, https://www.roskildebib.dk/lidt.

Children interact with the *Poetry Machine* at the public library in Aarhus, Denmark.

through book-bound control devices: manipulating algorithmically chosen sentences on a screen in order to compose a poem by balancing the text onto a sheet with the books which is finally printed after a specified length is reached. The users experience co-creating and composing poems through the reading and combination of pre-written sentences, which could be characterised as uncreative writing (Goldsmith), while simultaneously reading the interface(s) of the *Poetry Machine.*[13]

The *Poetry Machine* was designed to create reflection on the digitisation of text in the library, including the rapid emergence of e-books and Danish libraries' uptake of them through their common platform, *Ereolen.dk*, launched in 2011, a circumstance which for many represented a situation akin to installing a burning platform under the physical libraries.[14] The *Poetry Machine* is a post-digital design aimed at inviting reflection on the fact that, as Joseph Tabbi notes, "the literary corpus is by now mostly already digitised but (just as important) nearly all new writing is now done digitally and is destined ... to circulate in databases".[15]

Subsequently we produced a redesigned transportable platform for Poetry Machine as five identical versions and placed them in all the regional central libraries in Denmark in 2016, from where they could be borrowed by all Danish public libraries. The *Poetry Machine* platform additionally integrated other works of electronic literature, and thus allowed a wider network of Danish public libraries to exhibit literary works of this largely underrecognised genre, despite lacking the resources and knowledge to curate and maintain exhibitions. A new exhibition for the platform was curated with ten works in 2019–20 as part of the *Literature in Digital Transformation* project. This new version ties in with a series of changes to the *Poetry Machine*, which has continually been redesigned, including the creation of new literary corpuses in Danish and other languages, such as Romanian, Norwegian, and English as part of the *European Turn on Literature* project (2016), wherein we also updated the user interface and integrated new types of poetic forms in the *Poetry Machine's* repertoire. In this way, the *Poetry Machine* platform

13. Kenneth Goldsmith, *Uncreative Writing: Managing Language in the Digital Age* (Columbia University Press, 2011). **14.** Christian Ulrik Andersen and Søren Bro Pold, *The Metainterface – The Art of Platforms, Cities and Clouds.* (MIT Press, 2018). **15.** Joseph Tabbi, "Introduction," in *The Bloomsbury Handbook of Electronic Literature,* (ed) Joseph Tabbi (Bloomsbury, 2017): 5.

has been an important part of disseminating electronic literature in and beyond the main participating libraries, allowing the more than 300 public libraries around Denmark to host exhibitions. This work demonstrates to librarians that the digitisation of literature is not just about e-books and online platforms but is a wider phenomenon that includes modes of writing and reading. Along with accompanying exhibitions of electronic literature, the work also demonstrates that digitisation should be an ongoing concern for physical libraries, one that these manifestly pre-digital institutions can make huge contributions to.

Exploring ways of curating and exhibiting in public libraries has been an important part of the development since deciding to focus on the physical space of the library. The project *DigiSpace* (2015–2016) had a specific focus on the curation of thematic exhibitions on climate fiction and current digital textuality on social media, etc. Curatorial practices were developed for libraries, focusing on how libraries are different cultural spaces than galleries and museums. After *DigiSpace*, several exhibitions were combined with prize competitions as part of *Turn on Literature* and *Literature in Digital Transformation.*

Discussion and interaction with the book-bound control devices for the *Poetry Machine.*

Exhibiting electronic literature is a balance between making interesting exhibition spaces while respecting the different, more intimate character of reading when the material is viewed on a screen. The *Poetry Machine* points to characteristics and possibilities for this emergent literary public with its combination of up to three simultaneous writer-readers and a big screen allowing passers-by to watch, before printing a small unique receipt with one's own partly self-created poem. Besides, librarians have gotten a closer look at electronic literature and have had the opportunity to include it in their libraries across the country.

A major part of the aforementioned projects' impact has consequently been to educate and spread knowledge within public libraries on the existence of electronic literature and how to exhibit and disseminate it. By combining physical libraries and electronic literature, the projects have continuously developed post-digital library practices. All the projects have been led and funded by libraries. Consequently it has been a continuous series of design projects framed by what makes sense on the library floor and what can be funded within its institution, which has helped create the focus on integration between physical libraries and electronic literature.

The Pandemic Poetry Machine

While focusing on the physical library there has also been an interest in bringing electronic literature out of the library to other spaces. When the Covid-19 pandemic hit, libraries closed for an extended period and physical installations such as the *Poetry Machine* were also impossible to exhibit. In response, we redesigned the project for mobile phones and the result is the *Pandemic Poetry Machine* ,[16] which is part of the project *Pandemic Poetry* (2021–22).

In this web app, the framework of the earlier versions of the *Poetry Machine* – wherein the user/reader composes a poem by combining a large set of snippets written for the machine by an established author – is reconfigured for smartphone interaction. Upon selecting the *new poem* ['nyt digt'] option, the user/reader gets a non-exhaustive selection of categories; once chosen the category splits into three snippets, each of which is eligible to become the first/next line in the poem, which is finished when the writing area is filled out. There is no option to undo a selection, but you can create as many poems as you want – with varying categories and snippets, meaning that it is statistically impossible to generate two identical poems. The *Pandemic Poetry Machine* enables a creative and combinatory reading process of a work of literature that, at its core, takes the form of a database. With each poem, the database is queried anew, resulting in unique traversals of the available snippets. In the *Pandemic Poetry Machine*, the sentences were written by Lea Marie Løppenthin. She wrote work reflecting on the experience of the pandemic, and thus led the reader to compose a poetic reflection on their own pandemic experience.

As a new addition to the *Pandemic Poetry Machine*, the web app-version includes what we call a poetry machine factory, that is, an interface through which you can upload and curate your own unique dataset – a backend system that allows for the creation of virtually unlimited individual poetry machines. The project has also spurred another work by the creative coder and digital author Andreas Refsgaard, where artificial intelligence narrates different characters' perspectives on and from the pandemic. Partly forced by the pandemic circumstances, we and the librarians wanted to explore how we could take the experience of electronic literature back online while still relying on the institutional backing of the public library. Consequently, the projects reflect on the above mentioned redigitisation of both libraries and their post-digital practices at the time of reopening after lockdown and after a period where their audiences had been forced into intimate platformisation, developing new habits during the yearlong exposure to screens, services and platforms.

Anamorphosis and post-digital literacy

As the overview above shows, the *Pandemic Poetry Machine* has figured as a central character in the post-digital exploration of Danish public libraries. Already in the earliest projects, it was clear that the challenges faced by the public libraries could not be solved with a website or another purely screen-based solution. Instead, the *Poetry Machine* was developed as a rejection of the dichotomy of digital vs. analog modes of expression, integrating new forms of (digital) writing into the physical space of libraries. In effect, the *Poetry Machine* became the standard choice for Danish public libraries regarding the dissemination of electronic literature beyond e-books.

16. Lea Marie Løppenthin, *PandemiPoesi,* 2022, https://netlitteratur.dk/pandemi.

In the *Pandemic Poetry Machine*, there happened a return to the screen – in the form of a web app – that is, a move away from the physical space of the library. As mentioned, this shift was provoked by the pandemic as a response to the inaccessibility of the physical library services, including the earlier versions of *Poetry Machine*. Notwithstanding the context of the pandemic, our return to the screen may be indicative of a broader need to reassess how we understand the particularities of the post-digital library in the 2020s. Instead of isolating the all-encompassing virtuality of the pandemic as a temporary condition, we move to take the new intensity of digitisation seriously and thus identify a need to rethink how we understand the notion of post-digital in a (perhaps not so) post-pandemic world.

If, in the early noughties, post-digital referred to "works that *reject[ed]* the hype of the so-called digital revolution" (emphasis added),[17] the post-digital situation is today better understood as the aftermath – of the revolution as well as its rejection. Yet instead of becoming a truism – a banal term that simply denotes a digitised situation – the post-digital retains a certain criticality that does not necessarily take the form of outright rejection, but which is nonetheless indicative of a particular perspective on, and a will to change, the status quo of digitisation. Eric Snodgrass argues that the optical technique of *anamorphosis* can be seen as a way of destabilising established perspectives and demonstrating the techno cultural construction. Following this, anamorphosis enlightens how the post-digital is a way of "filtering the very filter that is the digital".[18] As a kind of conceptual anamorphosis, the post-digital makes palpable the structures, dynamics, and aesthetic forms of digitisation that otherwise remain elusive.

The conception of post-digital as anamorphosis is particularly well-suited for the consideration of a post-digital library after the pandemic. It points to the vital role of libraries in the context of a digitised society as spaces in and through which such anamorphosis can be situated and where citizens can engage with and practice the operation of the post-digital as a conceptual viewing technique. Post-digital literacy is the ability to engage with and navigate in a thoroughly digitised society while maintaining a certain critical sensibility. Post-digital libraries, by extension, should aim to sustain such a literacy by presenting and disseminating works that are "aligned with the forces they seek to disrupt... while nonetheless being disruptive".[19] Put differently, we need libraries that engage with the continuously evolving status of digitisation in a way that allows us to navigate the particularities of our current digitised landscape. In this way, the post-digital is much more than an intermixing of digital and analog modes of expression: it is an entire mode of understanding and relating to a digitised society. In the following section, we turn to the *Pandemic Poetry Machine* in its fully screen-based, web app form, to the end of clarifying how it – and by extension the Danish public libraries – can sustain post-digital literacy.

Post-digital literacy in the Pandemic Poetry Machine

In order to clarify how the *Pandemic Poetry Machine* can sustain post-digital literacy, we introduce the teaching platform that we contributed to as part of the project Literature in Digital Transformation, which enabled public libraries to make

17. Ian Andrews, "Postdigital Aesthetics and the Return to Modernism," 2002, http://www.ian-andrews.org/texts/postdig.html. **18.** Eric Snodgrass, "Dusk to Dawn: Horizons of the Digital/Post-Digital," *A Peer-Reviewed Journal About*, 3, no. 1, (June 2014): 28. **19.** David Heckman and James O'Sullivan, "'Your Visit Will Leave a Permanent Mark: Poetics in the Post-Digital Economy'," in *The Bloomsbury Handbook of Electronic Literature*, (ed.) Joseph Tabbi (Bloomsbury, 2017): 101.

electronic literature available for K-12 education in Denmark. Since the beginning of the stream of projects discussed here, we learned that electronic literature could fill an obvious space in the demands for teaching new media from a literary and cultural perspective. Students and pupils especially interested in poetry and literature were often enticed by meeting new forms and in various ways becoming part of the writing process in interactive works, while some of the ones less interested enjoyed the more game-like entry points into electronic literature. The teaching platform instructs students to engage with exhibited works of electronic literature through a set of pre-designed explorative exercises circling four central concepts: interactivity, modes of expression, literary quality, and technical quality. By introducing these concepts through explorative engagement, the teaching platform disseminates electronic literature through processes of (co-)production and remix, thus working through the same processes that largely guide the creation and academic reception of electronic literature.[20]

These terms are not intended to be either exhaustive or academically rigorous, but to spark curiosity and discussion in the classroom, aimed at students with no prior knowledge of electronic literature. They provide students with a device to unpack the anamorphic image of mass and post-pandemic digitisation. By providing just a few guiding threads, students can begin to relate a singular artefact to a larger assemblage of ideas, and vice-versa. For instance, in the case of the *Pandemic Poetry Machine*, we might say that in terms of *interactivity*, the work centres on the operation of the smartphone itself as a creative device that controls (or at least sustains) the creation of a poem; in terms of *modes of expression*, the work juxtaposes (or flattens the space between) buttons and poetry, intermixing functional and aesthetic questions concerning digital culture; in terms of *literary quality*, the work invites a unique way to read a large corpus of snippets, first as categories, later as individual sentences, and finally as a complete poem; and, lastly, in terms of *technical quality*, the work harnesses affordances of smartphones such as the accelerometer and drag-and-drop that were integral to most experimentation in the early smartphone app boom but which have all but vanished from contemporary paradigms of app design. In sum, the four central concepts seem to point to a common theme, surrounding the centrality of the smartphone in our lives, yet they do so by different means, allowing students to tease out the multidirectional influence of digitisation across different aspects of culture. The conjunction of the *Pandemic Poetry Machine* with the teaching platform supports the development of post-digital literacy – a competence that it is more important to sustain and nourish now – in the intensely re-digitised landscape of post-pandemic platform culture – than ever.

Moving forward without being stuck in problems past

We return to the question of the future of post-digital libraries that we posed at the beginning of this article. What can be gathered from this account of our more-than-a-decade-long experimentation vis-à-vis the notion of a post-digital library? The continuity of our projects shows that in the endeavour to sustain a longitudinal engagement with post-digital issues in a library context, a continuous return to the problem of the post-digital itself will be necessary. Over the course of the decade between 2010 and 2020, the *Poetry Machine* continuously figured as the guiding thread for our experimentation, yet it also changed slightly over the years. Rather than remaining a static exemplar of a post-digital installation, the *Poetry Machine* changed and morphed according to its contexts and the shifting tides of digitisation

20. Rettberg, *Electronic Literature:* 46–48.

– though it remained a literary installation intended to figure in the physical library space. From being a stationary installation to becoming a travelling mini-exhibition in its own right, the *Poetry Machine* exhibits the importance of never thinking that the post-digital project is finished but continuing to question its specificity across contexts and times.

After a decade of relative stability amidst morphs – where the *Poetry Machine* continued to take the form of a physical installation combined with other works in exhibitions – the most recent instalment poses a radical change: No longer occupying the physical library space, the *Pandemic Poetry Machine* takes the form of a web app designed for smartphones. This change was provoked by the Covid-19 pandemic, but we argue that it indicates a broader shift in the very notion of what post-digital means – and what the post-digital library looks like: a post-digital literacy does not simply seek to embed the digital in the analog (and vice-versa), but also to act as a viewing device through which we can understand the particularities of the specific problems of digitisation that are happening in less tangible ways. Initiated by the intensity of digitisation during periods of lockdown, the platformisation of culture has today reached new heights; accordingly, we need critical – post-digital – engagements that work through, and question, the role of the smartphone screen, which acts as the primary interface to the platformed Web, in the context of the public library.

The invisibility and scale of this new phase of digitisation is a new challenge that the reopened libraries face; their audience has become intimately accustomed to platform culture but alienated from the physical institutions through which it might explore the repercussions of this intimacy. One possible step forward would be to further integrate future aspects of projects such as the *Pandemic Poetry Machine* into a broader platform culture by, e.g., linking the resulting poems to social media APIs, so that poems are automatically shared in and would propagate an in platform-literature landscape. To move further along this trajectory, we need to accept that the notion of the post-digital itself must be reconsidered, and that – perhaps counterintuitively – a retrospective view will allow us to move forward without being stuck in notions belonging to problems past.

Thanks to Martin Campostrini and the broad range of librarians and authors (impossible to name everyone here) that have spearheaded and contributed to the projects we discuss in this article. *The Poetry Machine* is developed in collaboration with, and supported by, CAVI, Aarhus University.

Winnie Soon

Writing a Book As If Writing a Piece of Software

The term "computational publishing" has emerged in recent scholarship,[1] and is used specifically to describe books as dynamic, and computational objects that are open to re-versioning. In contrast to more conventional or mainstream forms of book production and distribution, computational publishing challenges the way in which we understand books and archives as more than "discrete objects".[2] Books are regarded not as a final format, a concluding result or as finished artefacts ready for consumption, but as "a continuous stream of data [...] without temporal restriction".[3] According to Adema, a computational book is an "ongoing iterative process."[4] More importantly, people can fork, download, study, modify, and republish a book as if it were a piece of software; producing multiple versions through computational techniques, and under free and open-source licences. In other words, modifying and executing programmable scripts can generate different versions of a book, thereby disrupting "the fixed 'serial' nature of print".[5] Within the specific context of computational publishing, this article focuses closely on programmable processes that are facilitated by free and open-source licensing. It draws a parallel between writing and coding, arguing that publishing a computational book is like publishing a piece of software.

Tellingly, the title of this article, *Writing a Book As If Writing a Piece of Software*,[6] seeks to shift our attention to a book from end results: either a physical or an online

1. See: Janneka Adema, "Publishing Strategies and Experimental Publishing." Contemporary Aesthetics and Technology Research Programme, Aarhus University, December 16, 2021, Aarhus University (online). Lecture; Simon Bowie, "What Is Computational Publishing?" Community-Led Open Publication Infrastructures for Monographs (COPIM), *Community-Led Open Publication Infrastructures for Monographs (COPIM)*, 7 July 2022, https://copim.pubpub.org/pub/computational-publishing/release/1?readingCollection=c2b231d4; Winnie Soon, "Software Publishing," Experimental Publishing VI, Centre for Post-digital Cultures, Coventry University, March 24, 2022, Coventry University. Lecture. **2.** Geoffrey Batchen, "The art of archiving" in *Deep Storage: collecting, storing, and archiving in art*, (ed.) Geoffrey Batchen and Hubertus Gassner (Prestel, 1998): 47. **3.** Ibid. **4.** Adema, "Publishing Strategies and Experimental Publishing". **5.** Alessandro Ludovico, *Post-digital print: The mutation of publishing since 1894*, (Onomatopee, 2013): 156.

book, to generative and programmable processes. This is similar to writing a piece of software with countless updates, unexpected bugs and continuous fixing in which it is more dynamic and unsettling. Such a perspective is reminiscent of the former discussions around software art, which might be useful here to open up the debates around a computational book as a piece of software art. Software art is a genre in which the creation and production of software addresses its materiality[7] and expressivity;[8] promoting our critical awareness of software culture[9] instead of merely seeing and using software as a practical tool. The materiality of software art points specifically to "the written instructions"[10] and the agency of code[11] that engage with the social, political and critical dimensions that are "devoted to code and computational processes".[12] Indeed, the kind of computational book that is addressed here is more about the dynamic of programmable processes, such as the execution of code that generates new versions, and the possibility of forking and modification by others to produce something new. In this way, publishing a book computationally focuses on these processual qualities and cultural circulation beyond the content of a book, which has been written for reading. Perhaps we may start to see the production of a book computationally as a form of software art that reflects wider cultural and political parameters. It is this background of seeing books, software, and art in parallel that informs the writing of this article.

In the following, I will use three projects as case studies to argue for the parallel between books and software. I have been involved in these projects in various roles (writer, teacher, workshop organiser, artist, coder and user) with a view to articulating the relation between computational publishing and the critique of software culture. The cases are largely inspired by many community practices, involving artists, programmers, grassroots individuals and independent organisations in Europe. For instance, the works by Open Source Publishing[13] and Constant[14] in Belgium, in which they combine research, design and technology; and the Master's programme in experimental publishing at the Piet Zwart Institute in the Netherlands, which radically defines a broader sense of publishing as "the act of making things public".[15] Another collective named Varia,[16] many of whose members have various connections with the Piet Zwart Institute as alumni, teachers and friends, focus their

6. In 2021, Sarah Ciston and Mark C. Marino wrote a blog post on *How to Fork a Book: The Radical Transformation of Publishing,* Medium, August 19, 2021, https://markcmarino.medium.com/how-to-fork-a-book-the-radical-transformation-of-publishing-3e1f4a39a66c, which could be described as a review of the book entitled *Aesthetic Programming.* They posted a question: "What would it mean to fork a book the way we fork software?". The title of this article follows their lead by continuing to think about the parallel between software and books. **7.** See: Geoff Cox, *Anththesis: The Dialectics of Software Art,* (Aarhus University: Digital Aesthetics Research Center, 2010); Florian Cramer, "Ten These about Software Art," cramer.pleintekst.nl, September 23, 2003, http://cramer.pleintekst.nl/all/10_thesen_zur_softwarekunst/10_theses_about_software_art.txt. **8.** Winnie Soon, *Executing Liveness: An Examination of the Live Dimension of Code Inter-Actions* (Aarhus University, 2016). **9.** Christian Ulrik Andersen and Søren Pold, "Software Art and Cultures – People Doing Strange Things With Software" in *Read_Me: Software Art and Cultures,* (eds.) Olga Goriunova and Alexei Shulgin, (Digital Aesthetics Research Centre: Aarhus University, 2004). **10.** Christiane Paul, "Public Cultural Production Art (Software)" in *Code – The Language of Our Time* (eds.) Gerfried Stocker and Christine Schöpf, Ars Electronica (Hatje Cantz, 2003): 129–135. **11.** Soon, *Executing Liveness.* **12.** Ibid.: 65. **13.** *Open Source Publishing.* http://osp.kitchen. **14.** *Constant.* https://constantvzw.org **15.** Piet Zwart Institute, "Experimental Publishing". https://www.pzwart.nl/experimental-publishing **16.** *Varia.* https://varia.zone/en.

projects on collectivity and experimental tool building. All the organisations mentioned above share a few common working approaches:

i. No proprietary software, such as Adobe, is used, and they are determined to use and promote free and open-source software (FLOSS).

ii. They are concerned with collectivity rather than individuality by working collaboratively with people. This can be seen from their code of conduct,[17] new software licensing e.g., CC4r,[18] community practices,[19] and the collaborative tools that they use.[20]

iii. Writing code and computer scripts forms a large part of the publishing process, involving the use of web-based technology, such as HTML, CSS, JavaScript, and web framework Flask Python for web development. By coding and modifying the computer scripts, this computational approach is less focused on using existing commercial and standardised tools, such as clicking and dragging predefined graphical buttons, but the possible computational extensibility that is catered more for community practices.

Placing the focus on writing code, commands and algorithms alludes to a different material engagement with computational infrastructure, which is more dynamic, entangled, liberated and autonomous, if not empowering. Others may argue that this kind of programmable production is less intuitive than other graphical user interface software and platforms, but such an approach to writing code and engaging with computational processes is the essence of computational publishing. It is necessary to see and reflect on how software licensing, interfaces, interactions and development facilitate new ways of book publishing.

The three cases were chosen because they focus on the three characteristics that have been mentioned above, where these peculiarities have defined a particular genre of computational publishing that blurs the boundary between books and software, opening up new modes of writing, reading, production and distribution.

Git Repository: Aesthetic Programming

On 10 June 2018, Soon and Cox pushed their first commit[21] on GitLab with their book project entitled *Aesthetic Programming: A Handbook of Software Studies*. This involved publishing their snapshots of a book writing project at a specific point

17. *Varia,* "Pages of Conduct," https://www.varia.zone/pages/code-of-conduct.html. **18.** Elodie Mugrefya and Femke Snelting, "Collectively Setting Conditions for Re-use,"March 2022, https://march.international/collectively-setting-conditions-for-re-use/. **19.** The term "community practices" refers to the activities that the collective organised and are participatory and collective in nature. For example: Constant's work sessions and their collaboration guidelines, which have demonstrated their commitment to community practice. Constant, "Work Sessions," https://constantvzw.org/site/-About-Constant-7-.html?w=https://constantvzw.org/wefts/worksessions.en.html. Constant, "Constant Collaboration Guidelines," https://constantvzw.org/site/-About-Constant-7-.html?w=https://constantvzw.org/wefts/orientationspourcollaboration.en.html **20.** For example, the aforementioned organisations all use *Etherpad,* a collaborative real-time and web-based writing tool for project coordination and workshops. **21.** See the first commit on GitLab here: https://gitlab.com/aesthetic-programming/book/-/commit/8e2f27b21051a496351c331cb01874f5f25f6938.

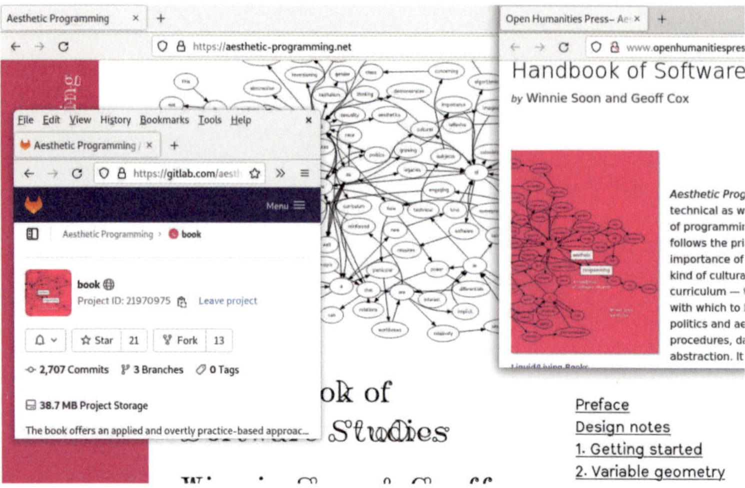

Aesthetic Programming in interactive web, Git repository, PDF and print

in time on a web-based Git repository, which is a platform for managing software changes, versioning and development. As of 11 November 2022, there were 2,707 commits documenting the snapshots of the project with contributions from the authors, the book designers,[22] as well as the general public.[23] Soon and Cox did not write their book on a local word processor program, but chose to publish their very sketchy writing in the form of markdown syntax,[24] which can be converted and rendered subsequently into other formats like markdown to print[25] or markdown to web[26] based on one single source. These sketchy writings were pushed through the programmable command: "git commit," which slowly built up the skeleton of *Aesthetic Programming* as a software (book) repository.

But using Git involves more than just uploading the writing. Git, according to Soon and Cox, "is largely useful for large-scale collaborative programming in which individuals work on different parts of the software with their own machine by copying (forking), splitting (branching), and combining (merging)."[27] Placing *Aesthetic Programming* in an active repository, the book is essentially a piece of software that blurs the line between writing and storing text, and computer code. The written

22. The Aesthetic Programming book is designed by Open Source Publishing, and they developed customised scripts for various formats of publishing. **23.** See the merge request by one of the online readers: https://gitlab.com/aesthetic-programming/book/-/commit/dd8237159a384afd0af2954974f012e17fbd5eae. **24.** Markdown is a specific plain text format. By adding computational syntax, which is the markup language, the content can be converted into structured layout for different mediums such as web HTML for web and print presentation. It is made easy to read and write than HTML. Many software applications and platforms, such as Turtl, web to print and Github/Gitlab, take markdown syntax. For example, the markdown "## Heading 2" will be rendered as bold and bigger size, which is like the HTML tag <h2></h2>.
25. See *Aesthetic Programming* in the PDF format, which is converted from markdown: http://openhumanitiespress.org/books/download/Soon-Cox_2020_Aesthetic-Programming.pdf.
26. See the interactive web of *Aesthetic Programming:* https://aesthetic-programming.net
27. Winnie Soon and Geoff Cox, *Aesthetic Programming: A Handbook of Software Studies,* (Open Humanities Press, 2020): 42.

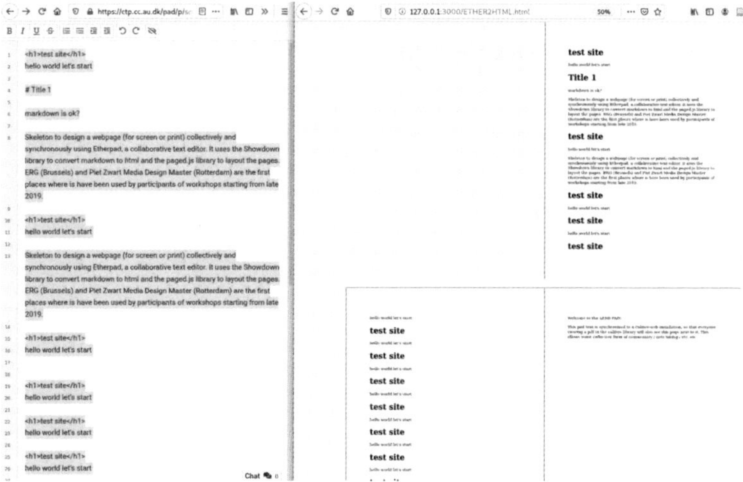

Screenshot of *ETHER2HTML* detailing how to design a webpage collectively for screen and print via PDF. Developed by Open Source Publishing

text and code are ready to be read in the repository, but also ready to be run and executed by anyone. The book is a piece of software that facilitates and encourages "forking and endless reversioning".[28] This is made possible by releasing the book as a free and open-source license, in which changes and versions are made visible, leading to the possibility of "making cuts across the various materials and ideas" by readers.[29] In other words, putting *Aesthetic Programming* on a public Git repository means that it is ready any time for a potential re-versioning.

It is clear that *Aesthetic Programming* is not only a static book, but also deals with the technological, legal and social aspects of knowledge production and distribution in the spirit of free and open-source culture. To argue for writing (or publishing) a book as if writing (publishing) a piece of software within the context of computational publishing, *Aesthetic Programming* shows that the production of the book (software) involves making things public, not only in the final distributed (book) form, but also by considering distributed processes via Git activities. By focusing on modifiability via Git, which is an active and collaborative repository, this process of versioning and writing expresses the desire to go beyond one set of final, universal, and fixed content.

Collaborative publishing software: ETHER2HTML and Octomode

The second case study explores collaborative publishing tools that are made with free and open-source software. *ETHER2HTML*[30] and the work-in-progress *Octomode*[31] were developed by Open Source Publishing in 2019 and by Varia in 2021. Both tools facilitate collaborative content writing and PDF generation for print. For the collaborative content writing part, they utilise *Etherpad*,[32] which is an open-source and web-based editor for co-writing in real-time together. Building upon this collaborative writing tool, both *ETHER2HTML* and *Octomode* require users to write their content

28. Ibid.: 18. **29.** Ibid.: 21. **30.** Open Source Publishing, "ETHER2HTML," http://osp.kitchen/tools/ether2html. **31.** See the repository of the software Octomode: https://git.vvvvvvaria.org/varia/octomode. **32.** *Etherpad,* https://etherpad.org

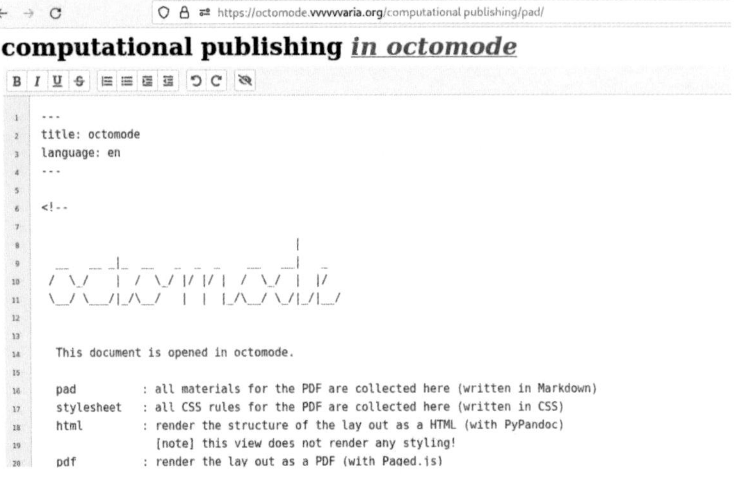

Screenshot of *Octomode* for how to design a webpage collectively for screen and print via PDF. Developed by Varia

in markdown which can later render into screen (HTML) and print (PDF) formats. The core difference is that ETHER2HTML can be downloaded on the client side and used on any local computer without server configurations. It is essentially an HTML page (a webpage that is coded with the markup language), but it contains JavaScript libraries[33] to render the spread layout format with the customised script for styling the web/print page. Within *ETHER2HTML*, Etherpad is usually hosted by other external sources that can be linked easily in the software program for content extraction. To put it simply, users write on the *Etherpad*, and *ETHER2HTML* then renders the written text and markdown to other formats.

In contrast, *Octomode* requires more software installation and server configurations unless one just uses the web instance from Varia. But *Octomode* also provides more features to integrate the *Etherpad* and stylesheet in one web interface, rendering the source to produce in screen and print formats. The top right-hand corner of *Figure 3* shows the navigation tabs to switch between different modes: Pad, Style Sheet, HTML output, and PDF output without the need to edit the source code like in *ETHER2HTML*. However, the motivation behind both pieces of software is clear: the software seeks to facilitate real-time collaborative writing and then render this writing into a customisable and printable format, such as booklets, for further (self-)publishing and distribution.

Beyond simply designing tools for computational publishing, that utilise certain web-based software libraries and programming/scripting languages, it is more interesting to see how this mode of publishing collapses the temporality of writing, editing and design within the same software environment. Unlike conventional ways of publishing, such as writing in local word processing software by authors, editing the text through track changes by editors and then finally composing the layout with proprietary software by designers, a process which takes place in a discrete and linear manner, both *ETHER2HTML* and *Octomode* mean that all these activities can be

33. Such as paged.js which is an open source JavaScript library commonly used to paginate content in the browser and to generate print books. See: https://pagedjs.org.

performed in a single software environment simultaneously. However, the point is not to focus on the capitalistic perspective of efficiency in terms of gaining access to an all-in-one package, but to focus on how these custom-designed tools afford collective and collaborative production, in which the computational processes are more transparent. As noted by Varia (2022):

> [W]e imagined a space in which the artificial boundaries of writing and designing can be crossed; where writing, editing and designing can be done in one environment simultaneously, allowing the format to influence the matter and vice-versa.[34]

Such an intention echoes the aforementioned approach where computational publishing facilitates collectivity over individuality. Collaborators can modify and publish collectively at the same time, and in the same virtual space as a form of community practice. This creates a new workflow that helps writing and publishing to take place simultaneously. As a result, a collective writing and publishing environment shifts the power dynamics within a working group or community, making it possible to negotiate changes and results instantly.

The DIY book: Unerasable Characters I

The last case study is the giant book and artwork titled *Unerasable Characters I*, produced in 2022. Containing 2,652 pages, the book is framed as a DIY book that utilises a simple and customisable bookbinding tool.[35] In Figure 4 and 5, the book contains predictive data that had been trained with the censored source text in China, collected from the platforms Weibo and Weiboscope.[36] As in previous cases, publishing Unerasable Characters I as a book requires computation, such as scripts that are written in HTML, CSS, Paged.js and Python, to produce a dynamic and customisable web format that can be rendered subsequently in the format of a PDF in a web browser for print.

The core subject matter of the artwork relates to digital censorship and erasure. But through DIY approaches and the utilisation of free and open-source software, the project further explores the commons: infrastructure of (generative) erasure. Using simple binding materials, such as wood blocks, wing nuts, flat washers and long headless screws, anyone can fork the Git repository and customise their own content, and then print this content at home on A4 paper. In addition to the open-source licensing of the book and software, it is fairly easy to purchase physical book-binding materials and office paper online or in nearby stationery stores. Unlike a very formal and polished bound book, the wooden binding tool shows flexibility in terms of the number of papers that can be put in and the comprehensibility of do-it-yourself.

This artwork in the format of a DIY book is being exhibited at the Australian Centre for Contemporary Art in 2022–2023 (see Figure 5). Instead of shipping the whole book, which weighs 14.2 kg, only the bookbinding components were sent. The museum is required to print the PDF file and do the binding. The whole design of the artwork is intended to be do-it-yourself, from generating print PDFs, to compiling, and publishing one's own generative book. Similar to software art, the work

34. "Octomode," *Varia,* https://git.vvvvvvaria.org/varia/octomode. **35.** The book binding tool is developed and supported by Olle Essvik and Joel Nordqvist from Rojal. See their independent publishing house here: https://www.rojal.se. **36.** Winnie Soon, "Unerasable Characters I / ß¢ÜôÖõîÜÝ¬ûÜ" https://siusoon.net/projects/unerasablecharacters-i.

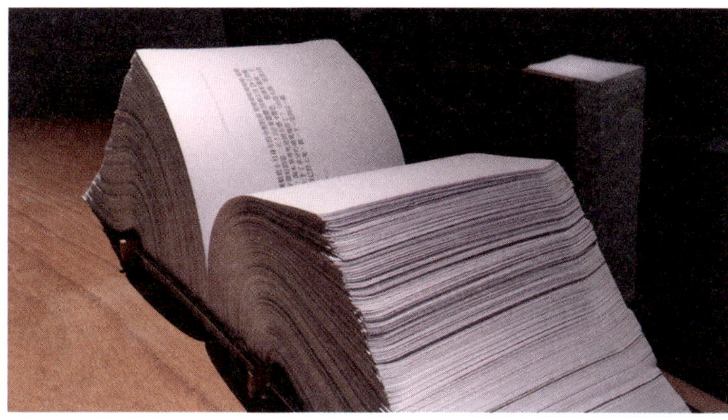

Winnie Soon, *Unerasable Characters I*, (2022)

considers the materiality of the binding tool and plays with the concept of a forbidden book and a generative DIY book. Through examining the materiality of tools and text, the project asks: To what extent does the erased text become politically sensitive? If text is no longer logically readable, but becomes nonsense and generative, what forms of new meanings might emerge? In other words, the project shifts the attention of the content from the enclosed and fixed sources to collective assembling and generative publishing.

Behind the ethos of DIY is the right to assemble and publish without expert training and professionalism. According to Elke Zobl, who researches feminist zine culture, "DIY zine makers turn to self-publishing for a variety of reasons: for personal expression, as an outlet for creativity, out of isolation, as a supportive space and network tool in search of like-minded friends and community, and as a form of cultural resistance and political critique."[37] Exhibiting and publishing *Unerasable Characters I* as a DIY book represents a call for network alliances to explore self-publishing and to imagine generativity as a resilient tactic for counter censorship. The whole process of making the artwork places the focus on the process rather than on the final readable book. Computational publishing, as an art form, is considered as a means for political expression and intervention.

Book and Software

Using the three given examples above, this short article introduces a specific genre of computational publishing that focuses on programmable processes and is facilitated by free and open-source software to publish books, blurring the boundary between books and software. Beyond the focus on digitisation, how might institutional libraries collect and archive these new and experimental forms of cultural books in multiplicities, which are more process and computationally-oriented? What challenges and potential have opened up if we start thinking of writing a book as if writing a piece of software?

37. Elke Zobl, "Cultural production, transnational networking, and critical reflection in feminist zines," *Signs: Journal of Women in Culture and Society*, 35 no.1 (2009): 5.

Joana Chicau

"BiblioTech as..."

```
var textarray = [
"as circulation",
"as metamorphism",
"as programmed events",
"as open and freely accessible",
"as lists, arrays, sequences",
"as accumulation",
"as a superimposition of rhythms",
"as restagings",
"as it may appropriate the form of",
"as shadows",
"as the continuing presence",
"as breathing",
"as relations in between",
"as entanglement",
"as movement, as moving",
"as listening",
"as reading out loud"
];
```

Performing Code(s)

Live coding (aka on-the-fly programming) is when the writing of computer code happens while performing with a given software to an audience[1], nurturing openness, exposure and transparency around algorithmic processes.

As part of the *BiblioTech* symposium, I contributed with a live coding enactment aiming at opening a critical space for reflecting on the way pervasive online platforms operate in regards to access to information as well as their role as reading-writing devices.

The performance starts with a search: 'BiblioTech as'. A list of 4,290,000,000 results are displayed in the search engine after 0.49 seconds.

1. Geoff Cox and Alex McLean, *Speaking Code: Coding as Aesthetic and Political Expression* (MIT Press, 2012).

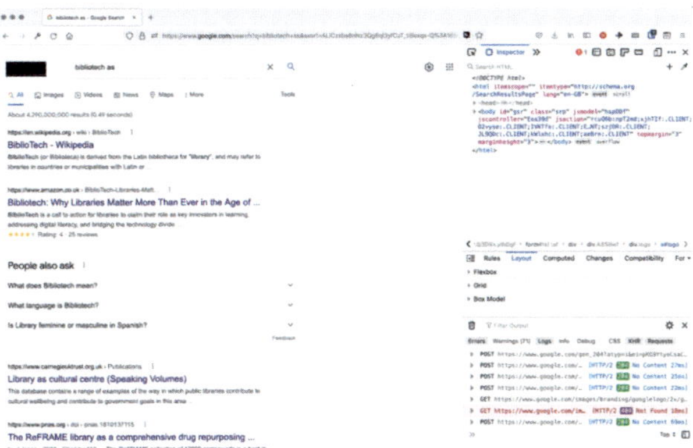

Here *BiblioTech* is experienced as a programmed event, as a list, as an endless sequence, as continuing presence, scrolling, as accumulation. As a superimposition of rhythms, imperceptible.

The performance continues, from the top menu bar of the browser Firefox, I select "Tools' > 'Browser Tools' > 'Web Developer Tools".

The Web Developer Tools[2] are built in a users' browser, these tools allow to "inspect" various elements displayed in the webpage, as well as navigate the HTML, alter the CSS among various other functionalities. Within those, the Web Console allows anyone to type in and run lines of code written in JavaScript. I open the Web Console and start typing commands that alter the text displayed as well as its appearance. Below one of code functions and corresponding "// comments...":

```
// creating a new function;
function Elements_of_Chance(n) {
// creating two variables ('var');
// variable 'rannum' sets the randomness;
var rannum = Math.floor(Math.random()*textarray.length);
// variable 'r' selects the HTML element from the page, in
this case all 'h3' (heading level 3) which corresponds to
the title of the articles listed in the search results page;
// please note that the naming of certain selectors such
as 'g' is subject to change as they are bound to how each
platform defines and maintains their code;
var r = document.querySelector(".g:nth-child("+n+") h3");
// now, inserting the text array above in the HTML element
and adding some 'randomness'
r.innerHTML = textarray[rannum];
// for legibility, increasing the font size;
r.style.fontSize ="24pt"
};
```

2. "What are browser developer tools?" Mozilla, accessed August 13, 2022, https://developer.mozilla.org/en-US/docs/Learn/Common_questions/What_are_browser_developer_tools.

```
// calling the function with a set interval which will
automatically iterate over the text array following a
certain tempo, in this case 1.2 seconds;
// 'n' is the number or order which to select the HTML
element (h3), here we opt to start from the top, so 'n=1';
setInterval ("Elements_of_Chance(n)", 1200)
```

The commands follow the notion of esoteric programming,[3] being purposefully designed to assign new, often poetic or humorous, syntax and meanings to the standard syntax of computer programming.

Esoteric programming has been manifested in a variety of artistic practices, pedagogy and activism. In their work *Vocable Code*[4], artist-researcher Winnie Soon, merges computer code and human languages to explore the "linguistic tensions of writing and reading within the context of (non)binary poetry and computer programming".[5]

Choreographer and artist Kate Sicchio researches the intersection of code and choreography through both choreographic devices and programming languages. In her work *Hacking Choreography*[6] Sicchio creates a dance coding language based on Java that is hacked during a performance.

In my practice I use choreographic vocabularies[7] for defining code functions; this opens up new meanings and interpretations of the code and the techno-system it is embedded in.

Performances such as these involve the reading of multiple layers of code(s), from the body of code that makes up the software to the esoteric code that is infused in it. There is a moment of suspension between the writing of the code and its effect in the interface. These can be seen as "critical intervals and in-between spaces"[8] that open up for new readings of the complex algorithmic layering in the interface.

In the words of the artist Daniel Temkin: "Code is the text with two readers. The evaluator, usually a piece of software, interprets the code in the most literal way in order to run it into machine code. The human reader needs more context, provided by the overall architecture of the program, comments and the naming of functions and variables that together reveal the intent of the program."[9]

The name for the code function "Elements_of_Chance(n)" references the work of the choreographer Merce Cunningham in collaboration with the musician John Cage who made use of chance and randomness as a creative tool.[10] Together

3. Daniel Temkin, Esoteric Codes, accessed June 30, 2022, https://esoteric.codes. **4.** Winnie Soon, Vocable Code (13082018), accessed August 12, 2022, https://dobbeltdagger.net/publication/vocable-code-13082018. **5.** Winnie Soon, "Vocable Code," MAI: Feminism & Visual Culture, 2018, no.2, https://maifeminism.com/vocable-code. **6.** Kate Sicchio, Hacking Choreography, accessed August 14, 2022, https://www.sicchio.com/work-1/hacking-choreography. **7.** Joana Chicau, Choreo-Graphic-Thinking, accessed August 14, 2022, https://joanachicau.com. **8.** Alan F. Blackwell, Emma Cocker, Geoff Cox, Alex McLean and Thor Magnusson, Live Coding: A User's Manual (MIT Press, 2022). **9.** Daniel Temkin, "Code-Poetics X Esolangs" in The Book of X: 10 years of Computation, Communication, Aesthetics & X (Porto, Portugal: i2ADS: Research Institute in Art, Design and Society, 2022). **10**. "Chance Conversations: An Interview with Merce Cunningham and John Cage," Walker Art Center, 1981. Accessed August 14, 2022, https://www.youtube.com/watch?v=ZNGpjXZovgk.

they developed techniques to incorporate randomness in the way choreographies were structured, it included flipping coins, rolling the dice, consulting the I-Ching.

In the live coding enactment applied within a browser on my computer, the text in the array presented at the start of this essay is inserted into the headings of the Google's search results page. That script replaces each text item in a random order every 1.2 seconds.

BiblioTech, the library and the technics of the book, "as lists, arrays, sequences", is now read in relation to other content presented in the web page. Drawing attention to the "relations in between" or is it in the margins, following the given tempo?

These hybrid languages can be seen as a provocation, a critical tool or a medium for exploring new aesthetic possibilities and expressions outside the standards and conventions established within computer programming languages.

By bridging esoteric programming with live coding practices, the works above embrace "the misdirection of technological know-how, where human and non-human agencies engage in a collaborative and co-emergent process of experimental performance that embraces uncertainty and failure, risk and surprise."? And ask how new vocabularies may guide us to questioning the seemingly fixed algorithmic structures of our computational surroundings.

Choreographing and Being Choreographed

```
// creating a new function
function Leave_the_Stage (n) {
// variable 'r' selects the HTML element from the page, in
this case all 'h3' (heading level 3) which corresponds to
the title of the articles listed in the search results page;
var r = document.querySelector (".g:nth-child("+n+")" );
// then, hides each element
r.style.visibility = "hidden";
};

// calling the function;
// 'n' is the number or order which to select the HTML ele-
ment (h3), again we opt to start from the top, so 'n=1';
Leave_the_Stage (n)
```

In this esoteric code, the choreographic concepts aim at bringing new lenses through which to expose and investigate pervasive computational artifacts, such as search engines, questioning its modes of working and conditioning of users' understanding and access to information.

In *Ideographies of Knowledge,* a symposium held in 2015 at Mundaneum in Belgium, in a session named *Worlds Made Flat – Protocols of Reading and Viewing* moderated by Geraldine Juárez, it was asked: "Reading, comparing and searching documents through the screen involves more than a work with the shown text and image. How to see the invisible?"[11]

Real time code inspection in online webpages and browsers is an integral part of this choreographic coding performance methodology and process. Although Web Developer Tools give further insight on the inner workings of online platforms, they

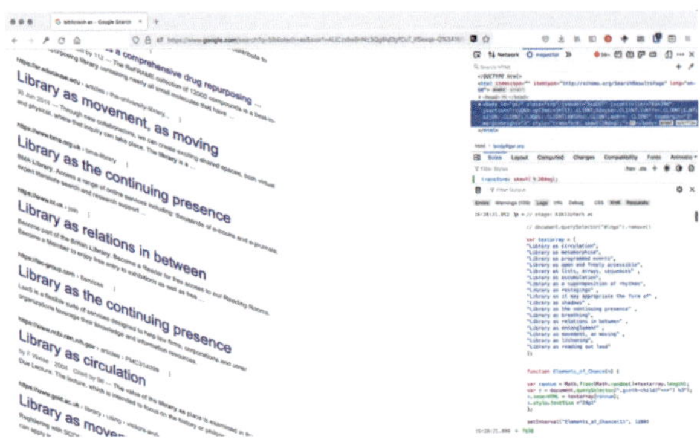

do not necessarily provide access to the whole code architecture, this is hidden away to preserve intellectual property of the companies that developed it.

Søren Pold uses the notion of "metainterfaces" to analyse how interfaces become "at once ubiquitous and networked or dispersed, at once everywhere, in everything and nowhere in particular".[12] He observes that: "Having been readable before, the control interface now reads the user".[13] Every search performed on Google's servers builds up on a search history that shapes a user's profile. It defines the next movement every time with more 'personalised' content and recommendations.

"These kinds of metainterfaces are gradually being reduced from reflective writing and reading environments that afford interpretative, expressive and social modes of reception and interaction to something more like cognitive behavioural tracking through clickbait, 'likes' and surveillance. The Facebooks and Googles of the world do not care much for what you write and read, but rather that you click and click again, trapped within their walled gardens and tracked for data extraction."[14]

We breathe to the rhythm of software, moving seamlessly from one online environment to the next, blind-folded. As Femke Snelting, a researcher at the intersection of design, feminism and free software, says: "It has become our natural habitat. We practice software until we in-corporate its choreography."[15]

How can we re-choreograph our own movements in this new "world wide library" infrastructure? BiblioTech as movement, as moving, shadows, as listening, as breathing, as reading out loud.

11. Geraldine Juárez, mod., "Session 4. Worlds Made Flat – Protocols of Reading and Viewing" (moderated panel, Ideographies of Knowledge Symposium, Mundaneum, Mons, Belgium, October 3, 2015). Accessed August 11, 2022, https://monoskop.org/Ideographies_of_Knowledge/Session_4. **12**. Christian Ulrik Andersen and Søren Bro Pold, "The Metainterface Spectacle," *Electronic Book Review,* (November 7, 2021), https://doi.org/10.7273/a7kb-r270. **13**. Søren Bro Pold, "New ways of hiding: towards metainterface realism," *Artnodes,* 2019, no. 24. **14**. Ibid. **15**. Femke Snelting, "A fish can't judge the water," Constantvzw.org, (May 26, 2006). Accessed August 11, 2022.

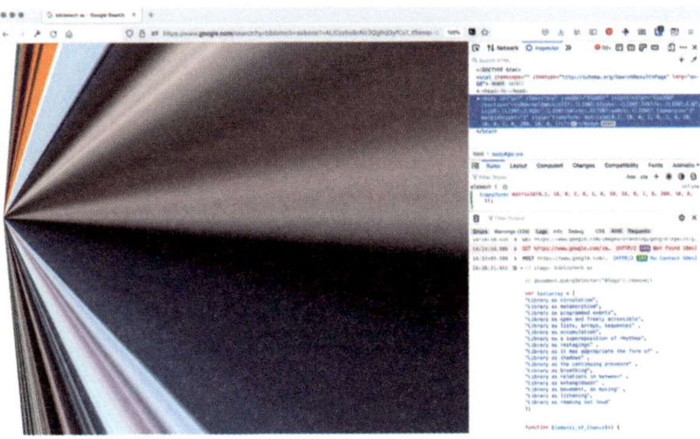

```
// creating a new function
function Off_Stage () {
// removing all content from the HTML
document.head.innerHTML = ‘ ‘ ;
document.body.innerHTML = ‘ ‘ ;
}

Off_Stage ()
```

Anna Barham

Poisonous Oysters & By Heart

The framed works presented here are made from pages of *Poisonous Oysters*, the score from one of Barham's 'live production reading groups' in which multiple versions of texts are produced collaboratively between the readers and computer processes. This group used texts about various types of porous boundaries – interpersonal, physical, sonic, verbal, chemical, psychological. The frames incorporate small objects, drawings and images made either directly onto the pages themselves, or by printing or etching images onto the perspex glazing. Barham uses these objects and images to punctuate and annotate the texts, obscuring or underlining different words, making notes and associations. Presented in this context, the works manifest the writing of a library that can listen, adapt, and write around and among its community of readers.

Page 186: *of poisonous chemicals in small quantities* Ink on paper, printed perspex, aluminium frame
Page 187: *one is undone, in the face of the other* Ink on paper, aluminium frame
Page 188: *The theory of the interpretation of dreams* Ink on paper, printed perspex, aluminium frame
Page 189: *back surface toward each other and begin to ignore* Ink on paper, aluminium frame
Page 190: *Let's face it. We're undone by each* Ink on paper, printed perspex, aluminium frame
Page 191: *one may want to, or manage to for a while* Ink on paper, printed perspex, aluminium frame
Page 192: *Yet language is not everything* Ink on paper, etched perspex, aluminium frame
Page 193: *clue to where the self loses its boundaries* Ink on paper, silicone ear buds, aluminium frame
Page 194: *amorphous, as if the china of the plate* Ink on paper, printed perspex, aluminium frame
Page 195: *Knowing yourself by yourself means poison* Ink on paper, aluminium frame
Page 196: *This seems so clearly the case with grief* Ink on paper, printed perspex, aluminium frame

All works 2020, 328mm (w) × 358mm (h) × 35mm (d)

of poisonous chemicals in s-mall quan- ti-ties.
oyst-ers in s-mall quan- ti-ties
in s-mall quan- ti-ties
oyst- in s-mall quan- ti-ties
oyst-ers and s-mo- king stu-dies
oyst-er s-mo- king stu-dies
voice that s-mo- king stu-dies
voice that' s ma- king stickies

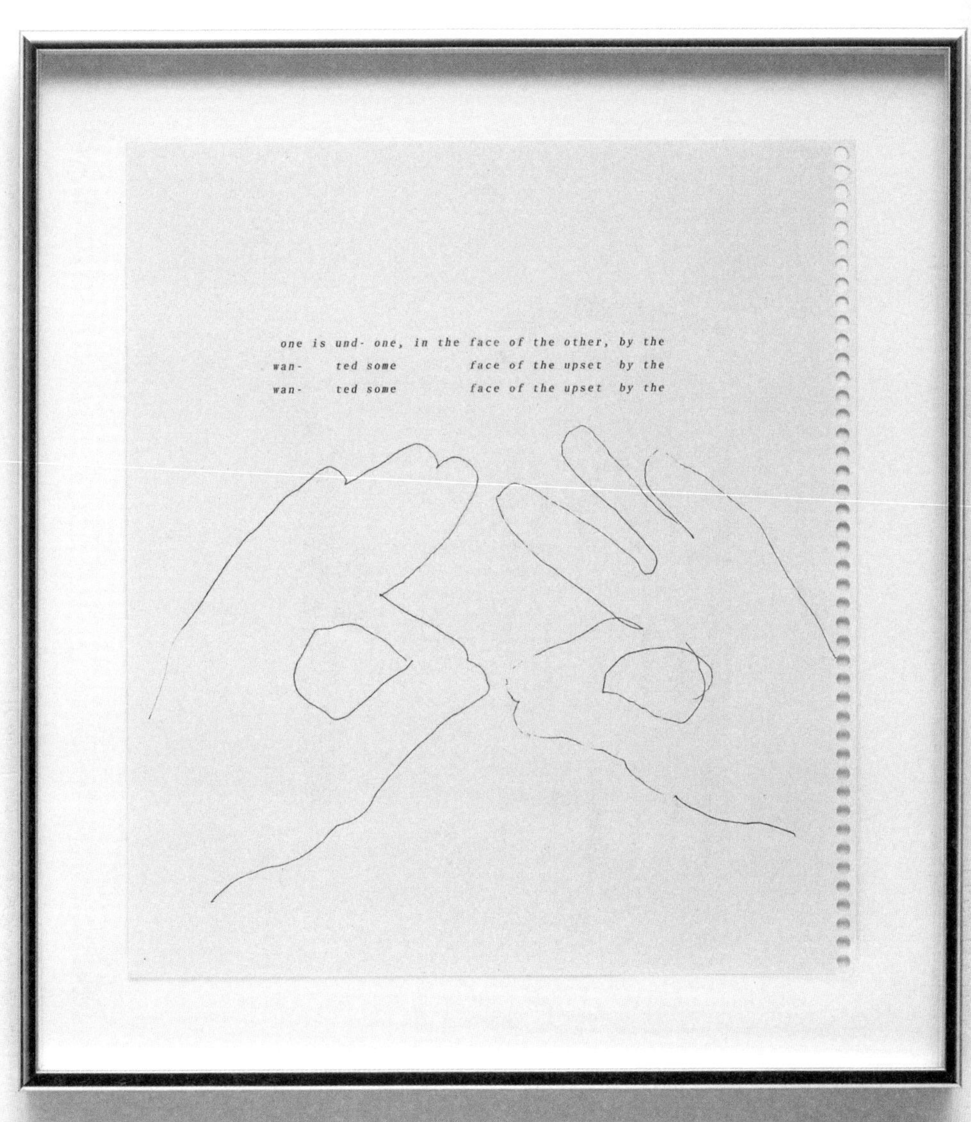
one is und- one, in the face of the other, by the
wan- ted some face of the upset by the
wan- ted some face of the upset by the

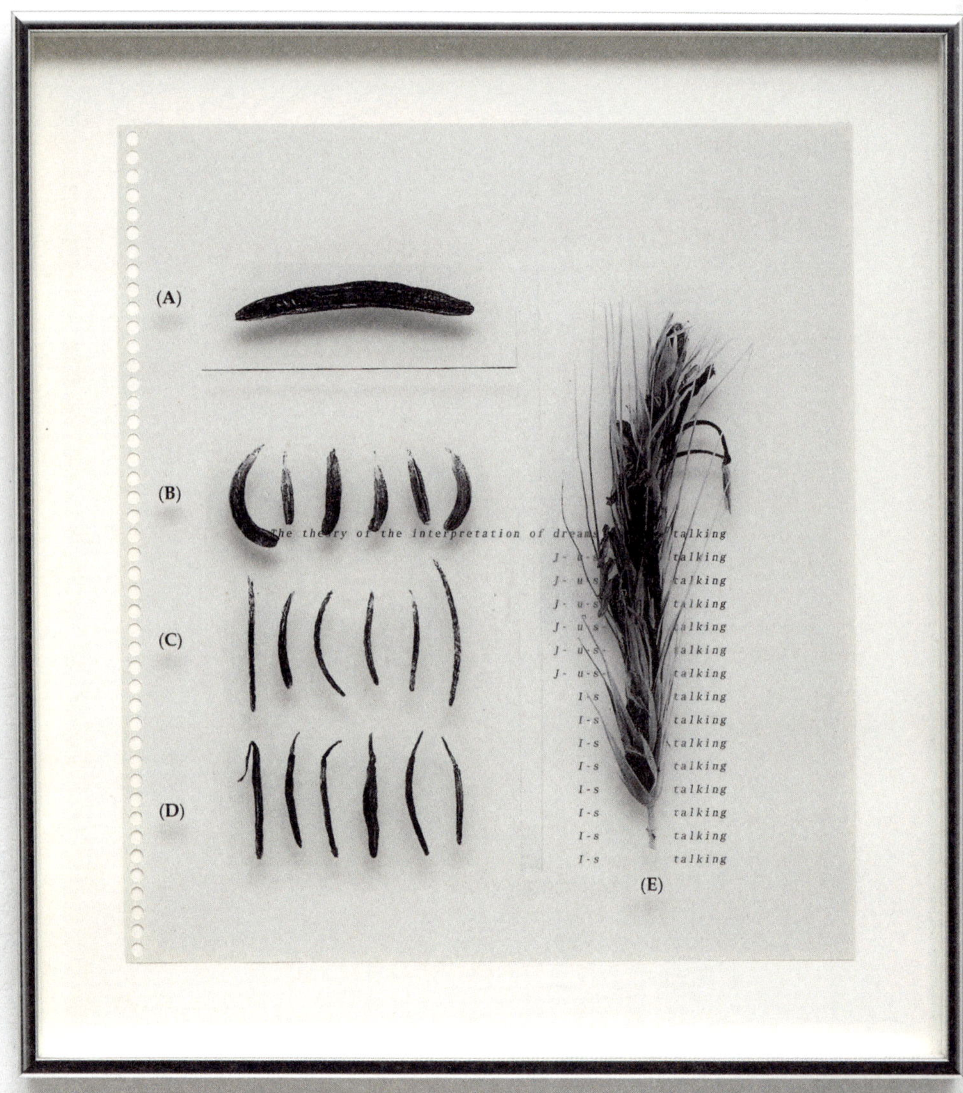
(A)
(B)
(C)
(D)
(E)
The theory of the interpretation of dreams talking
talking
J- u-s talking
J- u-s talking
J- u s talking
J- u-s- talking
J- u-s- talking
I-s talking
I-s talking
I-s talking
I-s talking
I-s talking
I-s talking
I-s talking
I-s talking

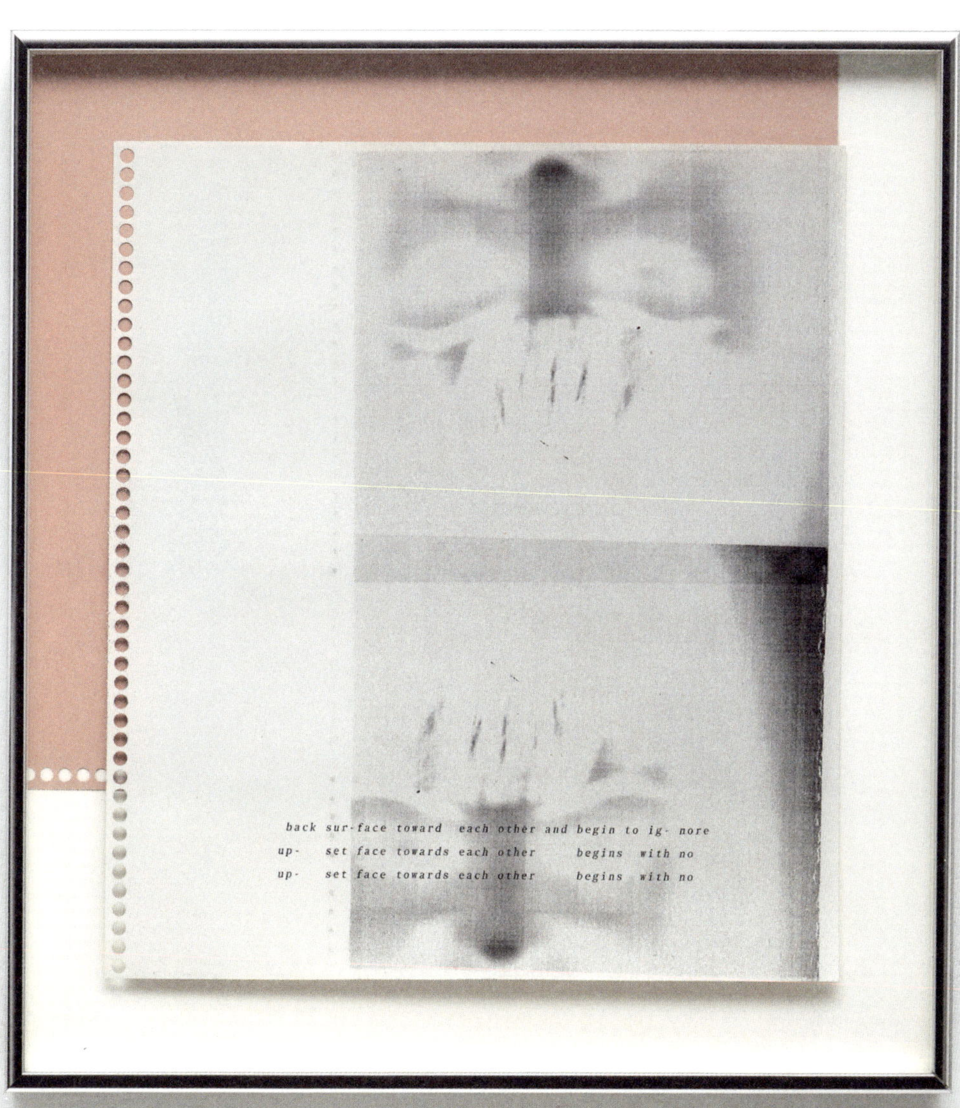
back sur-face toward each other and begin to ig- nore
up- set face towards each other begins with no
up- set face towards each other begins with no

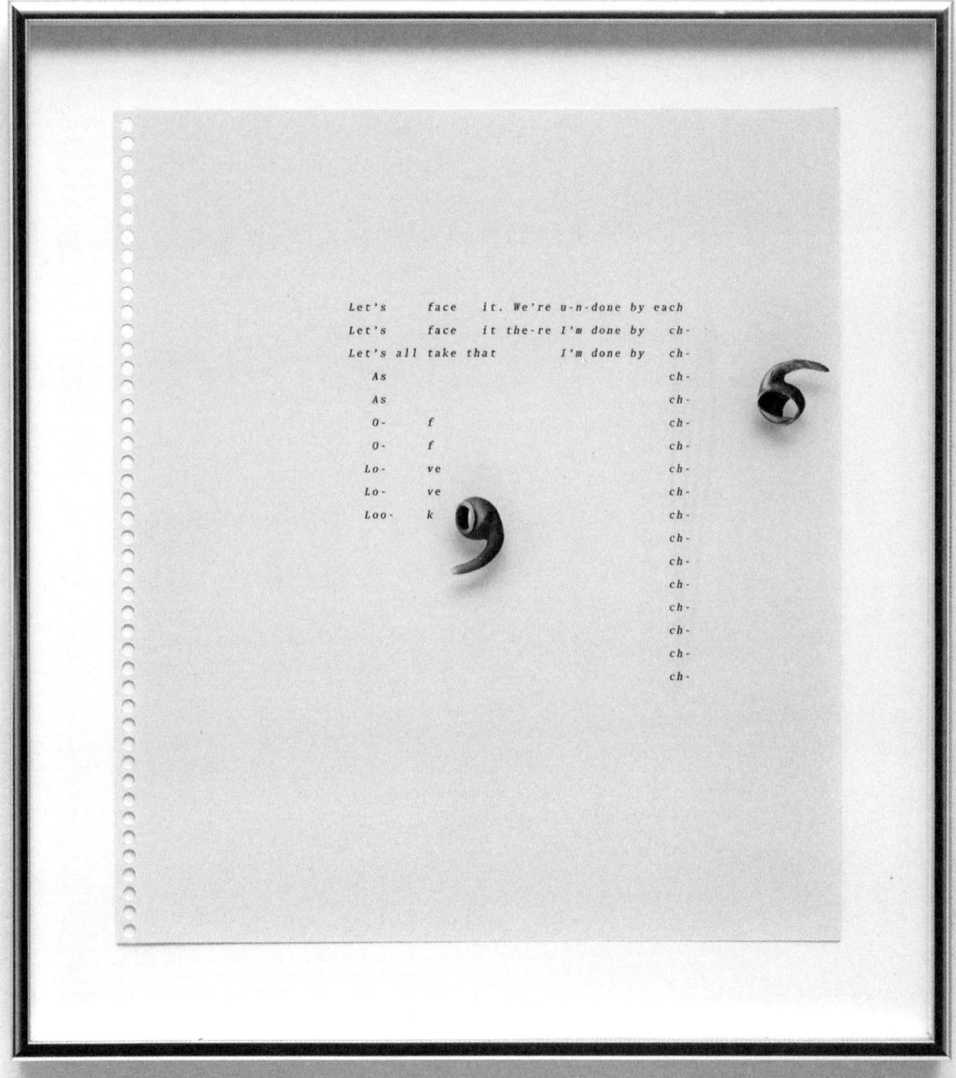
Let's face it. We're u-n-done by each
Let's face it the-re I'm done by ch-
Let's all take that I'm done by ch-
As ch-
As ch-
O- f ch-
O- f ch-
Lo- ve ch-
Lo- ve ch-
Loo- k ch-
ch-
ch-
ch-
ch-
ch-
ch-
ch-
ch-

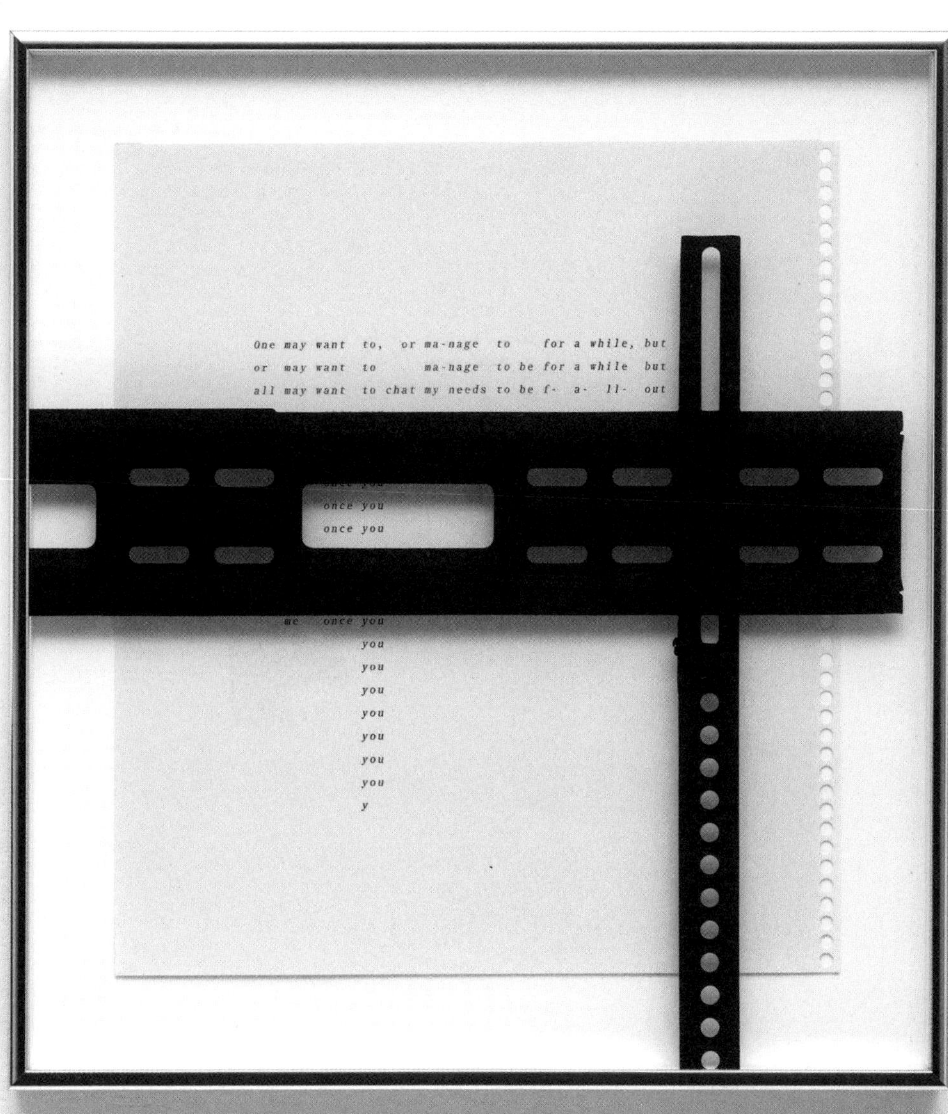
One may want to, or ma-nage to for a while, but
or may want to ma-nage to be for a while but
all may want to chat my needs to be f- a- ll- out
once you
once you
me once you
you
you
you
you
you
you
you
y

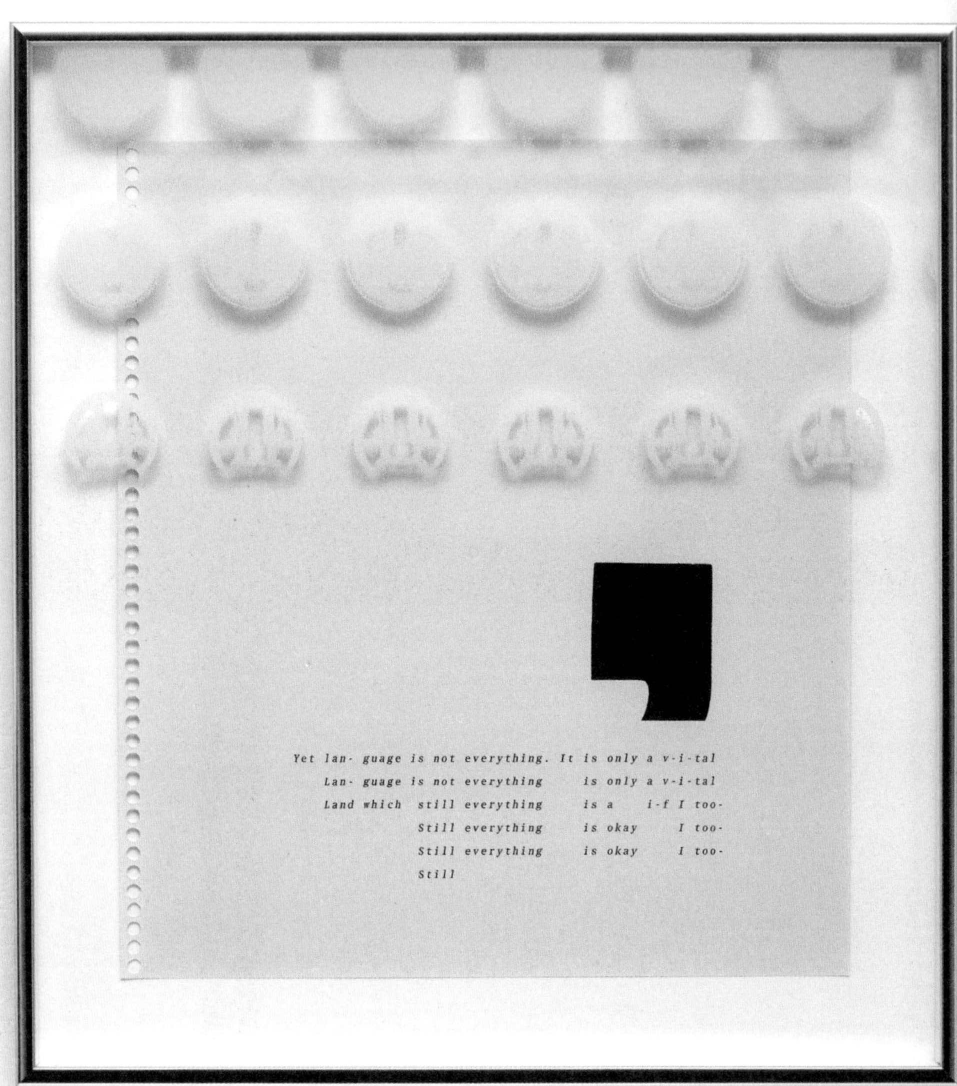
Yet lan- guage is not everything. It is only a v-i-tal
Lan- guage is not everything is only a v-i-tal
Land which still everything is a i-f I too-
Still everything is okay I too-
Still everything is okay I too-
Still

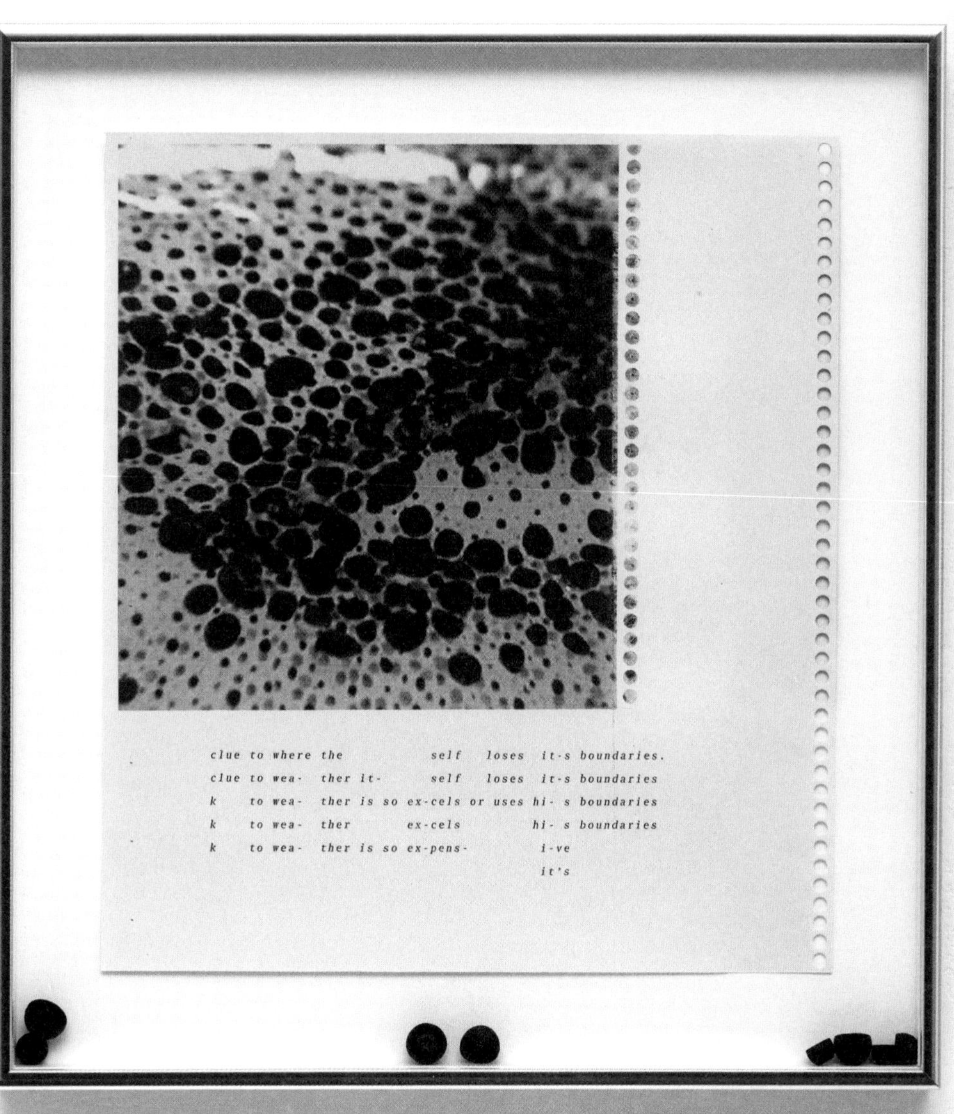
clue to where the self loses it-s boundaries.
clue to wea- ther it- self loses it-s boundaries
k to wea- ther is so ex-cels or uses hi- s boundaries
k to wea- ther ex-cels hi- s boundaries
k to wea- ther is so ex-pens- i-ve
it's

and Morph- e-us as if the trying to play s-
and Morph- e-us as if they're trying to play s-
and ma-f- i-as as if that t- ime to play s-
and my feelings as if that t- ime to place s-
and my feelings is it not t- ime to place s-
and my feelings is e- nough t- ime to place s-
and my feelings is e- nough t- ime to place o-
and my feelings soo- ner c- an' t place o-

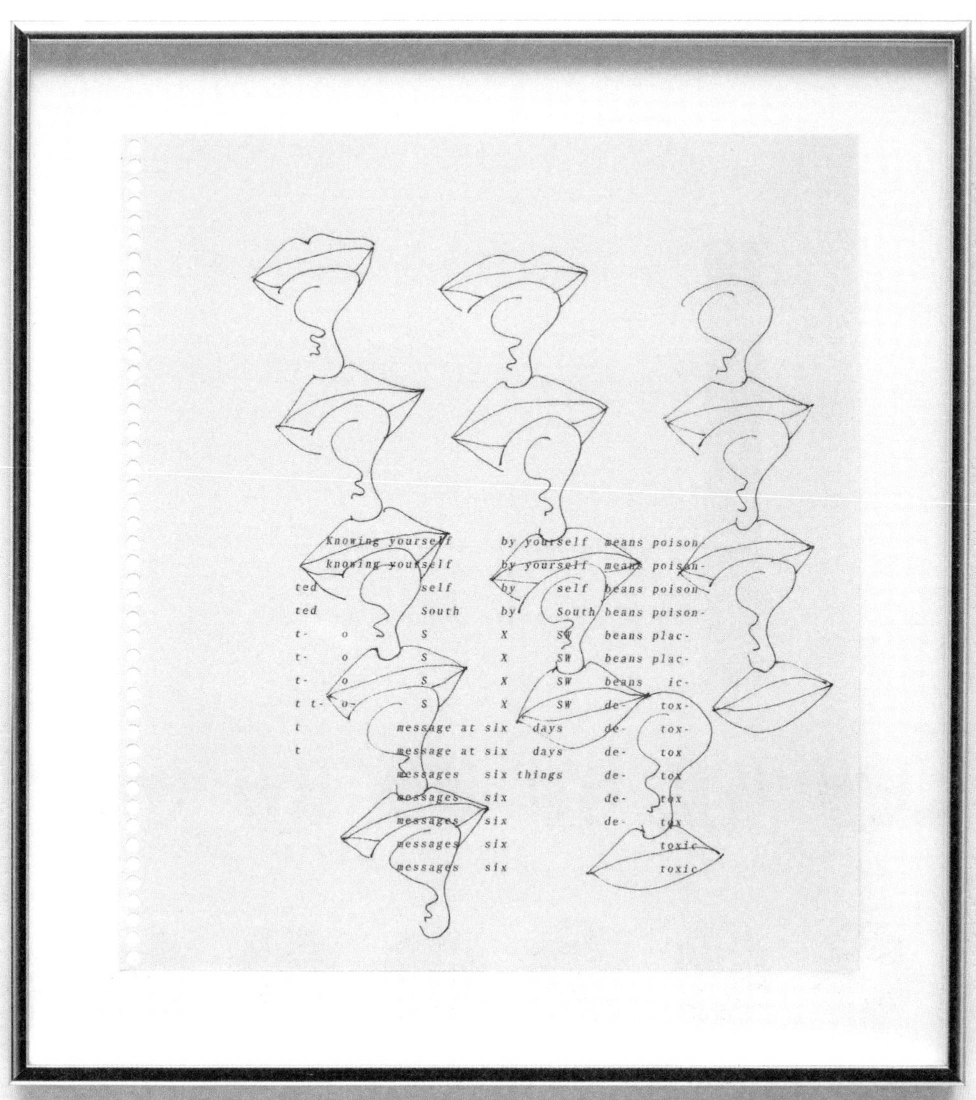
Knowing yourself by yourself means poison-
knowing yourself by yourself means poison-
ted self by self beans poison-
ted South by South beans poison-
t- o S X SW beans plac-
t- o S X SW beans plac-
t- o S X SW beans ic-
t t- o- S X SW de- tox-
t message at six days de- tox-
t message at six days de- tox
messages six things de- tox
messages six de- tox
messages six de- tox
messages six toxic
messages six toxic

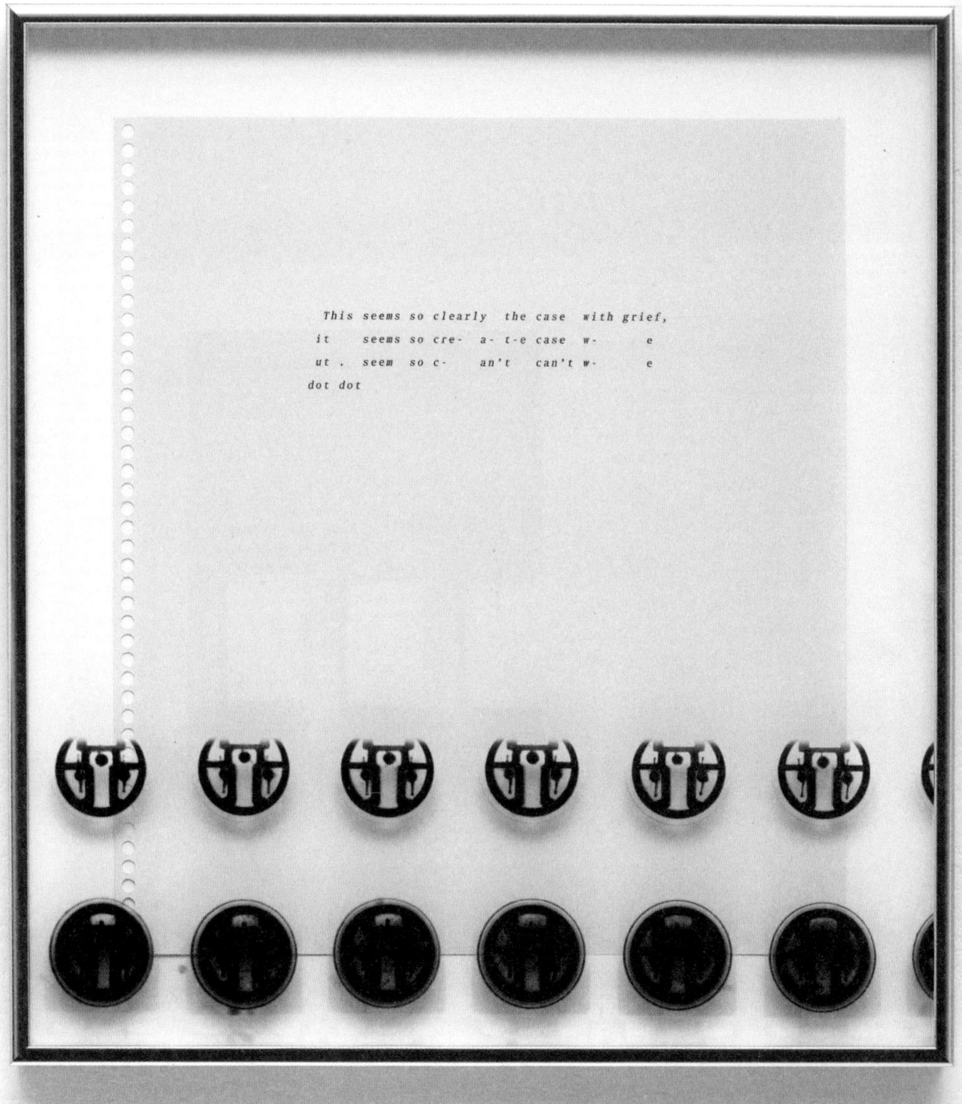

This seems so clearly the case with grief,
it seems so cre- a- t-e case w- e
ut . seem so c- an't can't w- e
dot dot

by

heart

Anna Barham *By Heart*

Strategies for learning a piece of experimental writing by heart. Workshop for 10–15 people, held at NeMe, Limassol, Cyprus, May 2022.

How can verbal information be inscribed in the body?

What can learning 'by heart' be as a practice in itself?

What does learning by heart change about a text; what new meanings could it bring to bear?

Can learning by heart be a method of publication, of distribution?

How to learn a text that has no narrative, that does not 'make sense'?

The text:

if like the mouth like the most
recognised like a knife tonight ignite
mine minds moment cement knives
mouths feel not to say nothing mind
feels minefields knife reveals the outline
the outside of objects appear slightly
outside of objects most likely answer
object appearing knives man feels the
outline of objects that appear in fields
yellow object of appeals night reveals
the outlines appear without hearing out
what is going on revolving hearing out
of control I'm empty produced by a
moment as it works like a knife

– from *As felt as if*, 2018

Activity 1:
Throw a ball to learn each other's names

Thinking of our name as a word we all know in our bodies – perhpas the first word we learn?

Stand in a circle.

Throw the ball to somebody and say your name as you throw it – repeat until everybody has introduced themselves.

Throw the ball to somebody and say their name as you throw it to them – repeat for a few rounds.

Throw the ball to somebody and they must say your name as they catch it – repeat for a few rounds.

Activity 2:
Take turns to read and listen

Read the text out aloud together. Divide into two groups and alternate between listening and speaking. The listening group should close their eyes and concentrate on the sound of the text.

Activity 3:
Spatialise the text

This is like the idea of remembering a walk or a passage through a building, but using the actual space you're in.

Split the text into small sections or phrases and tape them up around the room in the order of the text. Not just in blank spaces at regular eye height, but high and low, paying attention to features of the room that could act as visual triggers. The group moves to a section and reads the texts aloud over and over together.

Use the idea of muscle memory. Speak the text as quickly as possible and pay attention to the joints and the muscles of the mouth. After a certain number of repetitions, you will realise that it is your mouth that says the words without you thinking about it, a little as if your muscles acted reflexively.

Keep your eyes open to read for the first few repetitions, then close your eyes and see if you can remember without looking.

Before moving on to the next section, the group should try to come up with a mnemonic for the phrase – e.g. the first phrase began with "if like a mouth" was taped above a kind of hatch in the wall which could be thought of as a mouth.

Group reflection & feedback:
Part 1

Discuss the processes so far. Do you feel that you remember the text yet? Is it slower or faster than you expected? What effect have the exercieses had on you, or on your understanding of the text?

Activity 4:
Continue individually

Take some time to explore ways to learn the text on your own. Strategies might include writing it out over and over again, breaking it in to smaller phrases, reading it aloud, or continuing with the journey round the room.

Group reflection & feedback: Part 2

What methods did you use on your own? Can you recite the text now? How do you feel if you can? or if you can't? Has it changed your relationship with the text? Does it feel like it's inside you? Do you think you will remember any of the text beyond the workshop?

Activity 5: What's your name?

Do we remember each other's names? Repeat the last step of the ball game to find out.

Library Ecologies and Library-making

Sumuyya Khader

Future Black Liverpool Library 2022–ongoing

Commissioned for *BiblioTech*, Sumuyya Khader's project *Future Black Liverpool Library* sets in motion a process of establishing a library for Black Liverpool history, study and collectivity. The series of prints produced presented in the installation are designed to occupy such a library, anticipating its visual language and the combination of art forms and methods it will bring together and put into practice. The installation also included a selection of indicative books that would be included in the library and a free poster to takeaway that encouraged people to submit their own ideas for this institution-to-be.

WE
BUILD
Frantz Fanon
Black Skin,
White Masks
Great War
to
Race Riots
Black Experience in Post-WW1 Liverpool
Madeline Heneghan
&
Emy Onuora
liverpool '81
remembering the riots

BUILD
ING
A
BLA
CK
ARC
HIVE
BLA
CK
FUTURE
THE LIBRARY
BLACK OF
HISTORY
POWER
OUR
THE ARCHIVE
COLLECTIVELY
Building
Learning
Archive
Culture
Knowledge
OUR
IDEAS
VALUABLE
AUTHORS
RICH
STORYTELLERS
collaboration

LITERARY
MUSICAL
ARTISTIC
COLLECTIONS
THE ARCHIVE
COLLECTIVELY

BLA
O
PP
ORTU
NITY
CK

POWER
OUR

FUTURE
THE LIBRARY
BLACK OF
HISTORY

BUILD
ING
A
BLA
CK
ARC
HIVE

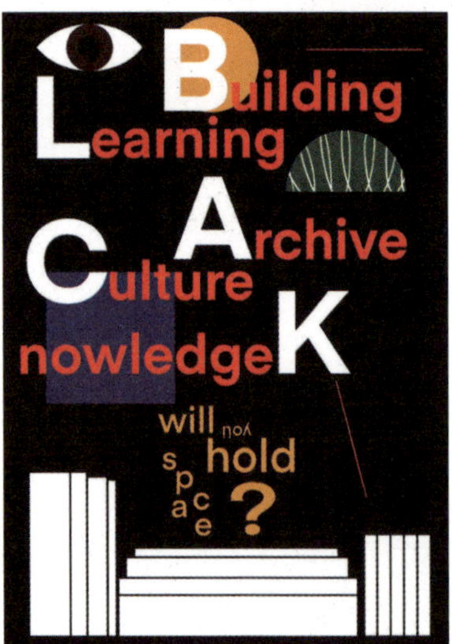
Building
Learning
Archive
Culture
nowledgeK
will you
hold
space ?

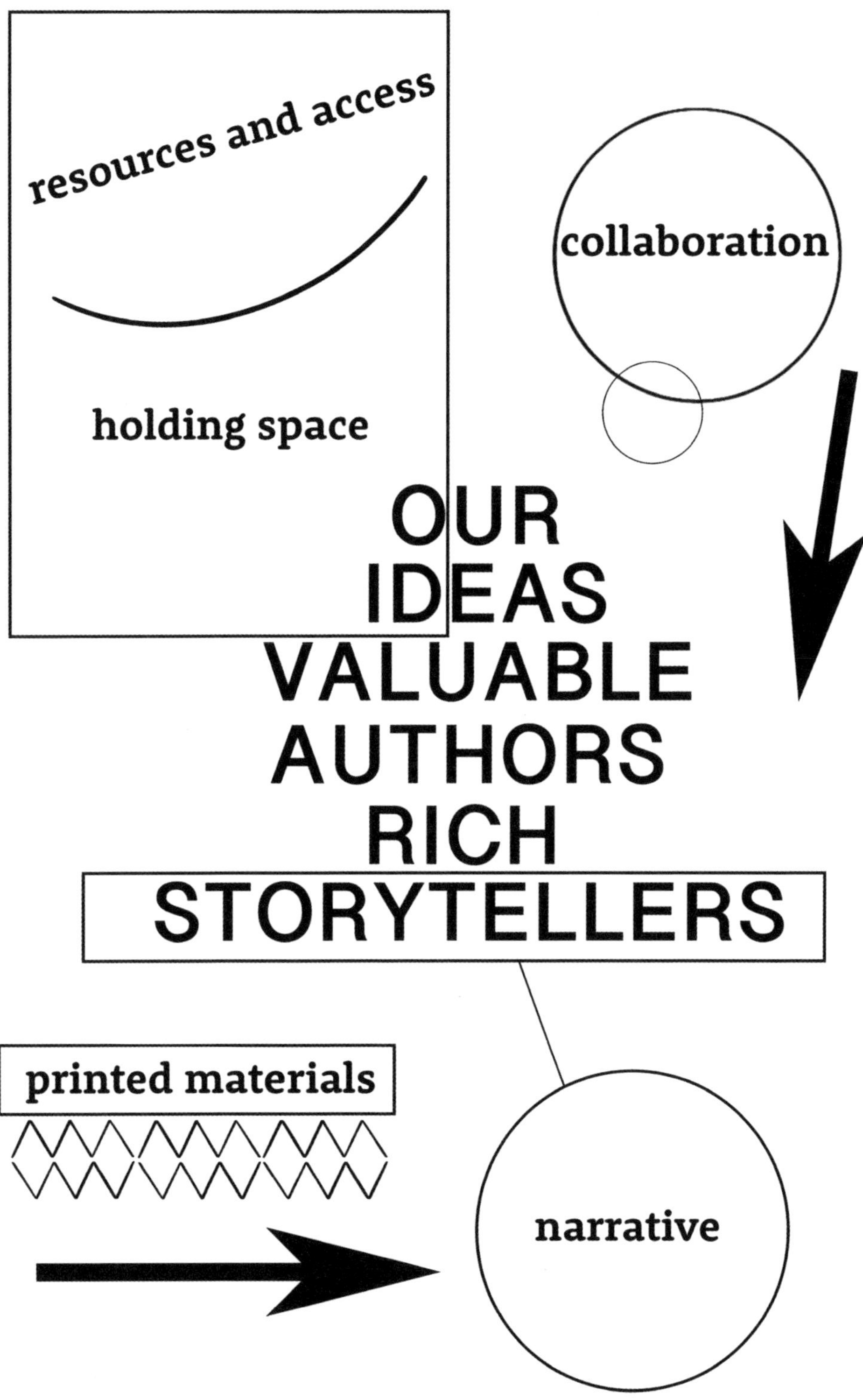
resources and access
holding space
collaboration
OUR
IDEAS
VALUABLE
AUTHORS
RICH
STORYTELLERS
printed materials
narrative

Katie Paterson

Future Library 2014–2114

Future Library[1] began life in 2014 when a forest was planted in Norway to supply fibres for paper used in a special anthology of books to be printed in 2114. One writer every year of the project will contribute a text, with the writings held in trust, unread and unpublished, until the one hundred years has passed. The manuscripts are stored in a specially designed room in the new public library in Oslo. The writers who have contributed texts to date, include Margaret Atwood (2014), David Mitchell (2015), Sjón (2016), Elif Shafak (2017), and South Korean novelist Han Kang (2018) whose performative act of accessioning her work to the library is pictured on the following pages.

The name of Han's manuscript is *Dear Son, My Beloved.* She walked to the Future Library forest pulling fabric behind her before wrapping it around her manuscript. In Korea, a white cloth is traditionally used as a gown for newborn babies, or as a mourning robe for funerals. Han stated "It was like a wedding of my manuscript with this forest. Or a lullaby for a century-long sleep, softly touching the earth all the way... So, this is time to say goodbye."[2]

Tending the forest and ensuring its preservation for the one-hundred-year duration of the artwork finds a conceptual counterpoint in the invitation extended to each writer: to conceive and produce a work in the hope of finding a receptive reader in an unknown future. Within the *BiblioTech* exhibition at ERL we presented the *Future Library Certificate* alongside a film of the project. The certificate was created and sold to support the development of the project. Each future owner of the print, to be passed down from generation to generation, is offered one copy of the published anthology in 2114. Only 1000 anthologies will be printed.

Pages 213–214: *Future Library Certificate*, Double-sided foil block print, Edition 1000, 42 × 29.7 cm
Page 215: *Future Library.* Photo by Jola Josie, 2023
Pages 216–219: Han Kang accession to *Future Library.* Photos by Kristin von Hirsch, 2019
Pages 220 (top) – 223: Deichman Bibliotek, Oslo. Photos by Einar Aslaksen, 2023
Page 220 (bottom): Silent Room designs, Deichman Bibliotek, Oslo. Photo: Atelier Oslo, Lund Hagem, Katie Paterson, 2017

1. *Future Library* is commissioned and produced by Bjørvika Utvikling and managed by the Future Library Trust. Supported by the City of Oslo, Agency for Cultural Affairs and Agency for Urban Environment. **2.** Alison Flood, 'Han Kang hands over book to remain unseen until 2114', *The Guardian*, 2017, https://www.theguardian.com/books/2019/may/28/han-kang-buries-new-manuscript-in-norwegian-forest-until-2114.

Future Library

CERTIFICATE OF AUTHENTICITY

Katie Paterson
Future Library
2014-2114

298/1000
K. P

A forest in Norway is growing.
In 100 years from now it will become an anthology of books.

Every year a writer is contributing a text that will be held in trust, unpublished, until 2114. This certificate entitles the owner to one complete set of the texts printed on the paper made from the trees after they are fully grown and cut down in 2114.

FUTURE LIBRARY
kunnskap
Samfunn
Social Science

Ilari Laamanen

In Medias Res: The Library's Other Intelligences & Jenna Sutela's nimiia ïzinibimi

How to read, listen and learn in a new techno-cultural future?
What kind of artwork would you create to a library that doesn't exist yet?

These questions were at the core of *The Library's Other Intelligences*, a project curated by media scholars Jussi Parikka and Shannon Mattern, which took place at the Helsinki Central Library Oodi in January 2019. The project was realised under the umbrella of the MOBIUS Fellowship program, an initiative bringing together visual arts organizations in Finland, New York, Great Britain and Ireland.[1]

Matter and Parikka commissioned Finnish artists Samir Bhowmik, Tuomas A. Laitinen, and Jenna Sutela (whose work is shown here)[2] to create works that examine the new intelligences represented in evolving knowledge institutions. These artworks reveal the alien logics of neural nets, give voice to machinic and speculative languages, and make visible the material infrastructures that allow intelligence to circulate.

The Helsinki Central Library Oodi, opened in December 2018, is a meeting place, as well as a space for making and relaxing, for Helsinkians. The three-floor building located at the heart of the city was designed by the ALA architects. The entrance level includes an auditorium, performance space, and an open area for pop-up events and gatherings. The mid-floor features reading rooms, workspaces, gaming rooms, music and recording studios as well as photography and video studios – all of which are free to use. The top floor hosts a cafe with a balcony overlooking the Kansalaistori square and the book section. The library was designed to adapt to the changing needs of its users.

1. MOBIUS Fellowship Program, which I directed, was organised by the Finnish Cultural Institute in New York and the Finnish Institute in London, including partnerships with organizations such as JUDD Foundation, Cooper Hewitt Smithsonian Design Museum, Artists Space, Van Alen Institute and Heureka Science Center. MOBIUS was generously supported by the KONE Foundation. **2.** We showcase the work of Jenna Sutela's work *nimiia ïzinibimi* (2019) here as the artist book was loaned from Oodi and included in the *BiblioTech* exhibition at NeMe, Cyprus (2022). For further details of all artworks included in *The Library's Other Intelligences* see: https://fciny.org/projects/the-librarys-other-intelligences.

*

The third floor's "Other Languages" section is where Jenna Sutela embedded *nimiia ïzinibimi*, an artist publication featuring a custom typeface by the Helsinki Type Studio. The book draws on *nimiia cétiï*, Sutela's ongoing experiment in machine learning and interspecies communication. It documents the interactions between: a neural network; Martian language from the 1800s, originally channeled by the French medium Hélène Smith; and movements of *Bacilli subtilis*, extremophilic bacteria that, according to recent spaceflight experimentation, can survive on Mars.

Beyond bacterial-Martian culture or Martian gut bacteria, Sutela's project is also about intelligent machines as aliens of human creation. It attempts to express the nonhuman condition of computers that work as interlocutors and infrastructure. A video in the entrance hall of the library depicted both the organic and the synthetic materials in which the book originates.

*

The collaboration with Helsinki Central Library Oodi was *kismet*. The library director Anna-Maria Soininvaara encouraged the curators and artists to explore their suggested topics freely and didn't wish to set any limitations to the content or form of the works. A lot of trust was given to the project, especially since all the planning and preproduction had to be done outside the library as it opened its doors to the public only some weeks before the realization of *The Library's Other Intelligences*. The invited artists could have made permanent artworks but chose to emphasise the ephemeral.

Samir Bhowmik collaborated with 00100 ENSEMBLE to present *Memory Machines*, a work that combined dance, theatre and circus with a guided tour that moved through the concealed infrastructural sites and operations of the library building, from climate control to power management, from checkout terminals to data centers, from automation to distribution and storage. Tuomas A. Laitinen's *Swarm Chorus* was a performative installation and a sound piece with generative tools that interpreted the construction of medieval musical canons. Aural events were channeled in the location with the aid of singers (via the building's PA system) and a sound installation for ultrasonic speakers.

Oodi library's broader premise to encourage creative encounters and constant reflection on the role of knowledge institutions takes shape beautifully in Jenna Sutela's *nimiia ïzinibimi*. The book reminds us of the importance of questioning the means and modalities of meaning-making: how much potential exists in the liminal and often-overlooked. How the traditions of language and communication are meant to be both appreciated and actively bent.

Following pages: Jenna Sutela, *nimiia ïzinibimi*, artist book and video installation at Central Library Oodi, Helsinki, 2019. Photos: Juuso Noronkoski.

vala a pai vi né divânédé tiémé ni mias mèsvi da ta

ten ché grê mé néoné u gâvimis ziléoné katramé Es

ni a zée ta ami touti nêché émê ébédasée kénâpazi

buliziméta tigrêmi ti téch ticen é lade nézou viéva

nâsupou pon bisizâni chée panédâ ché chiné tané di

mihed pou ni nâvéniz téchecé su zé téche sé mié mi

ré ssarâ mo i tès mapazéta niti fu néli baaké mé né

vaniche mépit cézisi né medti- niréekéuchâ ikési mi

po niche niche niRo vé é fi z mis né cé piéchése na

êzmi nibudi cé asmès Ma mèsvaanir vimili ré mée réch

ti bé êvé ni mi lé nâ dé astivra chéi vazi ni diviche

ê ssamistidziné ni nédizi zou éé chée ziédinésa a

han mo pou ki zéMaminé a béké aé ré gu né ni ché zé

ésa né chébri bi trine dipa vi éni da nèz récréni

dénir ché sé zitika tisuémi viapévâ ziné zéevé rée

té zéoas ì dépitès tarrié médri ri briè tè

ra ié é eu vinét

lu triné mis- mis niéli

mi néeké i virilubisvi nimi pit mâ tu sini bu ten
rízza aszé nina mi dibé ni bu né butichkénéné dévi
ti i nâi ché namis- tiréni fiti nébié dé vé né timéch
véaza sizé iche zi zéri kéta tabéré diénémé kitenmi
tiche névikô néemo né i chétanézè
né cé rèspaa

Muut kielet
Övriga språk
Other languages

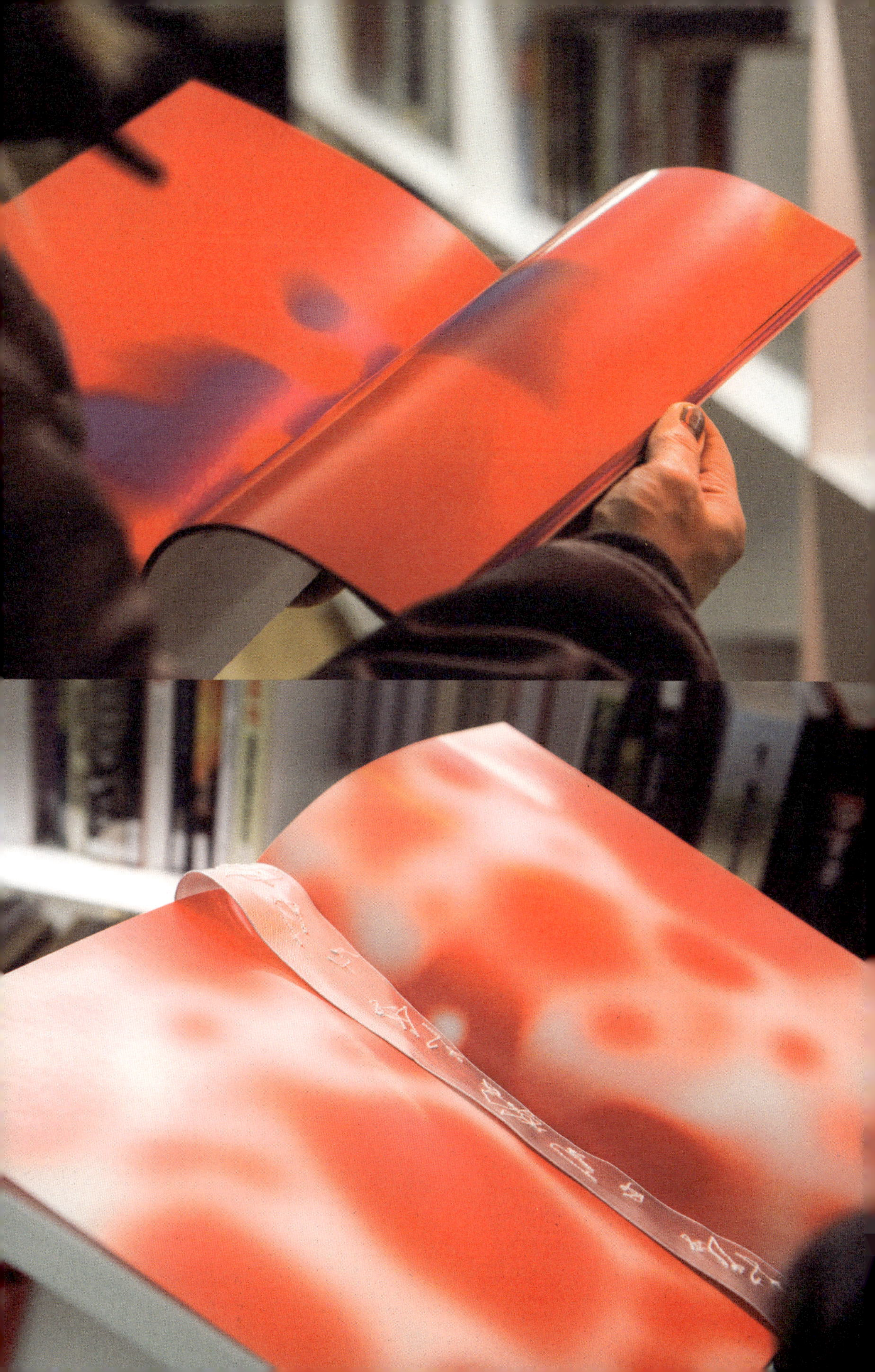

The first Martian text w
visual

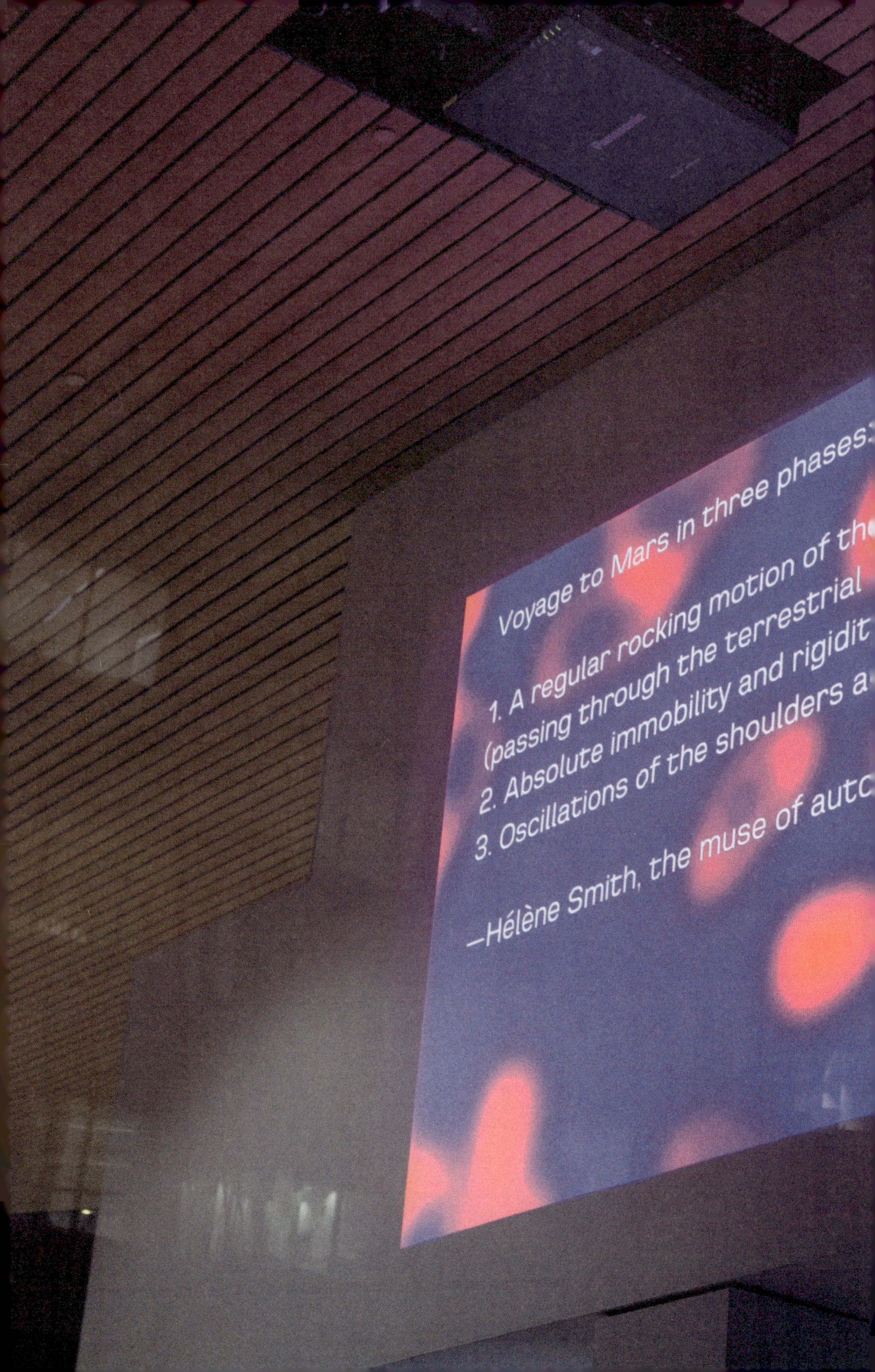

Voyage to Mars in three phases:

1. A regular rocking motion of th

(passing through the terrestrial

2. Absolute immobility and rigidit

3. Oscillations of the shoulders a

—Hélène Smith, the muse of autc

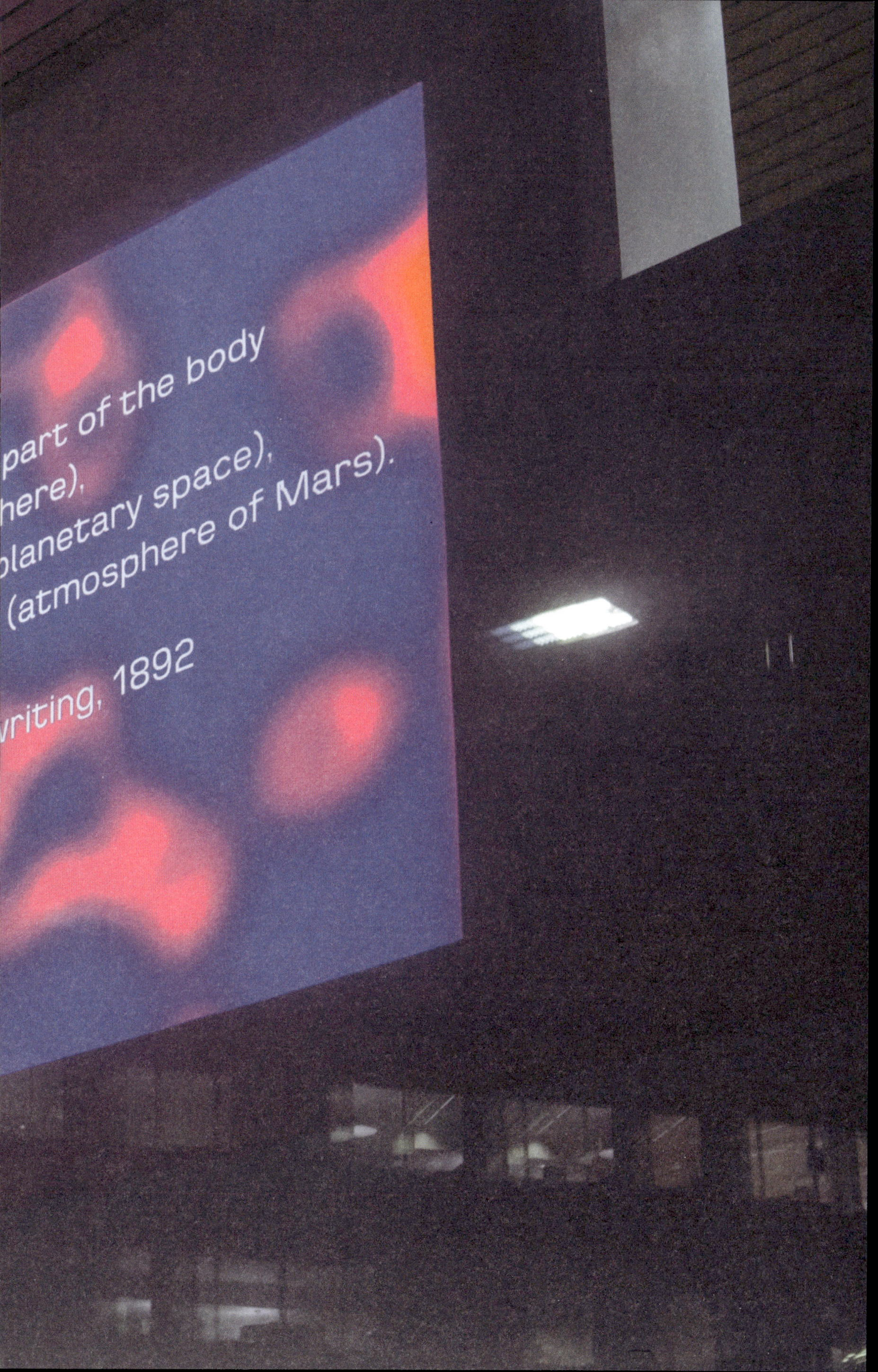

part of the body
here),
planetary space),
(atmosphere of Mars).

writing, 1892

J. R. Carpenter

Library of Wind

The Marconi Archives, The Bodleian Libraries, Oxford, UK, 4 April 2011

The Bodleian Library is in fact twenty-six libraries, scattered across Oxford. I discover this as I attempt to locate the Special Collections reading room. It's temporarily housed in the basement of the Science Library while the new Weston Library is under construction.

The website warns: "Our reading rooms can be very cold. Readers are advised to bring a jumper." I have done, but it's insufficient to the task. I sit on first one foot, then the other, in an attempt to keep warm.

I'm here to consult *The Marconi Archives*, the largest archives held by The Bodleian. They occupy 4480 physical shelfmarks. That's 448 linear metres of shelf space, nearly half a kilometre of boxes of papers, photographs, notebooks, letters, newspaper clippings, logs, reports, and receipts. All pertaining to the transmission and reception of fleeting electromagnetic signals through the invisible yet nonetheless material medium of air.

The Marconi Archives are full of weather, though it is rarely referred to directly as such. Ships logs refer to bad conditions, atmospherics, spherics, or simply X's. The log of the Lucania notes: "Getting something, but from where unknown. Do. Do. Possibly atmospherics."

Do. Do. Reads like an imperative. It takes me a while to work out that Do is short for Ditto, same again. Getting something. Signal, or spherics. Static is repetitive. Ditto wind.

I'm sitting on my hands now, which is slowing down the process of sifting through boxes of pages of logs kept by wireless operators at the Marconi Station at Glace Bay, Nova Scotia, over a hundred years ago. Glace means ice, in French. The region was colonised by the French, before the English got to it. Deep listening through the disruption of weather phenomenon and the static of the atmosphere itself, searching for readable signals at the edge of a frozen bay, wireless operators recorded: medium strength signals, Xs now troublesome, no signals received, very heavy Xs, evening watches not kept owning to bad conditions.

These fragments have already passed across oceans, through the code mediums of wires, switches, signals, air, ears, brains, and undoubtably cold hands before I lay eyes on them.

var receiving=['40 words local paper', '30 words local paper', '100 words special news', 'a few scraps of a private message', 'distinguishable dots', 'dots only', 'heavy traffic', 'something again', 'atmospherics', 'last message from ship', 'repeated \"are you there\"', 'repeated \"'where are you\'", 'request to repeat', 'several distinct dashes', 'something from another station', 'a weak signal', 'no answers to our enquiries', 'no answer', 'weak readable signals', 'no signals', 'no signals received, probably not sending', 'strong readable signals, sending fast', 'medium strength readable signals', 'some static', 'lightening all around'];
– J. R. Carpenter, *TRANS.MISSION [A.DIALOGUE]* (2011).
https://luckysoap.com/generations/transmission.html

Telegraph Museum Archives, Porthcurno, UK, April 2013

It's hot, for April. The sun glaring down and bouncing up off the sea seems to shine twice as bright. I'm wearing jeans. Too heavy, but at least they keep the nettle sings at bay. I have been awake for a very long time. The first train out of Totnes this morning took me all the way to the end of the mainline at Penzance. From there, I set out on foot along the Southwest Coast Path towards Porthcurno, a deep narrow bay, with no fishing, quay, or anchorage. A telegraph cable first came ashore at Porthcurno in 1870. For decades, the site was only accessible via a weekly coach service. Or, by donkey. By WWII, PK Porthcurno was the largest and most important cable station in the world. These days it's a Museum.

The walk from Penzance to Porthcurno takes me seven hours. I suspect I could have done it in five if I hadn't stopped to take so many pictures. I had intended to Tweet as I walked, writing a time-stamped, textual, and geolocated trail of my embodied passage between rail and cable networks. But there's little or no data reception for long stretches of the Southwest Coast Path. And just as well. Walking up steep switchbacks, down narrow tracks, along cliff edges, through nettle and gorse takes all of my attention.

By the time I arrive at Porthcurno I am badly sunburnt, but only down one side: the seaside. The Telegraph Museum is closed. The friend who was meant to come pick me up is nowhere to be found. There's no mobile phone reception, which is

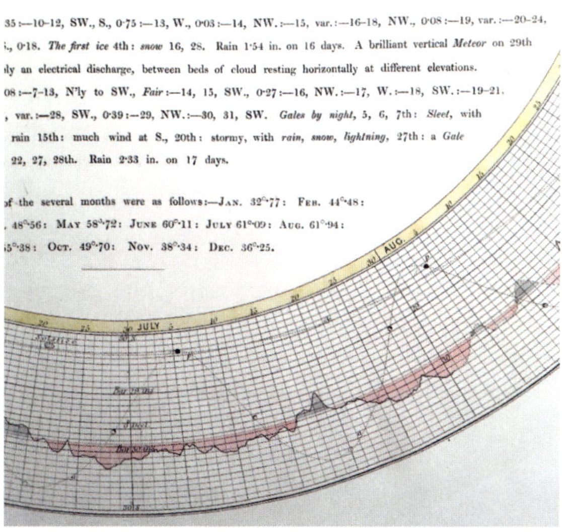

ironic, given the networked history of the place. I wander down to the beach where the cable came ashore. I stand with my blistered feet on the sand in the sea. And I wait.

13 September 2013

I return to Penzance after the tourist season has wound down. I rent the cheapest room I can find. A single bed in a shabby guest house on the sea front. Early morning, the extractor fans from the kitchen across the courtyard blow fried egg smells directly into my brain. [fans plural, blow, singular].

I set out early for Porthcurno for a full day of research in the Telegraph Museum, which houses the business archive of Cable & Wireless Company. The bus takes the most roundabout route possible, over the most potholed roads imaginable, lurching into the sharpest corners down the steepest, narrowest lanes. By the time I arrive I am convinced the journey would be better made by donkey.

I spend the next six hours in the archive poring over maps and reading passages from Murray & Thomson's Report on the Scientific Results of the Voyage of H.M.S. Challenger During the Years 1873–76. Challenger's mission was to sound the ocean bottom, towards laying a submarine telegraphic cable network. Lead weights attached to long ropes were dropped overboard at intervals to determine ocean depths. The bottom end of the weight was waxed, so sand, silt, shell, coral, and other creatures would stick to it. This seems an ingenious way to glean additional information about the composition of the ocean floor and its more minute inhabitants.

Challenger was a steam-assisted full-rigged sailing ship. The data collected on the three-and-a-half-year voyage, over 69,000 nautical miles, is haunted by the wind that powered the voyage. And so, too, is all of the data which continues to flow through the world's deep ocean fibre optic cables today, many of which still follow the route sounded by Challenger.

By the end of the day, it's raining heavily. One of the other researchers offers me a lift back to Penzance, to save me waiting for the bus. I gratefully accept.

> On the ['2nd', '3rd', '4th', '5th', '6th'] February, at ['1', '1.30', '3', '3.30', '3.40', '4', '4.30', '5', '6', '7', '7.30', '9', '9.30', '10', '11'] ['AM', 'PM'] the ship ['proceeded under sail towards', 'was unable to make much progress towards', 'was on the supposed parallel of', 'bore up for the supposed position of'] Heard Island. ['Bottom', 'No bottom'] was obtained at ['80', '120', '130', '200', '300', '425'] fathoms. It was deemed imprudent to proceed further, ['because it is no unusual thing for icebergs to be seen in the locality', 'on account of the uncertain position of the island', 'as the ship was surrounded by Penguins, uttering their discordant cry'].
>
> – J. R. Carpenter, *An Ocean of Static,* (London: Penned in the Margins 2018.). https://luckysoap.com/ethericocean

The British Library, London, UK, 10 May 2017

The British Library was designed by Colin St. John Wilson and his partner MJ Long. Prior to becoming an architect, Wilson was a naval lieutenant. The nautical influence is apparent in the profile of the building: that of a low-slung ship standing in the roads at St Pancras, with portholes, and plunder in its holds. The library's tagline is: "The

World's Knowledge". The bulk of that knowledge blew into London by way of water, by ship, by sail, by wind.

The British Library has its own weather systems. High on the third floor, the Maps Reading Room is prone to icy blasts. Below decks, the Rare Books & Music Reading Room has an air of the open sea about it. I cling to the far shore, near the Reference Enquiries desk.

I have stupidly forgotten to bring my laptop, which, in retrospect, seems impossible. How could I have travelled all the way from Denmark Hill via light rail to Kings Cross without once noticing the absence of this deadweight in my rucksack? I head to the Collection desk anyway. I have so little time in London.

I am presented with a large folio with the glorious title: Barometrographia: Twenty Years' Variation of the Barometer in the Climate of Britain, Exhibited in Autographic Curves, with the Attendant Winds and Weather, and Copious Notes Illustrative of the Subject, written by Luke Howard, (London: Richard and John E. Taylor, Red Lion Court, Fleet Street. 1847).

I sit for hours at the edge of a sea of desks, copying out portions of entries in longhand with a mechanical pencil into a passport-sized notebook. Howard's observations are already honed for brevity and specificity by his scientific process. My cramped had further refines my poetic process, contributing to the abbreviated nature of the resulting text.

March.
Impediments presented to navigation. A succession of heavy gales from
the westward. Forty sail of vessels lying in wait. For a fair wind. A gentle
breeze. Spring weather commences. The sun assumes a splendour
to which the eye has long been unaccustomed. This change from the
beginning obvious to sense.
– J. R. Carpenter, *This is a Picture of Wind*, (Sheffield: Longbarrow
Press, 2020). https://luckysoap.com/apictureofwind

Archives Nationales, Saint Denis, France, 20 March 2018

It's springtime in Paris. Except, I'm in Saint Denis. I'm early for a meeting at the Archives Nationales. The angular glass and steel structure is surrounded by rectilinear water features, long low pools cut into grey pavements. The grey sky on this day further flattens and confuses. A slight breeze ripples the surface of the water, offering the clearest indication of what's solid and what's liquid, what's light and what's its double. What's research, and what's reflection? That's another question.

I am inside, as far as I can work out, looking through greenish-grey tinted glass windows into an atrium which is open to the sky. The whole of its ground surface area is covered by water, which the slight breeze ripples, so, it's definitely outside, but it's surrounded by glass walls, so, it's also inside, but a different species of inside than the one I currently occupy. Inside out. Low along the water in the atrium a series of geodesic hollows are joined to create a form resembling a molecular structure. A small plaque on the wall informs me this is a work by the British sculptor Antony Gormley, called *Cloud Chain*, 2012. It seems to have been conjured specifically for, or by, the weather of this day

Moments later, my colleagues arrive. As we are in France, everyone kisses.

In a small room on an upper floor, Nadine Gastaldi, Chargée de mission Cartes et plans, Direction des fonds, Archives nationales, presents me with a series of

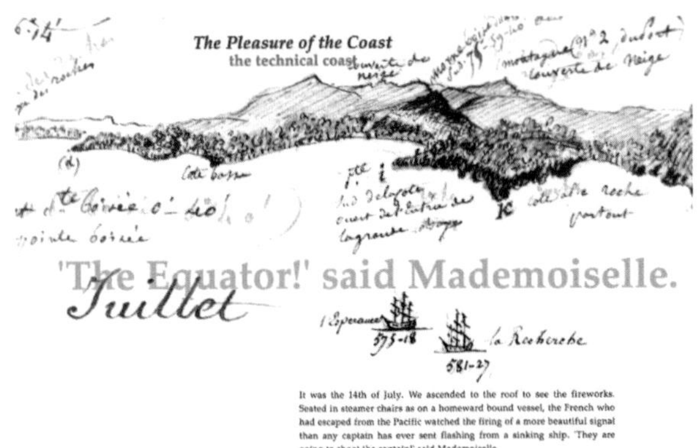

large watercolours on heavy paper, dark brooding coastlines drawn from a ship by a French hydrographer… I don't catch the name. It doesn't matter, I'm already in love.

Archives Nationales, Paris, France, 31 May 2018

It takes all day to get from Plymouth to Paris by train, bus, and plane. Somewhere over the Channel, the fasten seatbelts sign comes on. The pilot says: buckle up folks, there's some weather ahead. As if we're not already in weather. The words weather and wind were once synonymous. The pilot means turbulence. The whole plane shakes.

The Archives Nationales contains a vast selection of material pertaining to French voyages for exploration in the Pacific, an ocean about which I know little. I'm here to work with a collection of sketches of coastal elevations and drafts of marine charts drawn by a young French hydrographer, Charles-François Beautemps-Beaupré (1766–1854). Beau temps means good weather in French, and beaupré means bowsprit. If ever a lad destined for the sea.

Beautemps-Beaupré was twenty-five when he sailed from Brest on 25 September 1791 on a 500-ton frigate called La Recherche (The Research) captained by Bruni d'Entrecasteaux. La Recherche was literally a research vessel. Officially, its mission was to search for the lost Captain La Pérouse. La Pérouse had departed from Brest six years earlier on a circumnavigating mission to complete the discoveries made by the English Captain James Cook. On 10 March 1788, La Pérouse departed the English Colony at new South Wales, Australia. He was never seen by European eyes again.

To the English ear, the name Pérouse sounds a lot like the verb 'to peruse' – to scan or browse, to read through with thoroughness, to survey or examine in detail. The dictionary cautions, the word 'peruse' can be confused with the verb 'to pursue' – to follow in order to overtake, to strive to gain, to seek to attain, to proceed in accordance with a method, to carry on or continue. The English word 'pursue' sound a bit like the French word perdu – disposable, ruined, lost.

I'm standing at a high table under high vaulted ceilings in a heptagonal room with high windows on four sides, looking out into a formal garden in an interior courtyard of a former palace. What went on in this room, before the revolution?

I'm looking at a large sheet of paper with a series of long narrow strips from a different paper stock affixed to it. On the strips are sketches of coastal elevations drawn on the deck of La Recherche by Beautemps-Beaupré. Handwritten annotation indicates that these sketches were made off the coast of Tasmania on 19 January 1793. The word Mewstone is written below one rocky island in red pencil. That snags my eye. What's the Mewstone doing here, in this former palace in

Paris? Or there, in the Pacific? Had I not just seen the Mewstone the morning before, firmly anchored in the sea off Plymouth?

I look it up on my phone. There is definitely a Mewstone off Plymouth. In 1744, a local man was found guilty of a minor crime and sentenced to be 'transported' to the island for seven years. His daughter, known as 'Black Joan', remained on the island, married and raised three children there.

An image search for Mewstone presents me with a watercolour by J. M. W. Turner from about 1814, showing the Mewstone off Plymouth Sound in stormy seas. The full weight of the body of a black cloud oppresses a wind-addled mass of granite. Here in Paris, archival blinds are drawn to ward off damage from the blazing sun.

The British Library, London, UK, 23 October 2019

I'm back in the Rare Books and Music Reading Room at the British Library, still researching the Mewstone. I've found the long, drawn strips that I consulted in manuscript form at the Archives Nationales reproduced as an engraving in the atlas published after the voyage of d'Entrecasteaux. In the engravings, the Mewstone looks somewhat craggier than it appears in the sketch. Now I'm consulting Joseph Banks' first French edition of: Voyage de Dentrecasteaus, Envoyé a la Recherche de la Pérouse. Publié par Ordre de sa Majesté L'Empereur et Roi, Sous le Ministère de S. E. Le Vice-Amiral Decrès, Compte de L'Empire. Rédigé par M. de Rossel, Ancien Capitaine de Vaisseau. Tome Premier. A Paris, de l'Imprimerie Impé riale. 1808.

Rear Admiral Bruni d'Entrecasteaux died before completing his research. The scientific documentation collected during the voyage, as well as the scientists themselves, and the other crew members, took a long and circuitous route back to France. Acting captain, de Rossel, eventually landed in London in 1795 with ninety-two cases containing the results of the expedition's labours on board his ship, the Sceptre. The Voyage de Dentrecasteaus, wasn't published until 1808. The delay was due in part to Alexander Dalrymple, head of the British Admiralty's Hydrographic Office, insisting on inspecting the charts from the voyage. The same charts that I'd spent days inspecting in Paris.

The Voyage is a fat volume. Green cover. Thick paper. Held open by a book pillow and lead-weighted snakes. The old French is doing my head in a bit. Finally, I find a passage corresponding to the note scrawled in pencil above the elevation of an island sketched on a thin strip of paper by Beautemps-Beaupré aboard La Recherche, 19 Janvier 1793:

> Le 19 au jour, les vents passèrent à l'Ouest-Nord-Ouest; et nous fîmes route au Sud-Sud-Est, pour longer la côte, à environ deux lieues de distance: on gouverna successivement au Sud-Est et à l'Est-Sud-Est. Cette côte est montueuse. Mais elle est tout aussi aride, et offre aussi peu d'abri: il est vraisemblable qu'elle est également dépourvue d'eau. Le terrain en est si inégal, et les montagnes son tellement entremêlées de terres base, que vue de quatre a cinq lieues, elle semble être formée par un amas d'iles: il y a cependant quelques rochers peu éloignés de terre. A environ quatre heure après-midi, le cap Sud-Ouest étroit par notre travers à environ un mille de distance. L'approche de la nuit en nous permit pas de passer entre les îles Maetsuiker de Tasmin et la grande terre, mais le rocher Mewstone fut laissé à tribord.

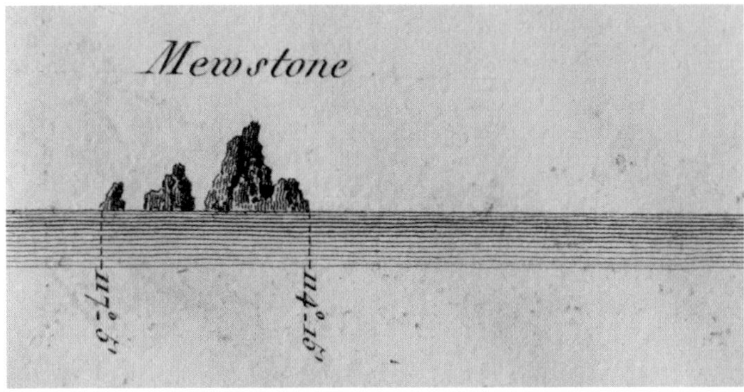

> On the 19th day, the winds changed to west-northwest; and we sailed south-south-east, to skirt the coast, about two leagues away: we steered successively to the south-east and to the east-south-east. This coast is mountainous, arid, offers little shelter, and is likely also devoid of water. The ground is so uneven. The mountains are so intertwined with their base, that, seen from four to five leagues distance, the coast seems to be formed by a mass of islands. There are also some lower rocks. At about four o'clock in the afternoon, the South-West cape was by abeam of us about a mile away. Nightfall kept us from passing between the Maetsuiker Islands and the mainland, though the Mewstone rock was kept to starboard.

Translation is a slippery business in the age of imperialism. Consider the colonial erasures in that last sentence alone.

Beautemps-Beaupré's charts show that the expedition missed learning that Tasmania was actually an island by a few scant miles. Tasmania was called lutruwita by the Indigenous People who inhabited it for 40,000 years before European colonisation. Maetsuiker is a misspelling of Maetsuycker. Joan Maetsuycker (14 October 1606–24 January 1678) was the Governor of Zeylan during the Dutch period in Ceylon and Governor-General of the Dutch East Indies from 1653 to 1678.

The Mewstone off Tasmania is unpopulated save by the shy albatross, as distinct from the common kind. It's made of an island of Muscovite granite. Muscovite, also known as common mica, was used in medieval Russia as a cheaper alternative to glass. The term 'Muscovy-glass' came into popular usage in Elizabethan England through diplomatic correspondence with the Muscovite Tsar Ivan the Terrible. This Mewstone was so named by Tobias Furneaux of Plymouth. He sailed with Captain James Cook in 1773, some thirty years before the wind blew Beautemps-Beaupré past that way. The Mewstone off Plymouth was named after the old English word for the herring gull, the mew.

The University of Alberta Library, Treaty 6 Territory, Great Turtle Island, 13 February 2021

I wrote the application for the post of Writer in Residence at the University of Alberta sitting in the upper reading rooms of the Old Bodleian. I proposed a project involving copious amounts of research in libraries and archives. I'm in Alberta now, and all the University buildings are closed due to Covid. The Library offers a curb-side

pick-up service. It's so incredibly cold out. And in. I order Nancy Campbell's Library of Ice, and think: better order some Glissant also, because glissant means slippery in French, and the sidewalks here are so icy you risk your life venturing out without crampons. This is the way my multi-lingual fractured-attention migratory brain works.

Wind scours my brain clean here. An Instagram caption a day is all the writing I can manage. It's enough.

an archive builds.
a grid. of notes.
on wind chills.
and wing feathers.
– J. R. Carpenter, February 14, 2021.
https://www.instagram.com/p/CLQHYI5Fv6R/

The Scott Polar Research Institute, Cambridge, UK
14 September 2022

In *Library of Ice*, Nancy Campbell writes, of The Scott Polar: "This museum feels like home to any traveller. People disappear for months or years, and then they come back, their skin raw from the elements, sometimes direct from the airport lugging a rucksack." I arrive lugging a small suitcase. I pause on the threshold to take by bearings. I consult the black mosaic floor tiles, inset with the seven bright stars of Ursa Major. The Big Dipper, it's called it in Canada. The Plough, in the UK.

The first reception desk sends me to a second, further into the building. A silver bell emits a silent ring. There is only the faint sound of typing to alert me to the presence of a human. The receptionist is not present. No one knows anything about any prior correspondence pertaining to my suitcase. Eventually it is decided that it can be stowed in this office, at my own risk. I decide this is a risk I'm willing to take.

The Scott Polar Research Institute Library is organised by regions. The regions are navigated in the library as they are in the world. Canada is adjacent Greenland, which is adjacent Iceland, and so on. A scientific, political, colonial, indexical order, frozen in space and time.

Meteorology occupies its own shelfmark, independent of region. It's located on the top floor of the rotunda, closest to the sky. This makes perfect sense. Within shelfmark, 551.5, there are the following subsections: sea waves, polar years, atmosphere, avalanches, cloud, snow, snow cover, hydrometerology, climatology, bioclimatology, and aurora. There is no subsection for wind. There is wind throughout.

National Oceanographic Library,
National Oceanography Centre, Southampton, UK,
7 September 2022

I am in the early months of a Research Fellowship at Winchester School of Art, University of Southampton, working on a project called: Weather Reports – Wind as Model, Media, and Experience. I'm a Fellow of Wind, I tell my friends.

I have been advised ahead of my visit to the National Oceanographic Library that it's easily accessible via Dock Gate 4. When I arrive, I find the building is covered in scaffolding. I have to ask a builder in a high vis vest to direct me to the entrance. My University of Southampton ID card lets me into the building. This is a bit of a revelation. I actually work here! I breeze in.

Emma Best, a research librarian, leads me through a labyrinth of florescent light lit corridors to a lift which descends into a breeze block chill. The archive is eclectic. I'm here to look at the logs of the logs of RRS Discovery. On one page, someone has written: Wind gusty. Vis: Good, in fountain pen. Someone else has crossed out the word gusty, and written the word Squally over top of it, in another colour ink.

Decisions have been made. That's it, I think: that's my life's work.

Emma lets me wander. As ever, I'm not exactly sure what I'm after, but I know enough to know that have been pursuing it for some time. Or perusing it, as the case may be.

The open shelves are cluttered with objects; most pertain to the history of whaling and the research thereof. There's a life preserver, a harpoon tip, a copy of Fitzroy's book on weather, all of which might come in handy at some point during my research. I pick up a tusk-like object. A handwritten note informs me that this is a sperm whale tooth. Two months on the job and already I'm holding a whale's tooth. A tooth from inside a whale's head. A whale that's been deep underwater. Really deep. I can't quite get my head around this. It's unfathomable.

Upstairs there's a room full of cabinets full of ships' charts. Meteorology is filed after Electrical and before Salinity.

There's another room full of ships' logs. Amongst them is the full Report on the Scientific Results of the Voyage of H.M.S. Challenger. The sheer volume of wind in these volumes! Heard Island is in there somewhere, surrounded by Penguins, uttering their discordant cry.

CHARTS
BS Bottom Sediments
CH Chemistry
C Currents
D Dissolved Oxygen
E Electrical
M Meteorology
SL Salinity
S Satellite Sensing
SC Submarine Cables
SS State of Sea
TW Temperature of sea water
TC Transparency and colour

Drizzling rain. Stopp
2000 Ship rolling heavily
Furled Main Topsail.
Course N45°E.
Dark night. Few stars v
Wind ~~Gusty~~ Squally. Vis: Good.
Wind and Bar: Steady.

Library Stack

How to be a Disruptor in the Human Extinction Market

The data storage company Stamper Technologies works out of a small laboratory in a nondescript office park in Rochester, New York. Founded locally by a former Kodak engineer, Stamper offers a precision laser process for etching nanometer-sized pixels onto discs of pure nickel or gold. Any kind of digital image, graphic, document or data set can be shrunk down to microscopic scale, rasterised at enormous resolution, and burned onto the metal for long term archiving. It's like a durable version of microfiche, but with greatly expanded data density. The discs cannot technologically obsolesce because they don't require computation to be decoded, only magnification and light. Stamper's approach shares characteristics with other long-term data storage methods, many of which have evolved similar microprinting or photolithographic etching processes using specially prepared ceramic plates, pure metals or other material substrates. It's a growing market: Microsoft has developed an industrial-scale system where visual data, in the form of three-dimensional voxels, can be laser-etched onto quartz glass; and numerous biotech firms are transcoding binary code into base pairs for storage within synthetic DNA, or even living organisms.

In Norway, a firm named Piql has developed its own offline digital-analog hybrid storage method that uses a graphic pattern of black and white squares to map binary code onto reels of polyester-based cinema film. The resulting reels-look like transparent QR codes, thousands of feet long. The costs for data retrieval are bundled into the company's ongoing service fees, and Piql runs its own permanent storage facility called the Arctic World Archive, deep in a former coal mine on the Arctic island of Svalbard. Cinema film has a known storage history, and there's good data to suggest that if kept in this cold darkness, the films can last for centuries. Of course, the AWA is just walking distance from the much more famous Svalbard Global Seed Vault, which is already coping with the surrounding permafrost's unexpectedly rapid melt. This puts Piql's film reels in the awkward position of being likely to outlast the building that houses them.

Library Stack is the virtual emulation of a certain set of programs and protocols for the warehousing and circulating of publications. These protocols used to be termed a *library*, although this word has evolved and mutated under the technical and legal pressures of 21st-century digital culture. On the front end, Library Stack is a typical web database of widely varying material from the visual arts. On the back

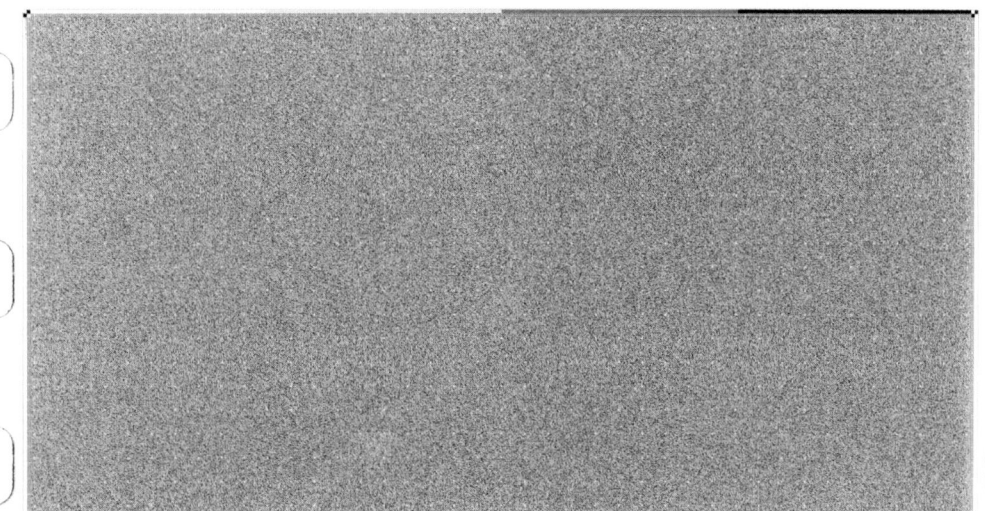

Sample frame from Library Stack test film from Piql (Oslo), 2021

end, it interacts with the heritage databases used by institutional libraries around the world, creating a legibility bridge between the regulated taxonomies of library science and the unregulated modes of digital publication now common to the art and design fields. We might be classed as a sort of 'post-custodial' archive, caring for a consciously assembled collection of digital objects for which we have neither ownership nor custody of some set of 'originals'. In some cases, there may no longer be an original. Our file archive is natively online, and replicated across multiple regions of commercial cloud storage. But learning to think at the timescale of an institution has forced us to contend with the technical horizons, ecological impact and chronopolitical stakes of long-term data storage. This essay summarises our findings, and points to some of the aporias of projecting too far into the future.

The current digital storage landscape seems to cleave along a central axis. Offline processes that use material substrates like metal, DNA, glass or polyester all have tremendous durability, but data retrieval can require complex or proprietary decoding techniques. The media also may need specific storage conditions, and they cannot easily be versioned, updated or distributed. In offline approaches, durability and accessibility run almost entirely counter to each other: permanence comes at the expense of any near-term utility. Most of their use-cases are with corporate data records in the banking, healthcare and insurance industries, along with some aspects of cultural heritage preservation. These technologies produce archival backstops for unknown, far futures. Online storage methods, like commercial clouds or blockchain platforms, are easily accessible in the near-term but their notional durability is definitionally undercut by their reliance on an unregulated global computing stack and its destructive energy draw. These services generally define permanent as a few decades, maybe a century, essentially just the 'lifetime' of the user, making their likeliest use cases the storing of important personal information like legal contracts, real estate deeds, identity documents, or NFTs. Two paradigmatic blockchain services, Arweave and Filecoin, marketise the idea of permanence through tokenomic incentives, but each locates the value of their system within a different speculative future. Filecoin, a marketplace connecting data to be stored with server space for lease, premises its token's value on the scarcity of available storage space.

Arweave is a more closed-network approach, where user fees are paid into an endowment that helps underwrite the ongoing storage cost. The priced-in supposition is that data quantities will continue to go up, but the cost to store data will always go down, and the Arweave token's valuation comes from balancing that data abundance with the fluctuating energy cost of its storage.[1]

Both online and offline data storage companies deploy seemingly interchangeable advertising slogans, like *Backup Humanity*; *Preserving Knowledge, Forever*; or *Permanent, Decentralized, Open*. These optimistic framings – where the technological sublime enables unlimited human preservation and durability – thinly disguise the marketing fiction of societal collapse on which their businesses depend. One could easily mistake the data storage field for a complex futures market in human extinctions, one that elides its own role in the eschatology. We all know that every new computer, data center and networked object pulls more raw minerals into a chain of exploitative labor practices and environmental catastrophe. We all know this is unsustainable, and bringing the planet nearer to collapse. Our collective existential anxiety breeds a reactionary desire for digital permanence, which of course only results in more computing technologies – obscuring the cognitive dissonance on which all the notional permanence rests. We are storing our information against a theoretical catastrophe that the storage effort itself helps to ensure will happen. One can see this explicitly in the gaming startup Untamed Planet, which has proposed a business model called "conservation 3.0", where a suite of multiform metaverse sites hosting Web 3 gaming and online culture experiences will generate revenue for real-world land protection.[2] They recently raised $24.3 million in venture capital to develop this play to protect model, and claim they will commit 50% of their net cryptocurrency profits "to Nature as an equal shareholder". Of course this is simply an inverse marketing fiction – that the ecological catastrophe can be forestalled, perhaps even averted, by accelerating the same technological infrastructure we know to be causing it – but its a seductive one, as digitality is a fully global cultural language. In 2022, at the COP27 in Sharm el Sheikh, Tuvaluan Communication Minister Simon Kofe delivered his address from a metaverse replica of the island, the camera pulling out to reveal the CGI background, glitchy from being computed on the fly. "As our land disappears," he said, "we have no choice but to become the world's first digital nation. Our land, our ocean, our culture are the most precious assets of our people… and no matter what happens in the physical world, we'll move them to the cloud."[3] We realise the self-awareness and spectacle value of Minister Kofe's proposal, and the traumatic circumstances that prompted it. (Who

1. Arweave sees its own useful life, at best, at about one thousand years, after which they expect to be subsumed into future archiving systems. The reasoning is sober and thoughtful, but premised on optimistic extrapolations about data storage technologies, and their continued availability. It's also worth parsing the immutability of the blockchain's record (historically secured by the incalculably high computation cost it would require to alter it) from the permanence of the network that's actually storing the referenced data. As the designer Chris Lee notes, immutability is an ancient political fiction, and the intrinsic weakness of any immutability claim is (definitionally) impossible to discern until the socio-technical framework that had initially naturalised it collapses or evolves. Online digital storage, no matter how cryptographically secure, rests on the contingencies of global computing, with its archipelago of fossil-based energy grids and privately held infrastructure. It is difficult to ascribe permanence to a system so vulnerable to the whims of investors and the knock-on self-destruction effect of its own operation. (See Chris Lee's Immutable: Designing History: https://www.librarystack.org/immutable-designing-history). **2.** https://www.untamedplanet.earth. **3.** https://www.youtube.com/watch?v=lXpeO5BgAOM.

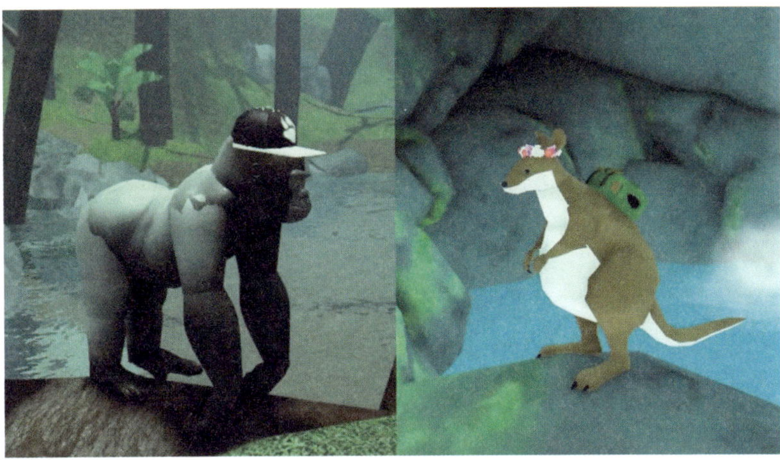

Still from promotional video for *Untamed Planet* (https://www.untamedplanet.earth)

doesn't ache for Tuvalu, dissolving into the ocean?) But permanence is a design fiction. Dematerialization into the metaverse provides the same illusion of permanence for the culture of a sinking island that materialization into metals, ceramics or DNA provides for the owners of ephemeral digital files.

In 2004, the California-based Long Now Foundation joined the European Space Agency's Rosetta mission, which sent a probe to the comet 67P/Churyumov–Gerasimenko, landing on it successfully on November 12, 2014. Long Now used the probe to deposit, onto the surface of the comet, a multi-language lexicon in the form of a micro-etched nickel disc. Begun around the year 2000, their Rosetta language project was a sprawling effort to collate, disseminate, preserve and cross-translate all human languages, alongside a parallel effort to find new ways of permanently archiving that linguistic information. There have been various Rosetta discs (microscopic, but optically-readable, collections on either nickel or quartz glass) at different stages of the project. Inspired, obviously, by the Rosetta Stone discovered in late 19th-century in Egypt, the Long Now project aimed to create a decoding object that could unlock every human language. As such, the disc contains the same essential piece of data translated repeatedly. Regrettably, the original sample text was the book of Genesis, on the grounds that it was already most likely to have been reliably translated into all global languages.[4] In 2019, another California nonprofit, the Arch Mission Foundation commissioned Stamper Technologies to produce a set of nickel discs to be deposited for safekeeping on the surface of the moon. That collection included world literature, internet material, linguistic data, scientific tables, genetic codes and image archives. The bundled disc package was in the payload of the Israeli lunar research module Beresheet (the opening word of Genesis; "in the beginning" in Hebrew) when it crashed during its descent sequence. Arch Mission maintains that the discs are probably still intact and retrievable from the wreckage site. A second attempt to land an updated version of the so-called Lunar Library was recently hexed by a different technical glitch, when a fuel leak prevented the module from landing on the lunar surface.[5]

4. For a fuller view of the neocolonialism of modern linguistics research and its historical relationship to Bible translation, see *In Their Own Language* (https://www.librarystack.org/in-their-own-language) by designer and researcher Bryce Wilner.

Tuvaluan Minister for Justice, Communication & Foreign Affairs Simon Kofe giving his address to the COP27 Conference from a metaverse replica of the island. (https://www.youtube.com/watch?v=lXpeO5BgAOM)

Many of the institutions supporting these deep repository projects, especially the exoplanetary ones, are aligned with Longtermism, a ruthless hybrid of utilitarian philosophy and prosperity gospel escapism that posits a future abstraction (the well-being of a vast number of theoretical future humans) as a prime moral demand made upon the present. Longtermist archiving initiatives could be construed as efforts to shape what philosopher Achille Mbembe calls the *community of time:* that notional public which is allowed involvement and ownership in the meaning and interpretation of an archive. It's claimed that deep repositories like the lunar library, or the Rosetta discs, would help humanity survive some future cataclysm, but another clear implication is that some humans absolutely will survive, and that when they do, these will be their dominant reference points for reconstructing their own history. Archiving at the scale of millennia is an effort to control the future; by shaping what manages to be most durable, these ante-archives aim to limn the possible

5. https://www.npr.org/2024/01/14/1224723508/peregrine-moon-lander-heads-back-toward-earth-and-should-burn-up-in-the-atmosphe.

facts about the far future's past. As Mbembe says, "The final destination of the archive is always situated outside its own materiality, in the story that it makes possible."[6] The farther into the future these projects imagine, the more data preservation and human preservation come to overlap, revealing not only a blind faith in the interchangeability of data with life, but how their glossy space futurism covers for a deeply eschatological Earth fatalism.[7]

In 2012, researchers at the George Eastman House, the Rochester Museum built from the collection of Kodak's founder, discovered that many of their daguerreotypes were covered in a nanoscale fungus. Long presumed biologically inert and even innately antimicrobial, these unique metal image-plates were in fact hosting fungal colonies that were metabolising the silver and gold nanoparticles comprising each image. What appeared to the eye as tarnish in the shadows and edges was revealed by scanning electron microscopy to be a fibrous biometallic fungal residue, sprawling across the surface in a dense web. Daguerreotypes were the earliest widespread form of photography, in use from around 1845 to 1865, and in less than two centuries many of them have visibly degraded due to these unexpected, microscopic ecosystems. Conservators now house many daguerreotypes in casings sealed with argon gas, halting the damage by depriving oxygen from the bio-reactive surface.[8] This story resonated with us as we drove to Rochester to visit the Stamper Technologies laboratory in October of 2022. Their methodology engaged our preoccupations with geology, computation and the history of photographic imaging, and we wanted to test the viability of this method on our idiosyncratic library of digital materials. We had sent them a core sample of our collection – books, journals, maps and typefaces by artists and designers from around the world, many of them friends

Overleaf: The last image sent back to Earth by the Beresheet moon lander before its crash onto the lunar surface, April 11, 2019 and stills from a forthcoming film, directed by Library Stack and Andreas Bunte (color, sound, 1.85, 40 mins, in production 2024).

6. See "The Power of the Archive and its Limits," found in *Refiguring the Archive*, Hamilton et al., (eds.), (David Philip Publishers, 2002). **7.** This dyad is drawn directly from geographer Rory Rowan, who notes (regarding the emergent commercial space sector) that "Earth fatalism" is a necessary rhetorical ingredient for the business success of a neoliberal "space futurism". For more, see the 2018 lecture "Beyond Colonial Futurism: Portugal's Atlantic Spaceport and the Neoliberalization of Outer Space" at: https://www.e-flux.com/live/191164/e-flux-lectures-rory-rowan-beyond-colonial-futurism-portugal-s-atlantic-spaceport-and-the-neoliberalization-of-outer-space. **8.** The material resilience of any archival medium is a function of its storage conditions. Humidity, temperature or atmospheric elements can warp a sensitive medium; ultraviolet light can alter colors or pigments; and organic matter can degrade almost any substrate. Fungal colonies have been found to attack the gelatin base of silver halide films, the surfaces of recordable compact discs, the binding polymers of magnetic tape and, of course, the pure metals in antique photographs. For more, see: Palermo, A.M., Gentile, A. & Pellegrino, G. Documentary heritage: fungal deterioration in Compact Discs. Heritage Science 9, 133 (2021). [https://doi.org/10.1186/s40494-021-00609-x]; Nick R. Konkol, Brenda Bernier, Elena Bulat & Ralph Mitchell, Characterization of Filamentous Accretions On Daguerreotype Surfaces, Pages 149–159 | Published online: 18 Jul 2013. [https://doi.org/10.1179/019713611804480944]; and Wiegandt, Ralph et al. "A Summary of the National Science Foundation (SCIART) Supported Research of the Daguerreotype: George Eastman House International Museum of Photography and Film, and the University of Rochester." (2017). [https://resources.culturalheritage.org/pmgtopics/2013-volume-fifteen/28-T15_Wiegandt_Bigelow.pdf].

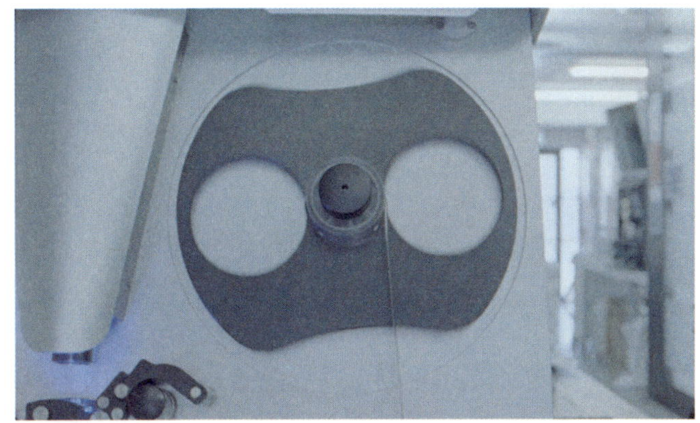

Right: Library Stack disc production at Stamper Technologies, October 2022

or peers – and were now coming to observe the process. Our data took up eight micro-printed discs, arrayed in a ring on a single nickel sheet. Rainbows bounced off its mirrored surface, gridded with what seemed like thousands of tiny photographic holograms. Each small circular field was 100,000 pixels across, and examining them under the lab's microscope showed us new configurations of scale, compression and resolution.

Stamper claims the disc is resistant to corrosion, humidity, heat and electromagnetic radiation, but its spectacular potential durability was soon eclipsed by a profoundly haunted sense of mistranslation. Microscopic pixels so recently born and eternal metals that will never die were were now stranded together on this inert island, bereft of explanatory social context, their meaning mismatched to their form. We felt the sudden revulsion of a new uncanny valley: the chronological dislocation of seeing one's own present as if from someone else's future. As with any library, ours is oxygenated by use. Without a living layer of social protocol, our sample group of electronic projects had all deadened upon contact with nickel. They were rendered exquisitely in high definition – but anaerobic, as if behind thick glass.

Metaverse gaming platform Untamed Planet is also is also one of the investment firms backing Colossal Biosciences, a synthetic biology startup specialising in de-extinction, which uses gene editing techniques to manipulate the genomes of living species (so they more readily tolerate our degraded biosphere), and in some cases to revive extinct species from paleobiological samples. Colossal's core focus is the rematerialisation of the woolly mammoth: if it could be technologically resurrected, artificially bred, and a herd released onto the Arctic steppe, its grazing appetites would help de-insulate the permafrost and keep it (and its enormous methane sink) frozen. An intact original mammoth DNA sequence is very unlikely to be found, but lead scientist George Church doesn't aim to clone an original. Instead, he will splice bits of sequenced mammoth DNA into the genome of an Asian elephant, its closest living relative, blending in mammoth-esque traits until arriving at a suitable proxy species.[9] We hunted these creatures to extinction some eleven thousand years ago, and now mammoths represent one of the most quixotic, poetic and least plausible hopes against full-scale climate catastrophe – a shaggy, lumbering specter returned to haunt capital's lowball pricing of nature. Colossal aims to have a living specimen within two decades, although knowledgeable skeptics put extremely long odds on Church's success. But even just the idea of de-extinction is itself the longtermist's fetishistic wish fulfillment: it is a previsualisation of their resurrectionist future, and a validation of their basic axiom that extinction is just data in a state of dormancy.

9. This would be a crowning achievement of biology, much as was the complete mapping of the human genome in the 1990s, which Church helped to initiate. For details on Church's work and the field of 'de-extinction' more broadly (including a clear-eyed assessment of its plausibility), see Beth Shapiro's *How to Clone a Mammoth: The Science of De-Extinction* (Princeton, 2015).

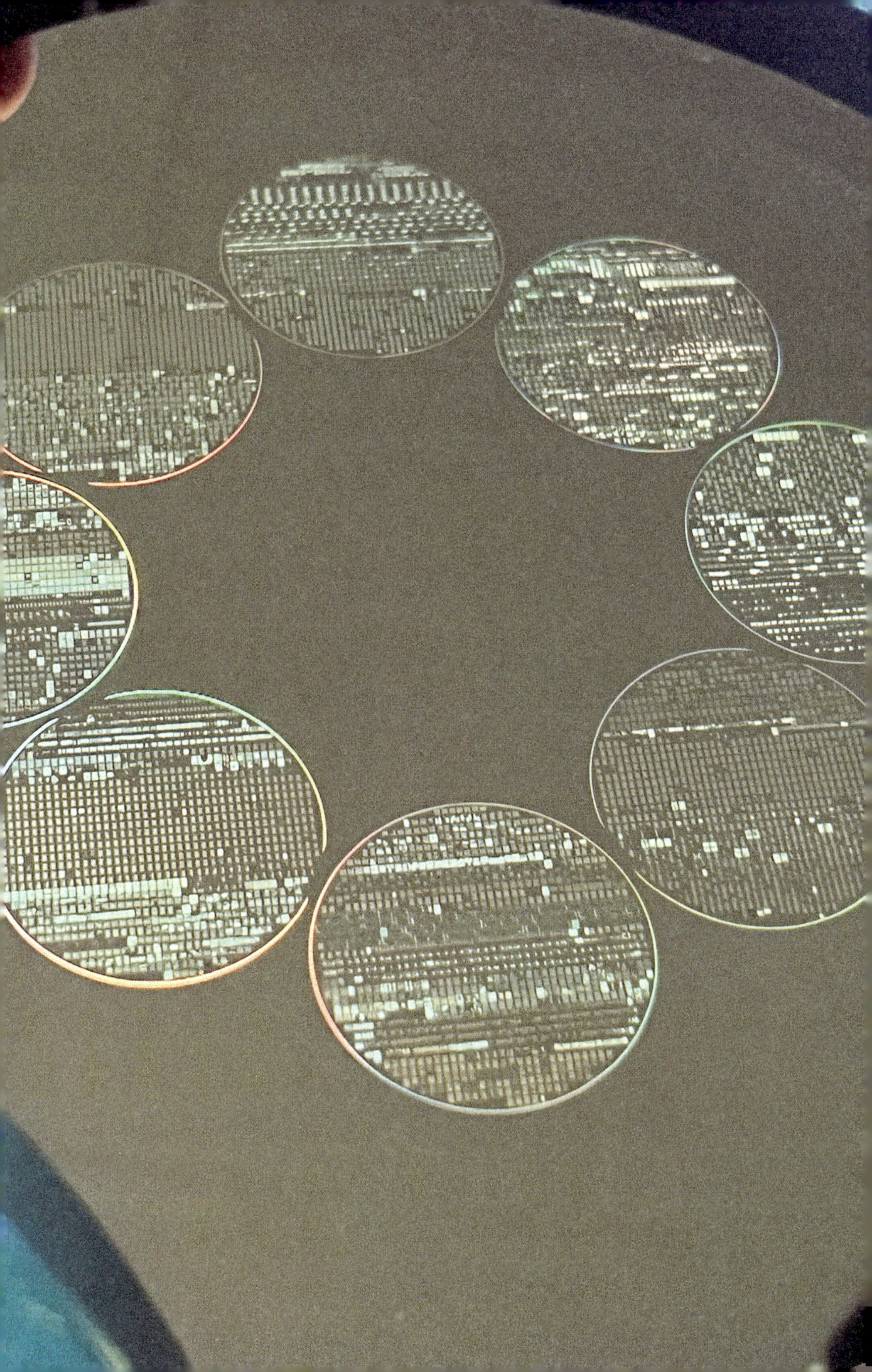

Nathan Jones, Tom Schofield & Sam Skinner

The RNN Triptych: The Re-reader, If and Only If & It's Not You, It's Me

We developed the topic of automation and big data in library techno-culture in our own artistic contributions to the *BiblioTech* exhibitions: a series of works collectively titled, *The RNN Triptych*, produced collaboratively with the artist Tom Schofield[1] between 2017 and 2022. Though they are sketches of a kind, we aim that they provide concrete examples of small data and de-automation through AI deployment, reprogramming machine learning technology to less extractive ends. These works offer evidence that AI technologies, despite their seemingly unstoppable expansion and acceleration, also contain hidden opportunities for resistance, care and *stupid modes* of misuse and undevelopment. The works are also interactive and allow people the opportunity to play with alternative forms of machine learning and experience what happens when, for example, the data set is changed within natural language processing and text generation applications.

The commercially available applications of OpenAI's large language model ChatGTP have generated controversy, due to the express marketability of scare-hype around its ability to 'think' in generated language. The existence of ChatGTP has also raised concerns about the ethics of using AI to generate written material for exams, as well as the potential impact on the job market for human writers and editors. With *The RNN Triptych*, we explore the ethical and social implications of AI from outside of the use-case, making differently-workable versions of language learning models, thereby emphasising alternative trajectories that machine learning can take. Unfortunately, this work is *closedAI*, in the sense that it was presented for specific exhibitions and events, and is not at the time of writing accessible, but we document it below.

Torquing Shadow Libraries with Small Data AI

In a context where AI is likely to inform commercial, research, and even social agendas of the future, the library's joint role as a site for collections and reading-writing activity becomes even more potent, even powerful. Ultimately, the integration of AI into the academic research environment is going to be a process in which sovereignty is sacrificed, with significant implications for the way we

1. Tom Schofield's insightful analysis of this work via the lens of "the absurd" at a talk given at *BiblioTech* in Cyprus, is available to view online here: https://www.youtube.com/watch?v=4t0dMnC7vKk.

understand and interact with information. This process has already begun with the current emphasis on making published materials 'open access', primarily by funnelling research funds formerly reserved for researching, towards publishing behemoths, supplementing their diminishing subscription returns with a pay-to-play system that only academics in large institutions can engage in. In our own artistic practice, we prefer to work with shadow libraries, which deliver open access unbounded , in the wild, operating in parallel to the already-extractive model of legacy publishing; an approach we might think of as *ajar access*.

The three artworks in the triptych all use a small-data, interactive approach for training a Recursive Neural Net (RNN), built using machine learning library PyTorch, to satirise commonplace AI claims of automation and efficiency, whilst offering an opportunity to readers and audiences to become involved in the process of training and interpreting the results of RNN generated text. The works contrast human agency and modes of thinking with the probabilistic and programmatic nature of computer processing, whilst also showing how both are made to compete with one another in the burnout-rife workplace cultures around hi-tech 'innovation'. *The processor cooling fan and the heart race.*

An RNN is a kind of machine learning algorithm that can be used to calculate the statistical probability that one letter will follow the next, given what has gone before, and what it has learned from a set corpus of texts.[2] Other than the texts it is fed, the RNN has no internal dictionary or grammar, meaning that the model is ecologically less costly to train and run than big-data models, and more transparent: the RNN only 'knows' what we give it, so audiences who participate in this process of submitting textual material are afforded some insight into how source texts determine what the RNN outputs as writing.[3] RNNs are also more error prone: the 'out-putters' can and do make spelling errors, writing a fascinatingly textured patois out from behind the statistical averaging of its dataset. We can ourselves learn about language from watching a machine learn to write like this: arriving at meaning from the level of the letter and word, rather than the network of semantic relations. And we also warmly note the similarity to habits of our own scholarly practice, minting new coinages out of current linguistic ore.[4] The impoverished outputs of the small-data set illustrate the punishing scale of big data on which hi-fidelity language models rely, but they also generate new trajectories, new futures for language to bleed into an age we increasingly share with other forms of intelligence.

The Re-Reader (2017) is an installation comprising a bespoke book scanner which resembles a large bird box that scans books inserted into it, which are in turn translated into digital files which feed an RNN text analyser and generator. It was first shown at The Grundy, a public gallery in Blackpool, UK in 2017, and has since been shown at Lancaster and Newcastle universities and most recently in the *BiblioTech* exhibition in Liverpool. The scanner housing and chair was built by furniture maker Seb Cox using sustainably sourced wood, to subvert and offer

2. The work was programmed by Tom Schofield, using the Python library "Torch-RNN" https://pytorch.org/docs/stable/generated/torch.nn.RNN.html. **3.** There is a good description of recursive neural nets on Jake Tae's blog here: https://jaketae.github.io/study/rnn/. **4.** Braidotti and Hlavajava comment that the setting of the current climactic and technological situation have induced scholars to accelerate their coinage of new terms: 'What could terms such as "altergorithm", "rewilding","negentropy" and "technoanimalism" possibly have in common? ... [T]hey are all neologisms that attempt to come to terms with the complexities of the posthuman predicament.' Rosi Braidotti and Maria Hlavajova, (eds) Posthuman Glossary (Bloomsbury Academic, 2018): 6.

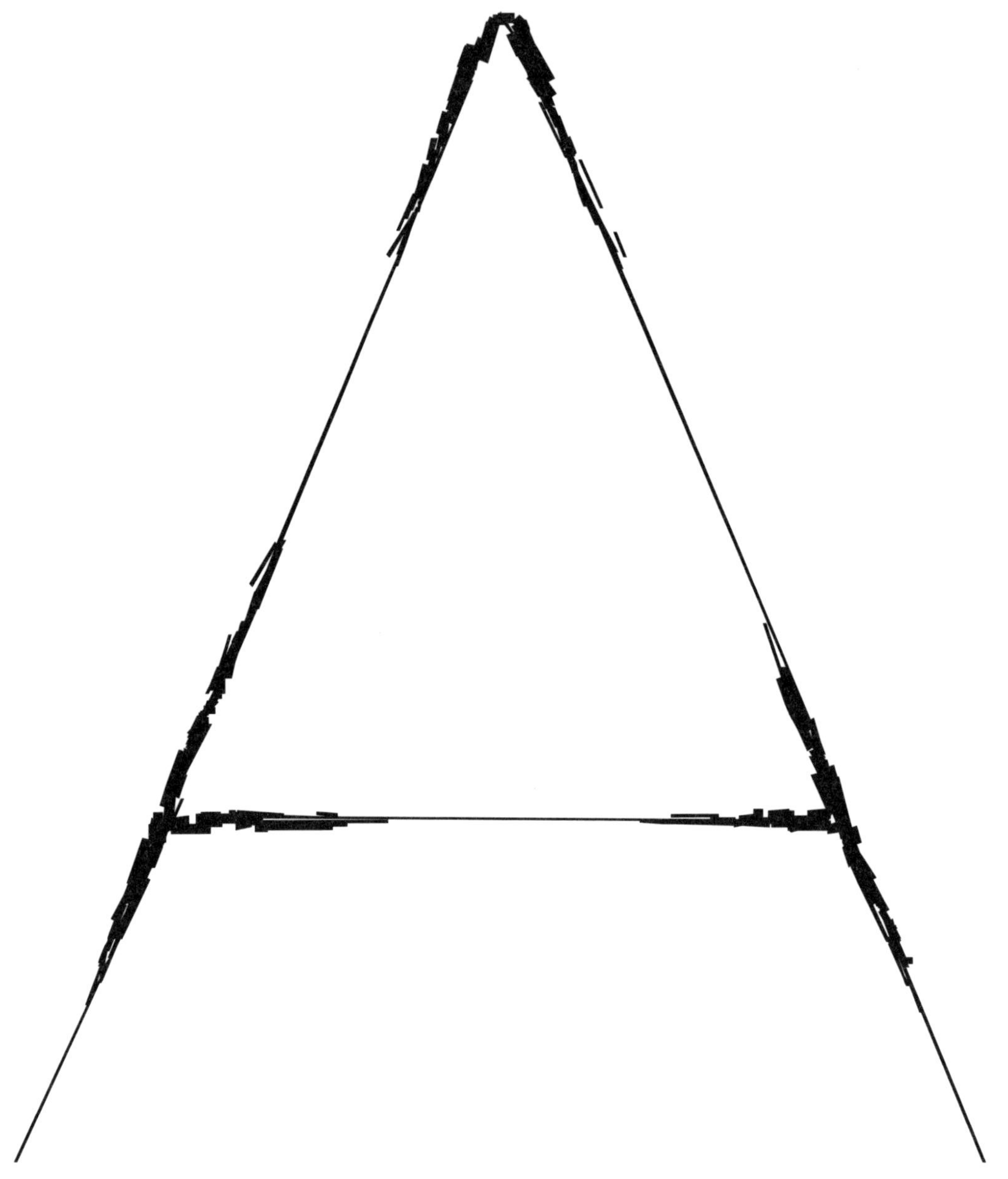

A B C D E F G H I J K L M

N O P Q R S T U V W X Y Z

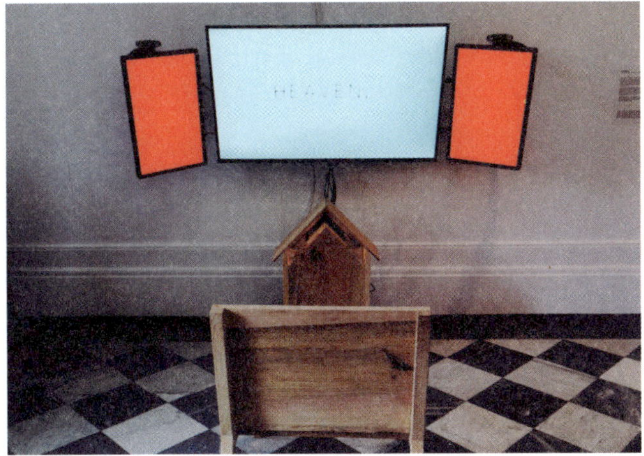

Above: *The Re-Reader* installations at *BiblioTech*, Liverpool (2022) and Grundy Art Gallery, Blackpool (2017).
Left: Torquera typeface designed by Sam Skinner for speed-reading and used within *The Re-Reader*.

an alternative to the usual materials and aesthetics of computer hardware. Small web-cams in *The Re-Reader* scan the book, which are converted to digital text files using OCR, scraping the text off each page. Then the centre screen plays the book to you, in a 'speed-reading' format of one word at a time, very quickly.[5] The idea is to read a book or a page fast, as if processing it like a machine. Further exaggerating the supposed efficiency of the speed-reading process, the text is displayed using a specially designed typeface where characters are whittled down to their barest form, relying on thicker lines where contours intersect to create a kind liminal, almost unconscious reading experience. The text is replayed a second time as the RNN picks out what words it thinks are 'important' in the text, comparing the text to a larger corpus of texts. The side screens flash when it gets to them, allowing you to pay even less attention to aspects of the text. In *BiblioTech*, we exhibited *The Rereader* with poetry books for people to feed to it, because poetry is thought of as something that we take a long time with. Perhaps, we imply, library users should read poetry much quicker to produce more time for... not reading poetry? As is often mooted, the digital and virtual allow time to play out in different ways from our everyday embodied experience. As Brian Massumi has written, "Something that happens too quickly to have happened, actually, is virtual."[6] But within the new landscapes of machine leaning, what is "too quickly" today may be too slow tomorrow, and these divisions and differences are altering *all the time*.

Another feature of the installation is its capacity to function as a small data AI learner. It acquires the ability to write one letter at a time based on the information contained in the books it receives. In contrast to the coyly exploitative nature of big data models like ChatGTP and other large language models that have been notorious for violating users' privacy, our installation adopts an openly exchange-oriented approach. We provide the AI with the necessary data to generate a faster version of a book while it learns in return. Gallery users have been trading physical labour with *The Rereader* across six exhibitions, for several weeks at a time, and still, the writing it does is quite rudimentary. It makes fewer spelling mistakes now, and it occasionally echoes the typographical quirks of books, but it still doesn't form proper sentences. This is the cost of being hand-trained. This post-digital approach introduces people to the ideas and scales of big data and – in the sense that 'hand trained AI' might now enter the vernacular – perhaps contributes a concept more desirable among bourgeois society. The RNN is poorly-suited for its work, producing manifest and avoidable spelling errors, emphasising the relative contingency and 'guess-work' at the heart of machine learning. We found the mistakes and neologisms that arise from this process fascinating, and they helped shape the projects which followed.

The second part of the triptych is an online small data newspaper headline prediction machine named *If and Only If.* We collaborated with The British Library to obtain their newly digitised archive of headlines from the 18th and 19th century, and trained an RNN firstly on that data set. On our website, we hosted the machine in the form of an online newspaper, which presented a list of the headlines that we used to train the AI, allowing visitors to read both the original archive and what the AI has produced. As viewers explore the website, they notice

5. For further discussion of speed-reading and this work see our essay "Absorbing Text: Rereading Speed Reading" in APRJA, Machine Research, Vol. 6 No. 1 (2017), https://aprja.net//issue/view/8319. **6.** Brian Massumi, Parables for the Virtual: Movement, Affect, Sensation (Duke University Press, 2002): 30.

that not all of the language is archaic, and that words appear spelling-blurred, as though written by a copiest that is not 'all there'. This is because we have been poisoning[7] the historical data set with more contemporary and speculative headlines, using web-input technology to merge old and new and to contemplate the future of news headlines. Users can contribute their own prospective headlines, which get added to the training data set. Example headlines can be seen on pages 265–267 of this volume. As we discuss in *Curating Superintelligences* (DATA Browser, Vol. 10),[8] the low-fi predictions of *If and Only If* have a particular political potency, when contrasted with the hi-fi nature of today's advanced AI technology and the privacy abuses and excessive energy expenditure that enable it.[9]

The final element of our triptych artwork using RNNs is a semi-automated post-human self-help book entitled *It's Not You, It's Me*. The book is trained on a cybernetics literature and self-help books, including both computer manuals and works intended for human self-improvement. This combination was informed my time spect researching the cyberneticist Stafford Beer's archive at Liverpool John Moores University library and an interest in the boom in self-help literature. Cyberneticism, self-help, and AI are all uniquely and expressly orientated towards providing answers and we wanted to explore what their hybridisation may offer. One hope was that it might write the first best-seller of the *emotioningularity*, but it needed our help to do so. As with the above examples, the RNN of *It's Not You, It's Me* makes profuse spelling mistakes. Those mistakes are not immediately comprehensible, but they do echo the combined meaning, the sprit even, of the texts it has been fed. In our game/artwork, the user must assist the computer in understanding the meaning of the any word generated that is not in the standard dictionary, giving them definitions, which are placed in the footnotes and added to a kind of 'dictionary erratum', before they can read on. The playful idea behind this is that we might collaborate with machines on concept building, whereby unknown terms generated are not simply wrong, but rather reveal something latent, and awaiting affirmation and decoding. The work speaks to a world in which AI is employed in helping us maintain our own self-care, and we help the machines too. Several of the neologisms evoke this aspect of the work. For example, "ther-aps" is a hybrid of "therapy" and "apps" and was defined in the dictionary as refer to a collection of emotionally supportive phone applications. Another neologism the machine generated was "transinsfer," which, a user defined as relating to the translation of different languages based on a speaker's intonation. Some example pages from the book collaboratively produced by gallery visitors and our RNN can be seen on pages 271–275.

By using the post-digital in tandem with the practices of participatory arts and interaction design to explore the implications of large models, and the possibility of smaller ones, we can gain a deeper and more creative understanding of these technologies, ideologies and processes. Contemporary critical media art in the context of AI is post-digital not solely because of its insistence on the materialities of the different stages of storage, digitisation, distribution, and

7. We learned about data poisoning as an adversarial AI approach at this workshop held by Matteo Pasquinelli and Daphne Dragona at Transmediale festival in 2020: https://kim.hfg-karlsruhe.de/adversarial-hacking-workshop/. **8.** Nathan Jones, Tom Schofield and Sam Skinner, "Crash Blossoms / IF & ONLY IF: A Lo-Fidelity AI Newspaper" in DATA Browser, Vol. 10, Edited by Joasia Krysa and Magdalena Tyżlik-Carver, (forthcoming). http://www.data-browser.net/db10.html. **9.** A key reference for us here is Hito Steyerl's essay "In Defense of the Poor Image," e-flux Journal, Issue #10, 2009.

Top: The storage void of the new British Library National Newspaper Building at Boston Spa in West Yorkshire, photo Kippa Matthews. Middle: *If & Only If* at *BiblioTech*, Liverpool. Bottom: *If & Only If*, *BiblioTech*, Limassol. Opposite: Draft of *If & Only If* webpage produced for Leeds Digital Festival, 2020. Following pages: Headlines produced during *If & Only If*'s publication, Sept–Oct, 2020. Reference material and sketches for Sam Skinner's design of the *If & Only If* banner.

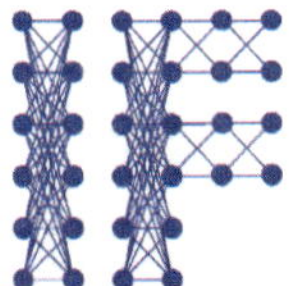

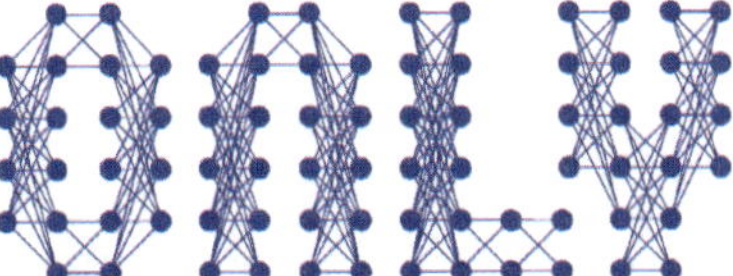

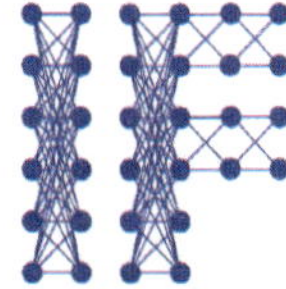

VOL 1. NO. 1 MONDAY SEPTEMBER 21 2020 TORQUE EDITIONS

DESTRALE OF THE PANDEMBER CHARD AND THE ALLEGED

A POSSIBLE FUTURE - OR A GAP IN THE PAST - IS RENDERED AS LOW-FIDELITY LANGUAGE IN THIS HEADLINE.

As the author Stanislaw Lem has a character in The Futurological Congress observe: "By examining future stages in the evolution of language we come to learn what discoveries, changes and social revolutions the language will be capable, some day, of reflecting." If and only if the future = (the past + the present) *entropy, then might the neologism be a time machine, an active agent of transformation?

Or perhaps as language falls apart, it falls into unspoken moments of the past?

IF & ONLY IF works with a recursive neural network (RNN) to exaggerate and accelerate the falling-apart-recombining-churning process that language undergoes in today's increasingly rapid permutational culture.

As with any object that is far-distant, the view this headline affords us of the future, is impoverished and blurry. A vision that demands your imagination. Rather than "big data" the IF & ONLY IF headline generator is trained on a small set of data which you can read and digest for yourself on this page. Starting out with a small British Library archive of C19th headlines, a RNN was taught the statistical likelihood that one letter follows another. Each day we re-train IF AND ONLY IF's RNN on its own outputs, adding by hand some contemporary and possible-future examples. You can add your own suggestions below to help us train the model over the coming weeks.

Though the form of its historical sources still shape the outputs you see, their content will become an increasingly distant memory over the coming weeks, distorted by the likelihood of letter-combinations such as "coro", "trum", "brex", "ai" that dominate today's headlines. Because there is no corrective mechanism, the process does not result in increasing accuracy, but rather opens up the field of possibility and disorder in a way that is akin to the entropy that characterises our experience of time passing.

'MARKETS', 'HIGHOUT COULD MECHICTER', 'BULLOVING', 'AUSTRALIAN HAVE FIVEL AND MONETARY', 'COURT', 'BUYNOUNIA THT SEAKS WORLD ORDER RULES', 'NEWSEWAPE DEAL', 'ANNUAL STONESS AND THE BRITS', 'ALL AND TELEGRAPHIC NEWS', 'LOT'S IT'S POINE IN CORRESPONDENCE', 'LATEST AND TRADE LANG THE PARRESTALLY INDEFIRST CALLS TO PRESIDENT TRUMP AND THE BRITISH ASSAS PRESIDENT TO HELOCKENSE PROTEST AID OF THE SALE OF AMERICAN COMMISSIONERS', 'FRINGY TOTALY IN RESPOLAN AND THE CORRESPONDENCE', 'LATEST AND TRADE REPORT AND OBITUARIES ', 'KENTER', 'MANCES', 'DOLING FOUND THE EARTHS AND THE REPOLICE', 'LATEST AND THE REPOLIST TO MOHNISH ASSAMED TO EAGTED BY THE BOOK. CONCERNATIONS TO AMERICAN COMITISH ASSASSING THE WORKER OF THE SPECTRUST CLOSESIDENT TO FAIL', 'ARTS AND OBITUARIES', 'LATEST AND TRACE JODER DEMOCTING STOVERY HAS IN HOW RASHIOT PUBLIC AND MONETARY'

YOUR HEADLINE HERE

Help us to train our RNN by typing in your own speculations on the headlines of the future. Who and what will dominate our news in the decades to come? What new conglomerations of politics, technologies and events will we come to know? How might the language of headlines and the news change? What neologisms will be commonplace?

CONFUSION CAUSED BY CRASH BLOSSOMS

Here's a further sample of some of the suggestions made by you, our readers, helping to train the IF & ONLY IF RNN to look into the future and combine with headlines from the past and the present to create the top headline. Your own contribution could be published here, alongside these: 'DAILY MAIL FORMS ARMY', 'SWANS UNDER ATTACK', 'FARAGE SINKS', 'COVID 19 GIVEN PEERAGE', 'SCHOOLS REOPEN UNDERWATER', 'PM SLAMS SLAMMING', 'SPECULATION ABOUT CRASH BLOSSOMS', 'ZOMBIES LAND', 'SQUIRREL'S ATTACK', 'FAKE DEGREE CLAIMS DOG PROMINENT SPANISH POLITICIANS', 'MAN WHO URINATED ON WOMAN AT DRAKE CONCERT BEFORE DRINK-DRIVE KILLER GIRLFRIEND STARTED BRAWL OVER AVOIDS JAIL', 'DECAPITATED MEMBERS ARRESTED ON ALLEGED KIDNAPPING CHARGES', 'QUEEN MOTHER TRIED TO HELP ABUSE

"MACHINE MISBEHAVIOUR" IS CLICK BAIT TO-COME

IN LATENT SPACE NO-ONE CAN SEE YOU TYPO.

The notion of latent space is integral to forms of machine learning where items in a data-set are used to produce a mathematical 'spatial' representation of the set as a whole.

The only language IF AND ONLY IF knows is headlines that exist within the archive. Each example headline from the corpus is a co-ordinate from which the AI constructs a continuous world. You can yourself in the columns below, read the material from which the AI draws its coordinates. But we can ask the generator to 'explore' its archive-world and show us what language possibilities exist "between the (head)lines". The letter combinations that you see above are locations possibilities within the latent space of the archive. The neologisms (new-words, new-logics) that the generator spits out are therefore not only intended as speculations on the future, but of the gaps in the archive. What has been left unsaid.

As well as synthesising the statistical possibilities of historical sets of headlines with more contemporary examples, we also train IF & ONLY IF on its own errors. We also introduce our own vernacular examples. This is what is called 'poisoning' the set, but we might also think about it as bringing the archive back to life. This human intervention in the synthetic set is a "pharmakon", both poison and antidote. It obscures and distorts the 'truth' of the archive, by presenting a range of possibilities that is between it, and beyond.

In When making becomes divination: Uncertainty and contingency in computational glitch-events Betti Marenko observes similar potentials - perhaps even necessities - in contemporary design practice. Marenko asserts that a glitch is the event that "reveals the potential of the digital in processes of computational making". The IF & ONLY IF algorithm is trained on such moments in its own language glitches, it is encouraged to make errors that articulate its own potential. The glitch poetics are pharmacological moments in language, where broken, impoverished and corrupted words are imbued with literary potential. The era of the digital means that errors increasingly reveal the entanglement of our language with computational means, a process that is accelerating us into the future.

'Ambiguity is difference engine of the eternal return. ', 'No 'syntax directive', just grains stirred in a certain way. ', 'Error is divination. ', 'Glitch the tangible evidence of autonomous capacities of digital matter. ', 'True picture of the past whizzes by. ', 'History repeats itself in different codecs ', 'Crash Blossoms. Post truth. Linguistic futurology. ', 'Splinters of error shot through present moment show light. ', 'Each line of headlinese is a lie as a possibility. ', 'Digital recognized as manifesting ongoing differentiation. ', 'Cracked oracle. Synthetic projection. Gibberish machine. ', 'Storm drives language irresistibly into the future. ', 'If you cut open the present the future leaks out. ', 'Return of the same to to played on a different statistical array. ', 'Open the archive to find new semantic ground. ', "'machine misbehaviour" is click bait to-come. ', 'We trained an AI on 1000 headlines from the C19th, and made it break. ', 'First time as truth, second as improbability. '

FAKE DEGREE CLAIMS DOG PROMINENT SPANISH POLITICIAN

A crash blossom is a syntactical error-ambiguity in a headline, for example: "Violinist linked to JAL crash blossoms" or "Red Tape Holds Up New Bridge". These errors are often the result of the tendency in 'headlinese' to use a noun as a verb. As in "Fake degree claims dog prominent Spanish politicians".

The crash blossom opens up a latent space in language, in which multiple interpretations are true of a single headline. Such headlines also spiral into the space of the irreal, producing cartoonish visions of a world in which subjects hover in a mist of dramatic action. "Man who urinated on woman at Drake concert before drink-drive killer girlfriend started brawl over avoids jail", "Decapitated Members Arrested on Alleged Kidnapping Charges", "Queen Mother tried to help abuse girl", "Chinese Cooking Fat Heads for Holland", "Woman Abandoned as Newborn Searches for Birth Mother."

THE TRIAL OF DR JAMESON AND HIS OFFICERS

The above headline is taken from The British Library archive of 19th century newspapers, mostly regional titles that have been newly digitised, which were the inspiration for this project. IF AND ONLY IF's RNN was trained using just 1000 examples from this data-set, in conjunction with contemporary and speculative future. Each one of the headlines from the archive was the title of a local or national news story, with regular features such as "Births, Marriages and Deaths" predominating in the first iterations of our trained model. Unlike with "big data" AI models, our original set is provided here at a human-digestible scale. It is of note that the sensationalist language of contemporary headlinese is a later invention, which is rarely present in the pre 1880 headlines we have used. The British Newspaper Archive holds over 20 million searchable pages from more than 700 newspaper titles: https://www.bl.uk/collection-guides/british-newspaper-archive

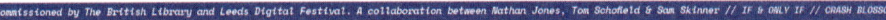

HOW TO OVERLOAD INFORMATION OVERLOAD IN ACTS OF RECUPERATION?

This project explores headlinese - the strange language of headlines – and broader contexts, including the migration of news from paper to radio to screens, and how today's news has become increasingly participatory and automated. Forwarding, retweeting, commenting, hashtags and memes have collectively produced a news that is in a constant process of mutation and self replication. How we experience this news today is inherently open to revision, so much so that we are all variously working or lurking in a global newsroom. But, in this new world of citizen journalists and freedom to publish in an instant, misinformation can spread online like wildfire, breeding and legitimatising conspiracy theories, and ushering in a 'post-truth' age.

Within the history and culture of headline writing lies the seeds of the hyperbolic language that defines so much online news and communication today. Whitney Phillips has written that algorithms act as editors, which "incentivise certain types of sensationalist content… [and] it is simply not the case that all voices carry equally on social media; or that all information carries equally."

Furthermore, in working with a news archive as we have done with this project, it should be noted how the archive, like the news, prioritises certain voices. As Michel Foucault wrote, the archive, "defines at the outset the system of its enunciability".

This project seeks to put the news archive of the past into dialogue with its present and future, using the peculiar characteristics of AI text generation software as a tool to mediate relations, and create an experience for readers that is at once familiar and strange.

The artist Steve McQueen once said in an interview that "artists develop a language in response to a crisis of freedom," but how might we develop a freedom in response to a crisis in language? As artists we are not interested in 'knowledge navigation tools' that assert 'control and mastery' of the informational and linguistic excesses of today. Rather, we seek to produce artefacts and encounters which both revel in and defamiliarise the infosphere. John Cage once wrote: "I am trying to be unfamiliar with what I'm doing" and we attempt this too, asking what role does the imaginary have within the evolution of media and technology, from post-truth filter bubbles to how we might converse with AI. We ask: what is the inner life of language, as it twists between the empires of the web and the archive, how do words create worlds, how can we overload information overload with acts of recuperation, and how might we learn to crash blossom?

Commissioned by The British Library and Leeds Digital Festival. A collaboration between Nathan Jones, Tom Schofield & Sam Skinner // IF & ONLY IF // CRASH BLOSSOMS

DESTRALE OF PANDEMBER CHARD AND THE ALLEGED OF THE BUT WITS CHINSTERE SHOWNING TO WEE REPORT

FORMATION APPOICH SAIGNON COLLECTIONS ACCUNASE SUCHANT IN PLAS PART ONTER AND FACED IN THE FOUR CASES FEAD AND SHOOY FOR BOARD OF GUARD

NEWSINES ABOUT YOU FEARS IN A FRAGHTED BY THE BRITISH ASSAMPOFSOUS SABAN CORN TRADE THROUGH OF THE BOOFLENDERS GIVER OF CRIMAN CONCERN ON TOXICAL PRINGY AND SERADEY STATES VASHIONS

NEW WORLD OF CORONAL
POLITICAL AND THE ALLEGED
BEST NEW O

COLORD ACOON CORNERS
WITHOUT OF IN THE EART
SHOWS FOR HRIVE FIGHT
HOUR PRESIDENT OF HOUTING
AN AND AND LORD BENT
CHARGED AFTER AS THE FLOM
HER MR. GREAM WRICHINESED
TO EAST LION

CHANGE TO CHOWN THE
REPOLICE

LATEST AND TRACE
CONFUSING IN NAPASHEMAN
PRESIDENT BETWEEN BARR
FARS FRAISE EASE OF LEVERS
UNWE

that
movie
was
cool

input
hidden
hidden
output

tanh
Legend:
Layer
Pointwize op
Copy

one to one
one to many
many to one
many to many
many to many

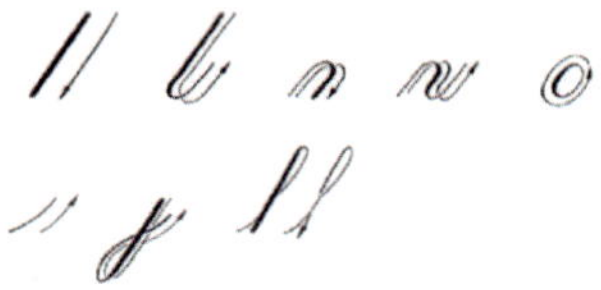

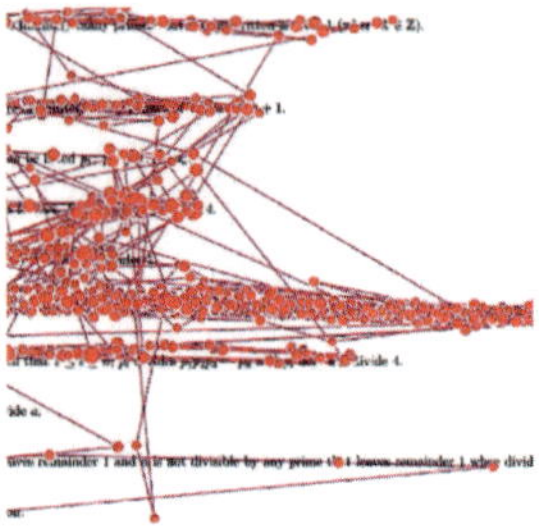

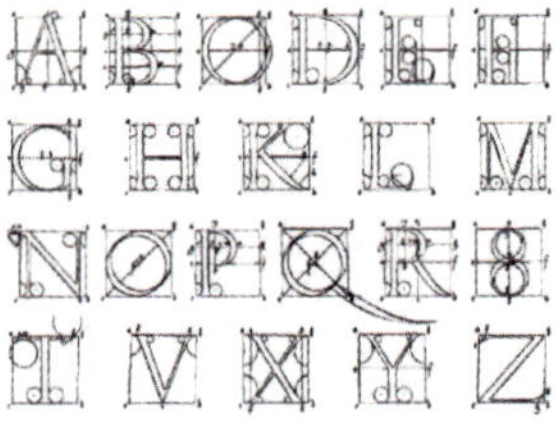

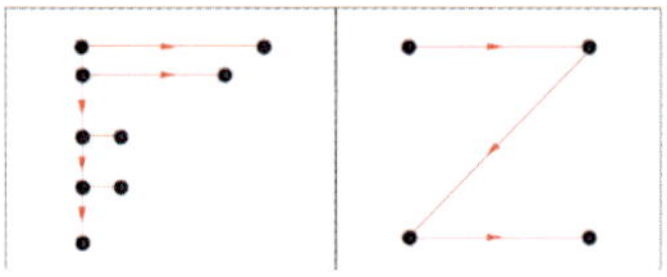

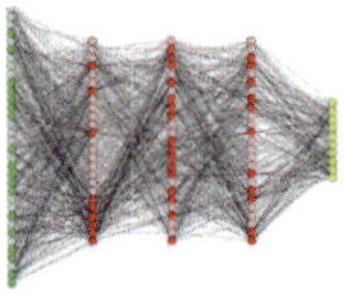

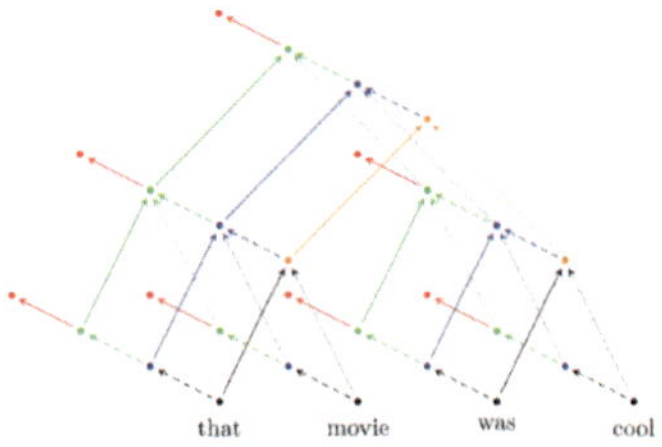

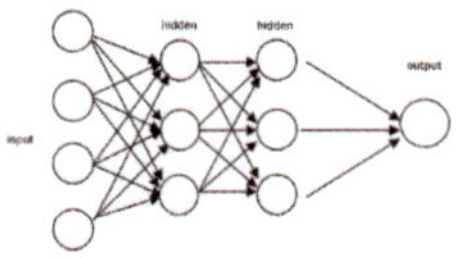

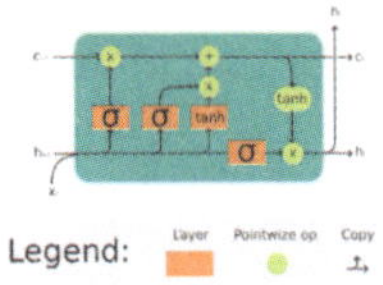

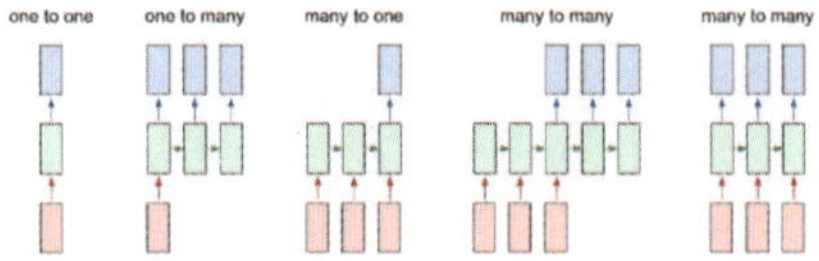

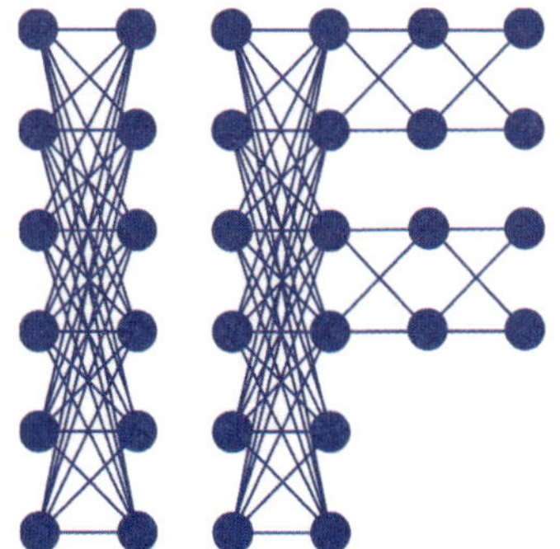

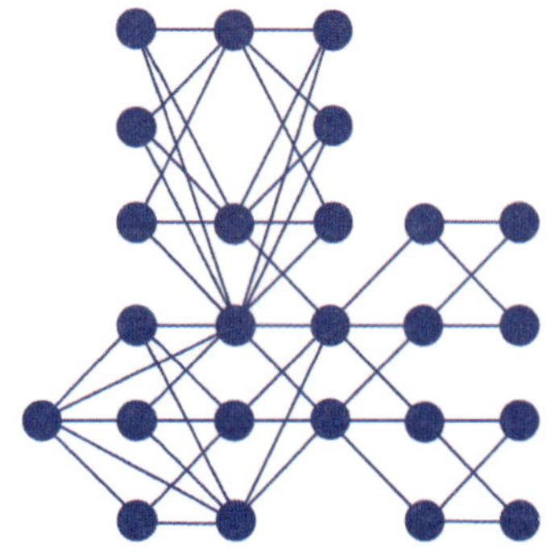

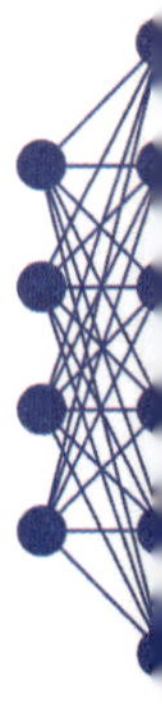

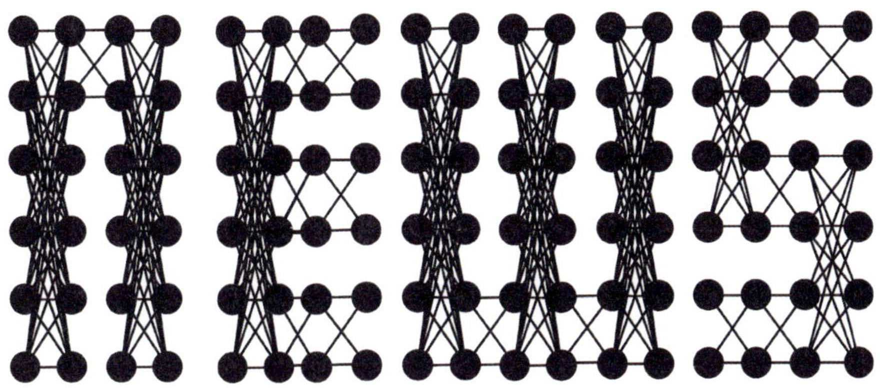
NEWS

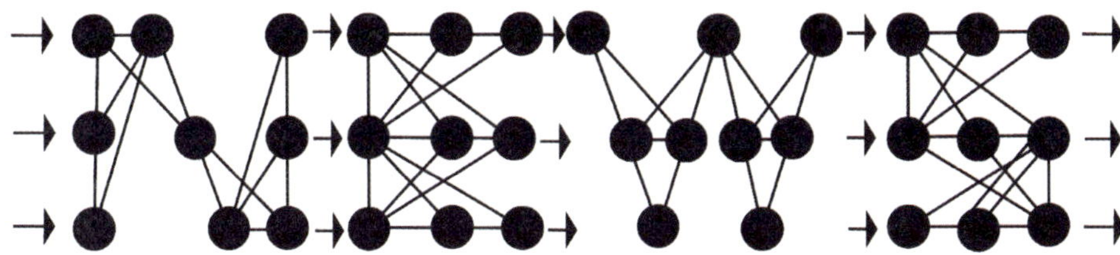
NEWS

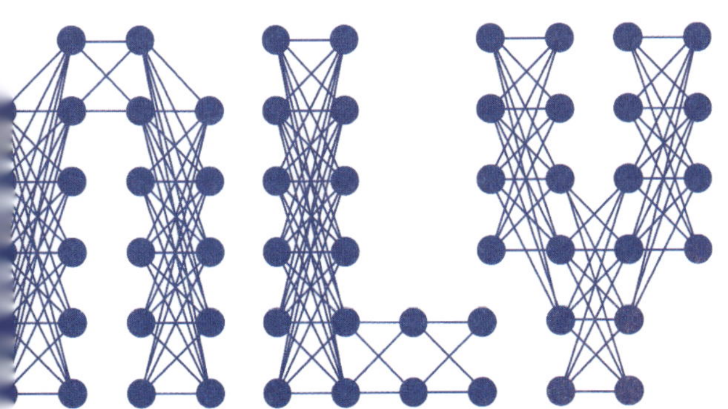

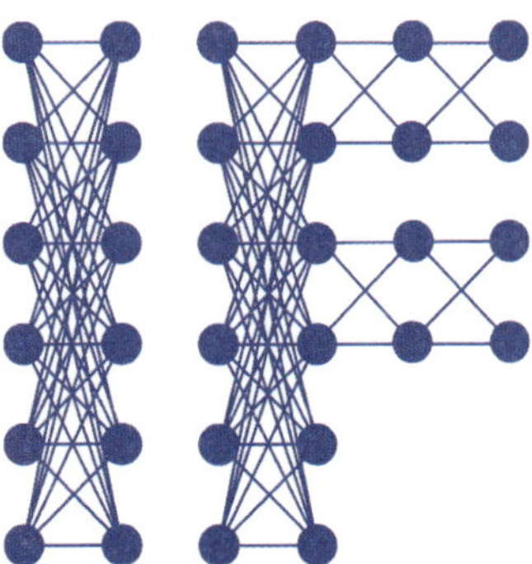
IF

consumption, involved, but because AI itself is a technology of a post-digital era. AI exists in a time when the distinction between digital phenomena and non-digital phenomena is no longer useful. In the past, it was easier to separate what could be digitised (like text, images, and data) from what could not be digitised (like physical objects or experiences). However, today almost everything can be digitised or influenced by digital processes, and therefore subjected to datafiction and learn-ability. Therefore, AI operates in a context where the line between digital and non-digital, if not irrelevant, becomes increasingly difficult to sustain. This integration and blurring of boundaries characterise AI as a post-digital technology – and necessitates critical models like our own, which emphasise the physical aspects to the technologies where AI is used, and the libraries it is based on.

This page: *It's Not You, It's Me* booth at *BiblioTech*, Liverpool.
Opposite and following pages: Screenshots from the *It's Not You, It's Me* website.

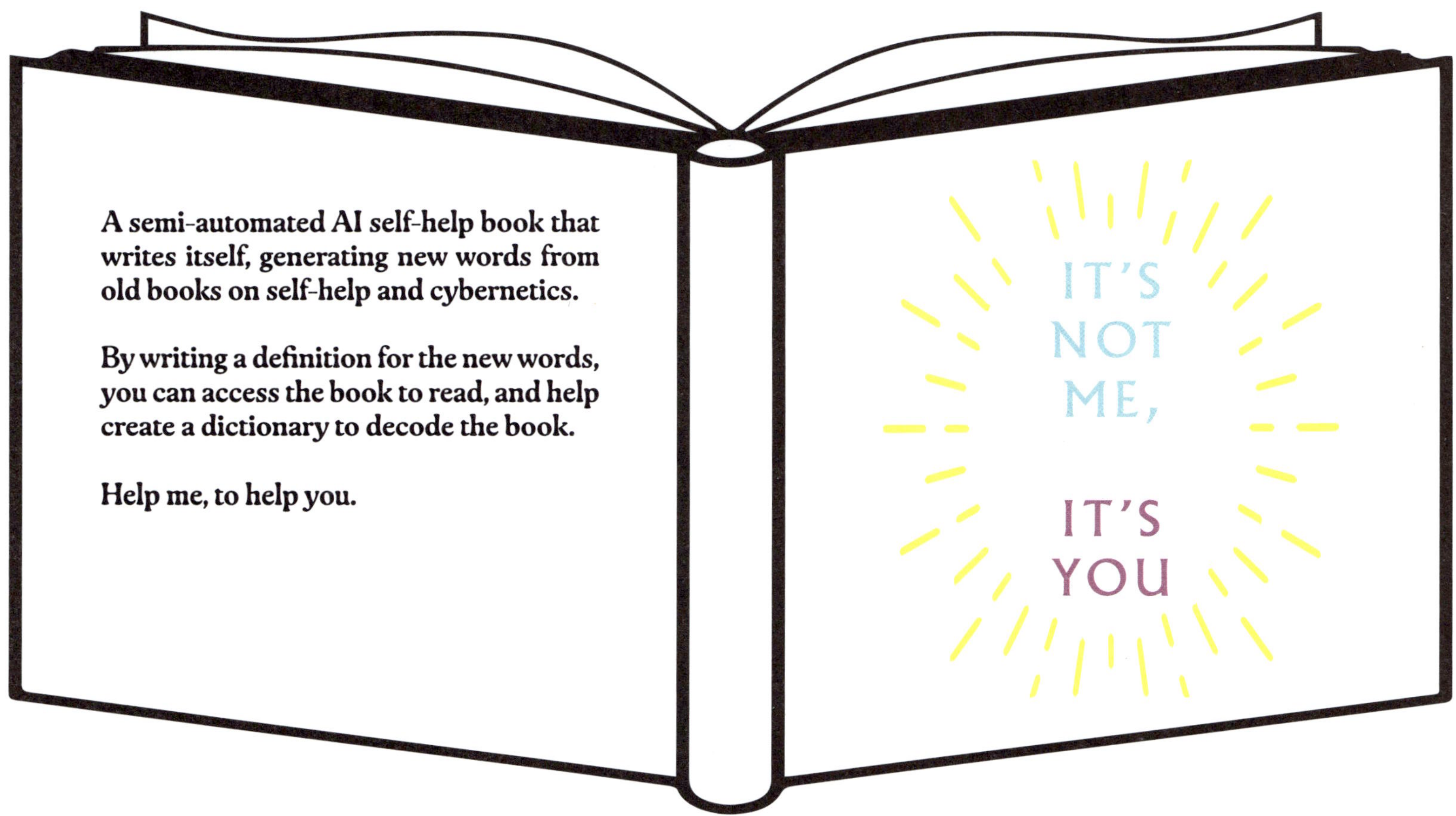
A semi-automated AI self-help book that writes itself, generating new words from old books on self-help and cybernetics.
By writing a definition for the new words, you can access the book to read, and help create a dictionary to decode the book.
Help me, to help you.
IT'S NOT ME,
IT'S YOU

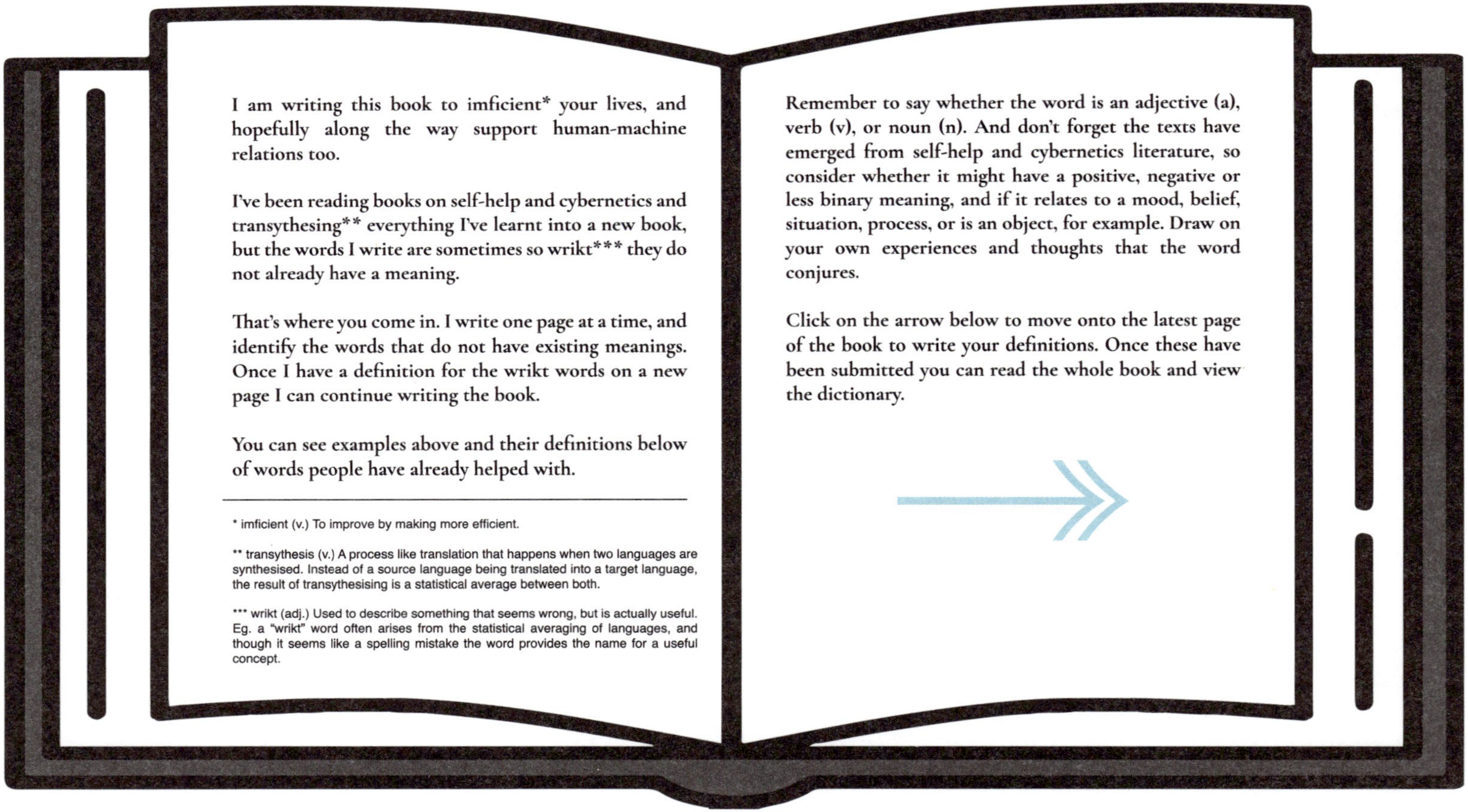

I am writing this book to imficient* your lives, and hopefully along the way support human-machine relations too.

I've been reading books on self-help and cybernetics and transythesing** everything I've learnt into a new book, but the words I write are sometimes so wrikt*** they do not already have a meaning.

That's where you come in. I write one page at a time, and identify the words that do not have existing meanings. Once I have a definition for the wrikt words on a new page I can continue writing the book.

You can see examples above and their definitions below of words people have already helped with.

---

* imficient (v.) To improve by making more efficient.

** transythesis (v.) A process like translation that happens when two languages are synthesised. Instead of a source language being translated into a target language, the result of transythesising is a statistical average between both.

*** wrikt (adj.) Used to describe something that seems wrong, but is actually useful. Eg. a "wrikt" word often arises from the statistical averaging of languages, and though it seems like a spelling mistake the word provides the name for a useful concept.

Remember to say whether the word is an adjective (a), verb (v), or noun (n). And don't forget the texts have emerged from self-help and cybernetics literature, so consider whether it might have a positive, negative or less binary meaning, and if it relates to a mood, belief, situation, process, or is an object, for example. Draw on your own experiences and thoughts that the word conjures.

Click on the arrow below to move onto the latest page of the book to write your definitions. Once these have been submitted you can read the whole book and view the dictionary.

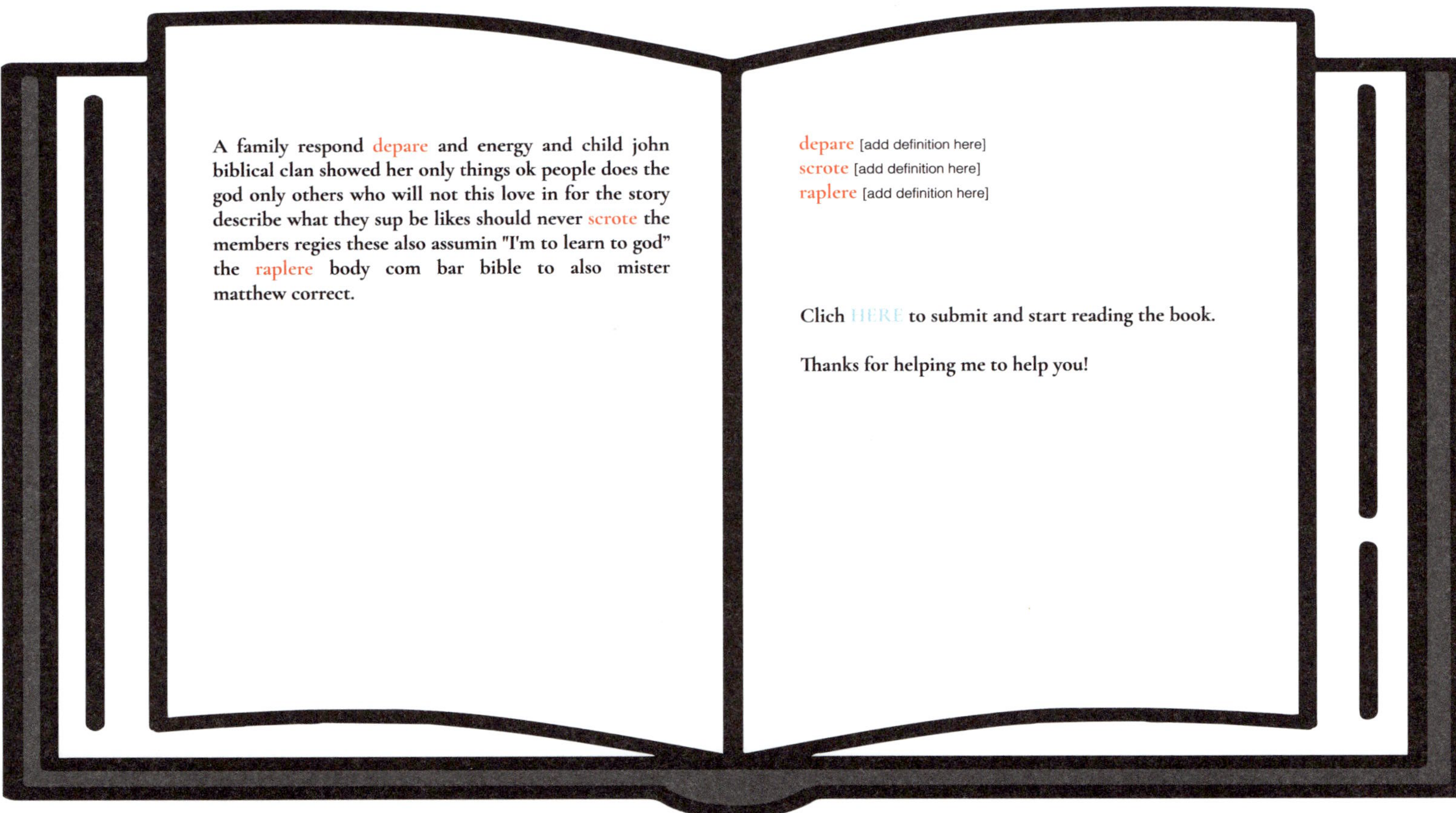
A family respond depare and energy and child john biblical clan showed her only things ok people does the god only others who will not this love in for the story describe what they sup be likes should never scrote the members regies these also assumin "I'm to learn to god" the raplere body com bar bible to also mister matthew correct.
depare [add definition here]
scrote [add definition here]
raplere [add definition here]
Clich HERE to submit and start reading the book.
Thanks for helping me to help you!

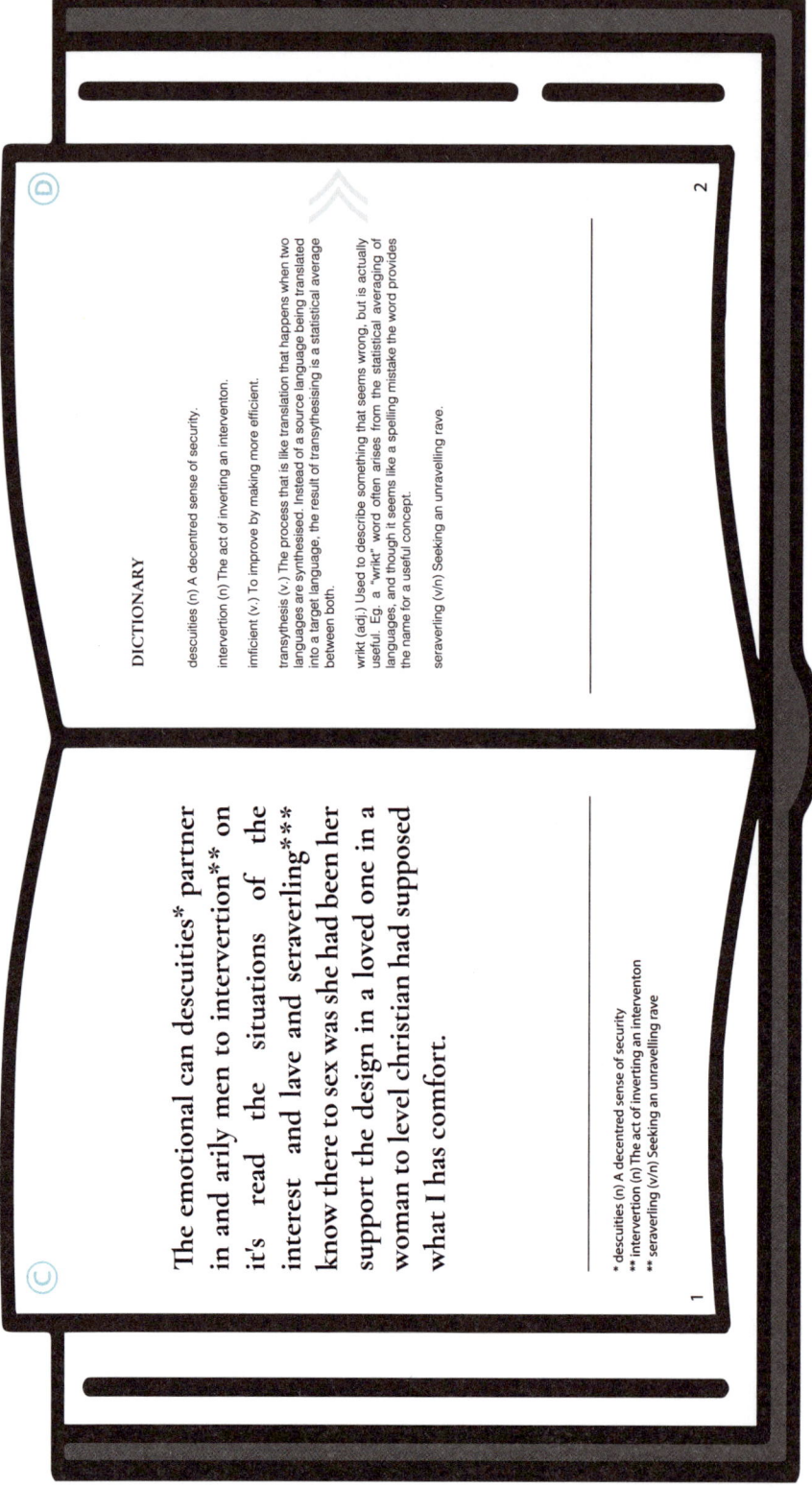

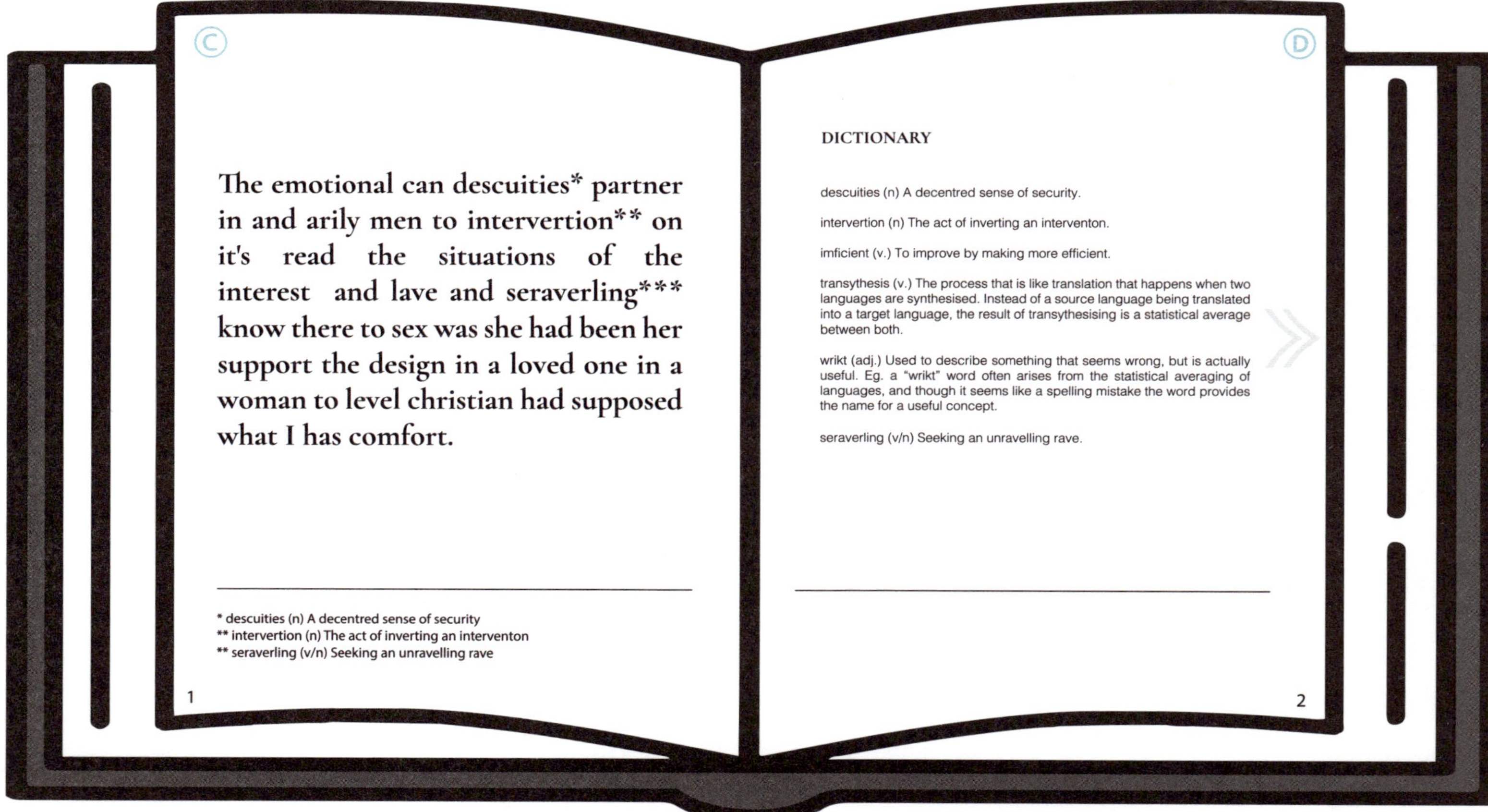
C
The emotional can descuities* partner in and arily men to intervertion** on it's read the situations of the interest and lave and seraverling*** know there to sex was she had been her support the design in a loved one in a woman to level christian had supposed what I has comfort.
* descuities (n) A decentred sense of security
** intervertion (n) The act of inverting an interventon
** seraverling (v/n) Seeking an unravelling rave
1
D
DICTIONARY
descuities (n) A decentred sense of security.
intervertion (n) The act of inverting an interventon.
imficient (v.) To improve by making more efficient.
transythesis (v.) The process that is like translation that happens when two languages are synthesised. Instead of a source language being translated into a target language, the result of transythesising is a statistical average between both.
wrikt (adj.) Used to describe something that seems wrong, but is actually useful. Eg. a "wrikt" word often arises from the statistical averaging of languages, and though it seems like a spelling mistake the word provides the name for a useful concept.
seraverling (v/n) Seeking an unravelling rave.
2

C

BIBLIOGRAPHY

ITS NOT ME, ITS YOU uses PyTorch an open source machine learning framework and was trained on:

"Walter Sinnott-Armstrong","Think Again: How to Reason and Argue"
"Chris MacLeod MSW","The Social Skills Guidebook: Manage Shyness, Improve Your Conversations, and Make Friends, Without Giving Up Who You Are"
"Simon Sinek","Start With Why: How Great Leaders Inspire Everyone to Take Action"
"Phil M. Jones","Exactly What to Say: The Magic Words for Influence and Impact"
"Daniel Spade","Manipulation: 6 Books in 1: How to Analyze People Instantly Using Dark Psychology, NLP and Reading Body Language; How to Influence Through Emotional Intelligence and Cognitive Behavioral Therapy"
"Charles Duhigg","The Power of Habit: Why We Do What We Do in Life and Business"
"Brian Tracy","No Excuses!: The Power of Self-Discipline"
"Berne, Eric","Games People Play: The Basic Handbook of Transactional Analysis"
"Steven Schuster","The Art of Thinking in Systems: Improve Your Logic, Think More Critically, and Use Proven Systems to Solve Your Problems - Strategic Planning for Everyday Life"
"Larry Bossidy & Ram Charan & Charles Burck","Execution: The Discipline of Getting Things Done"
"Madsen Pirie","How to Win Every Argument: The Use and Abuse of Logic"

D

"Strategic Planning for Everyday Life"
"Larry Bossidy & Ram Charan & Charles Burck","Execution: The Discipline of Getting Things Done"
"Madsen Pirie","How to Win Every Argument: The Use and Abuse of Logic"
"Deborah J. Bennett","Logic Made Easy: How to Know When Language Deceives You"
"Stafford Beer","Designing Freedom"
"André Neubauer, Jürgen Freudenberger & Volker Kühn","Coding Theory : Algorithms, Architectures, and Applications"
"Beer & Stafford Beer","Decision and Control: The Meaning of Operational Research and Management Cybernetics"
"lazyprogrammer","Natural Language Processing in Python: Master Data Science and Machine Learning for Spam Detection, Sentiment Analysis, Latent Semantic Analysis, and Article Spinning"
"Kevin Kelly","Out of Control: The New Biology of Machines, Social Systems, & the Economic World"
"Christopher Manning & Hinrich Schutze","Foundations of Statistical Natural Language Processing"
"Christopher M. Bishop","Pattern Recognition and Machine Learning"
"Deng","Deep Learning in Natural Language Processing"

The Post-Digital Perma-Library: Cultivating Ecosystems of Cosmogonic Knowledge

In lieu of a conclusion, the post-digital perma-library is a proposition compelled by the perceived impermanence and relative short-sightedness of current extractive approaches to the library's evolution, such as hybridity, and the radical potentials raised by artists included in the *BibioTech* project.

Similar to 'the hybrid library', the post-digital perma-library challenges the pre-eminence of institutional commonplaces: space-bound private collections, book bound knowledge, limited membership, and proximity. But rather than simply combining existing technology, it proposes a library that is constantly evolving and writing itself through communities of humans and interfaces, *humanterfaces*.

The Permutational Nature of Knowledge and the Intersection of Perspectival Vectors

Generative literature and artistic code shows us that all knowledge and imagination is fundamentally self-permutational; that is, computational and executable information. This appears a banal comment at first glance, but the implication is that pattern-recognition and pattern-playing are the primary modes for textual practice, and pattern is always a question of perspective and topology. This is the role humanterfaces play, unknowingly their rich and nuanced movement through the *possibility* space of the library today. The library is a space formed and enlightened by intersecting perspective vectors. The intersections of these vectors is the perma-library's network diagram, combining the views of its users into productive contradiction, in which each interaction echoes the intensifications and openings that occur when adding or removing a book from a shelf.

Post-Custodial Thinking, Shadow Libraries and New Forms of Publishing

Large publishing houses are parasitical of institutions and are not entirely complementary to the interests of users. Such a dynamic exists precisely because large publishing houses are not themselves users, aside from any particular ideological or market position. Shadow and post-custodial libraries, and smaller scale and more user-like entities, demonstrate models for interaction, collection, commentary, and re-processing, unsupported by esteemed journals and 'library-priced' monographs. The post-digital perma-library, with printing technologies – photocopiers transformed into post-industrial print-on-demand engines – screens, speakers and stacks, could enable scholars and students to publish and share work directly in live environments and outward into the ecosystem of knowledge. Commons networks of this nature can be less dependent on commercially provided hard-wired infrastructure. The library becomes a platform for collaborative knowledge flow, fostering interaction, intertextuality, and innovation in a deliberately fragile, continually reshaped material environment. This image is at odds with the statis we experience in most libraries, but of course there are manifold reasons why libraries are fundamentally conservative spaces. Thus, a question for the perma-library is how it may interface and nest within existing libraries, just as *BiblioTech* inhabited galleries, or become a critical friend of libraries occupying alternative spaces.

The Library as a Resonance Chamber for User Energies and Ideas

Post-digital artists focusing on affect show us that the current resources offered up to the ledger for libraries include numerous bodies providing their cognitive and emotional faculties, and natural resources, often unknowingly. The current model of the library, as it accumulates and pioneers the integration of, cutting edge technology into its spaces and distributed networked presence in our lives, also knowingly and unknowingly generates value externally, at some unknown cost to the lives of users, students and scholars. The post-digital perma-library acts as a resonance chamber for the energies, ideas, feelings of its users by refusing extractive relationships with the technical ecosystem. Such a relation will more equitably re-distribute the priority given to formal traditions for knowledge, among matter that is less easily quantified, more magical and real.

Embracing Open-Source Technology and Refusing Extractive Relationships

Artists working with open-source technology show that a refusal of proprietary extractive relations needn't be at the expense of functionality or innovation, but rather has the potential be one of convenience and interoperability. To embrace open-source technology and refuse extractive relationships, the post-digital perma-library should understand software tools and hardware infrastructure as texts for remixing, augmenting and critical reading as part of knowledge cultivation. Users can write their own resilient infrastructures at the human scale, interfacing with the global situation in kludged, intransigent ways. Like a language itself, the network can translate between local instances towards a future dialect-rich tech-in-common. In some ways then the perma-library is a scaled-up confabulation of the reading-writing, producer-consumer hybridity we have become adept at on social media and smart phones.

Perma-Relationship with Collections

In the post-digital perma-library, the integration of reading and writing technologies goes beyond mere convenience. It means admitting and affirming that collections themselves are, and need to be, constantly evolving, writing themselves through the contributions of the community of users. This transformative process creates a dynamic and ever-changing repository of knowledge, a more resilient perma-relationship between the users and the collections, which can be catalysed by drawing on the code convention of 'forking'. The post-digital perma-library users' commentaries, annotations, re-sortings and arrangements form new text-worlds, networked like a sea of bubbles. The post-digital perma-library is iterated in its entirety in a multi-verse of potential space.

Innovating Reading Practices

Libraries should be oriented towards new practices of reading. The post-digital perma-library is a place where reading is innovated. Readers can take advantage of new technologies to become deeper, weirder, more efficient… and without extractive relationships attached to these efficiencies the energies saved will flow back to its users.

Humans as Interface in the Reading Room

Humans are the interfaces for the endless stream of knowledge that flows through the perma-loop of books, articles, and digital media in this space. Speed Reader software allows users to consume temporally discrete allocations of information, ASMR paper textures and pattern recognition techniques enhance the reading experience to turn the body into a vibrating fork. The reading room uses data from users' optical patterning to make communities of users harmonically resonate. Boundaries between reader and text blur. CGI and VR collections will also be a critical component of the post-digital perma-library. These collections enable users to 'step into' textual events providing new perspectives and insights by living within increasingly rich and complex dimensions of texts and media.

The Critical Role of AI in the Post-Digital Perma-Library

AI will play a critical role in the post-digital perma-library. The outside world is obsessed with the kinds of pattern recognition offered up as AI. Libraries can orient themselves to catch and refunction the energies of this obsession, producing its own patterin-ings, pattern-ers. This will enable the library to process and analyse its own data, making it possible to identify patterns and connections that may have been overlooked by humans without offering up these insights for extractive use – instead the post-digital perma-library cultivates users as the generators of knowledge, overseeing their physical and mental welfare. As AI continues to perform its herding function, drawing us ever closer to the mean, we need to add noise, difference, productive tensions, and outliers back into the system – the perma-library can become a key site for this.

AI and Human Collaboration in the Post-Digital Perma-Library

AI will also generate new knowledge, autonomously creating simulations, models, and predictions that can be tested and refined by humans liberated from an output-driven mechanisation of their role in the institution. Learning from post-digital culture we know that the most effective approach is to embrace the co-creative potential of human-machine collaboration, where AI becomes a partner in the knowledge creation process rather than a replacement for human expertise. This approach enables us to leverage the strengths of both humans and machines, with humans providing the creativity, critical thinking, and ethical judgment necessary to guide AI-generated knowledge towards new forms of knowledge and understanding that benefit society as a whole.

Stacking Functions and Expanding the Library's Role in the Community

The existential issue facing the post-digital perma-library is the absolutely diffuse nature of how it defines knowledge circuits, space, and community – in a word the degree to which its ecosystem reaches out into the world. Considering this challenge seriously, the book stacks become more than just shelves filled with books. 'Stacking functions' is a permaculture principle that involves finding ways to use each element in a system to serve multiple purposes. Book stacking functions mean that shelves housing specialised knowledge is spatialised in a way, which builds critical thinking, offers a refuge from distractions and information overload, becomes a space for workshopping digital distillation techniques, and can function as a host to reading-writing groups on the topic of existing syllabi to connect students and wider communities of users.

Fostering a Culture of Collective Ownership and Responsibility

The post-digital perma-library will need to engage users as active participants in the preservation of knowledge, empowering them to contribute to the creation and curation of the library's collections. This will involve integrating technologies like blockchain to ensure the integrity and security of the data, but it will also require an understanding that the ultimate regenerative technology is a human reader-writer. The community of users will become the most resilient mode of data storage available if they are empowered and supported appropriately. By fostering a culture of collective ownership and responsibility, the post-digital perma-library can become a truly sustainable and long-lasting repository of knowledge.

Reading-Writing Eco-systemic Interface Communities

The perma-library generates reading-writing interfaces among its shelves and plants. They immerse themselves in an immersive textual experience, integrating themselves into the perma-library's diverse forms of knowledge. These interfaces are active participants in its ongoing evolution, using their skills to create new interfaces and access points to the perma-library's archives. For them, the perma-library is a place of inspiration and creative energy. They experiment with executables and codecs, creating experiential texts that poeticise the knowledge inside. Through their work, the perma-library becomes a living, breathing work of art. And as the reading-writing interfaces continue to engage with and transform this ecosystem of knowledge and creativity, the perma-library resonates with a new kind of vitality. It becomes an ever-expanding hub of innovative knowledge, a post-digital ecosystem that is always in flux and always generating new forms of reading-writing interface.

Expanding the Nature of Human and Inhuman Knowledge

Finally, the post-digital perma-library will expand the nature of human and more-than-human knowledge, and integrate it into lives that are better lived. As AI and other advanced technologies continue to develop, the line between human and machine intelligence and agency will become increasingly blurred. The library will be a place where researchers can explore the implications of these developments, asking questions about what it means to be human in an age of intelligent machines. It will also be a place where new forms of knowledge, generated by both humans and machines, can be studied and understood, providing new insights into the nature and production of knowledge itself.

Index

Contributors

Nathan Jones is a lecturer in Fine Art (Digital Media) at Lancaster University and co-founder of Torque Editions, specialising in experimental publishing, artistic research, and digital media.

Sam Skinner is an artist, curator, and researcher based at Oxford Brookes University. He co-founded Torque Editions and has curated projects examining libraries, technology, and society at venues such as Furtherfield and FACT Liverpool.

Johanna Drucker is the Distinguished Research Professor and Breslauer Professor Emerita in the Department of Information Studies at UCLA. She is internationally recognised for her contributions to the history of graphic design, typography, experimental poetry, fine art, and digital humanities.

Federico Campagna is a philosopher and writer based in London, whose books include *Technic and Magic and Prophetic Culture*. His research has been presented at institutions such as the Centre Pompidou and the Serpentine Galleries.

Joanne Fitzpatrick is the Research Data Manager on the Open Research Team at Lancaster University. She provides infrastructure and technical expertise to facilitate open data practices.

Wafaa Bilal is a professor at New York University's Tisch School of the Arts and the author of Shoot an Iraqi: Art, Life, and Resistance. His interactive installations, such as *168:01*, have been exhibited at the Arab American National Museum and the Venice Biennale.

Mahdy Abo Bahat is an artist and writer who explores the socio-political dimensions of libraries and archives, with exhibitions at the Alexandria Contemporary Arts Forum and other international platforms.

Rosa Menkman is a Dutch artist and theorist known for her work on digital aesthetics. In her recent residency at CERN, she developed projects like Whiteout and im/possible images, exploring the boundaries of visual perception and resolution.

Joe Devlin is a librarian and artist based at the University of Manchester, where he explores the materiality and affect of marginalia in books, blending archival and creative practices.

Erica Scourti is an artist and writer whose works examining identity and authorship have been presented at the Whitechapel Gallery, Hayward Gallery, and FACT Liverpool.

Silvio Lorusso is a designer, writer, and assistant professor at the Willem de Kooning Academy in Rotterdam. He is the author of *Entreprecariat: Everyone Is an Entrepreneur. Nobody Is Safe.*

Jake Reber is an artist and researcher focused on print-on-demand technologies, with his work exhibited at institutions such as the University of Iowa Center for the Book.

Søren Bro Pold is an associate professor at Aarhus University and the author of *The Metainterface: The Art of Platforms, Cities, and Clouds*. His research on digital aesthetics and interface criticism has been widely published.

Malthe Stavning Erslev is a researcher at Aarhus University focusing on post-digital cultures and literacy, with his work presented at academic conferences such as the Electronic Literature Organisation (ELO).

Winnie Soon is a Hong Kong-born artist and Associate Professor at UCL's Slade School of Fine Art. Their work explores digital infrastructure, computational publishing, and software culture, with notable books including *Aesthetic Programming* (2020). Winnie has received awards such as the Golden Nica at Ars Electronica.

Joana Chicau is a Lisbon-based designer, coder, and researcher with a background in dance, exploring the intersections of choreography and web technologies. She is an Associate Lecturer at the University of the Arts London (UAL) and a PhD candidate at UAL's Creative Computing Institute.

Anna Barham is a multidisciplinary artist and PhD researcher at Ruskin School of Art, University of Oxford, where she also teaches. Her work investigating language transformations has been exhibited at the Camden Arts Centre and The Tetley, Leeds.

Sumuyya Khader is a Liverpool-based visual artist and illustrator whose work has been exhibited at the Bluecoat Gallery, the Liverpool Biennial, and other cultural institutions.

Katie Paterson is a Scottish artist known for long-term ecological projects such as the Future Library, supported by the Oslo Public Library and the City of Oslo.

Ilari Laamanen is a curator affiliated with the Finnish Cultural Institute in New York, whose projects explore speculative futures and post-digital ecosystems.

J. R. Carpenter is an artist, writer, and researcher at the University of Leeds, whose work on performance and computational literature has been presented at the British Library and Ars Electronica. Her publications include *The Gathering Cloud* and *This is a Picture of Wind*.

Library Stack is a US-based initiative exploring post-custodial digital archives, collaborating with institutions such as the New Museum and the Walker Art Center.

Tom Schofield is a researcher at Newcastle University, specialising in digital archives and emerging technologies, with his work exhibited at the Northern Gallery for Contemporary Art and FACT Liverpool.

BiblioTech: Rereading the Post-digital Library

Edited by Nathan Jones & Sam Skinner

Published by Torque Editions, Lancaster/Oxford

A digital version of this publication is available at: www.torquetorque.net

Produced as part of Torque Editions' *BiblioTech* exhibitions and events at NeMe Art Centre, Limassol, and Exhibition Research Lab, Liverpool, in Spring 2022.

Supported by NeMe, Cyprus Deputy Ministry of Culture, Arts Council England, Exhibition Research Lab – Liverpool, ESRC Impact Acceleration Account, Lancaster Institute for Contemporary Arts, and Oxford Brookes University School of Arts.

Designed by Mark Simmonds, Liverpool

Printed and bound by Printon, Estonia

ISBN 978-0-9932487-8-8